# OIL BURNERS

## by Edwin M. Field

**Macmillan Publishing Company**
New York

Collier Macmillan Publishers
London

SJHP,
F454o.
1987

FOURTH EDITION

Macmillan Publishing Company
866 Third Avenue, New York, N.Y. 10022
Collier Macmillan Canada, Inc.                                          ʼ

Library of Congress Cataloging-in-Publication Data

Field, Edwin M.
    Oil burners.

    Includes index.
    1. Oil burners.  I. Title.
TH7466.O6F5      1984      697′.07      83-22308
    ISBN 0-672-23394-0

10 9 8 7 6 5 4 3

Printed in the United States of America

357 p. : ill. ; 22 cm.

# Foreword

The purpose of this book is to help everyone interested in oil burners to gain an understanding and practical working knowledge of the theory, construction, installation, operation, testing, servicing, and the repair of all kinds of oil burners, domestic and industrial.

Included in this book are the general electrical hookup and wiring diagrams of automatic control systems. Great emphasis is placed on how the ignition system operates, such as transformer action; high-voltage transportation, which includes various electrode assemblies; and the operational sequences of limit controls, thermostats, and various relays.

Various other topics, such as combustion chambers, drafts, chimneys, oil burner housings, drive couplings, fans or blowers, burner nozzles, and fuel pumps, are covered to provide the maximum amount of information. Steam and gravity hot-water systems are also included, along with forced and gravity warm-air systems.

Oil storage tanks are discussed; this includes underground, inside, and tandem tanks. The inclusion of troubleshooting charts throughout the book can assist the serviceman in making the proper diagnosis and the correct adjustment or repair.

Suggestions are made throughout the book about ways of conserving energy and cutting equipment operational costs.

# Contents

# CHAPTER 5

# CHAPTER 6

# CHAPTER 7

# CHAPTER 8

# CHAPTER 9

# CHAPTER 10

# CHAPTER 1

# Introduction

In its simplest form, the heating story begins with the raw petroleum product and concludes with the generation of heat and energy. Between these two points is the distillation and fractionation process of the petroleum product into usable fuel oil as we know it and the combustion process. This process includes the knowledge and techniques necessary to effectively produce the ultimate end product of our labors—controlled heat and energy.

## PETROLEUM

Petroleum is known as rock or crude oil. The word comes from the Latin words *petro* (meaning rock) and *oleum* (meaning oil). The product contains about 85 percent carbon and 14 percent hydrogen. The balance is composed of elements such as sulfur, oxygen, and nitrogen. Petroleum is a mineral found under the crust of the earth in "fields" scattered throughout the world. In 1858 the first well ever drilled to find *oil* was successfully completed. Since that time, thousands of uses have been developed for the product. However, crude oil in its natural state is rarely of practical use; the oil must be refined. There are over 300 refineries doing this job today throughout our nation. These plants turn out approximately 8 million barrels of oil daily, with a quarter of a million different oil companies involved in distributing the various products produced as a result of the refining process. Fig. 1-1 shows, in simplified form, a modern rotary-well drilling rig.

## Distillation and Fractionation

Technically, the first process of petroleum refining is called *distillation*. This was the first method used to separate crude oil directly into usable products, such as kerosene and gasoline. This process is still used today to separate the various fractions of hydrocarbons in the crude oil into workable groups. The distillation process separates these fractions into groups whose boiling points fall within given temperature ranges. The products of distillation are then further separated by a process called *fractionation*. As shown in Fig. 1-2, the oil is first heated to a high temperature by pumping it through long rows of steel tubes in a furnace. After this process, the crude oil enters the lower part of a closed, vertical tower, call a *fractionating column*, where part of the product is vaporized. The unvaporized portion, called *residue*, is drawn off from the bottom of the tower. As the vapors rise in the tower, they bubble through perforated trays, each designed to hold just a few inches of liquid. At the same time that this process is taking place, a stream of gasoline (called *reflux*) is pumped into the top of the tower and flows down over the trays. This reflux provides a cooling action, which condenses the heavier hydrocarbons. In turn, the hot vapors cause the reflux to vaporize. As this process continues, different *fractions* of crude oil condense on different trays. The heavier fractions (with higher boiling points) condense on the lower and hotter trays. The operation continues with different fractions of crude oil condensing on different trays.

8

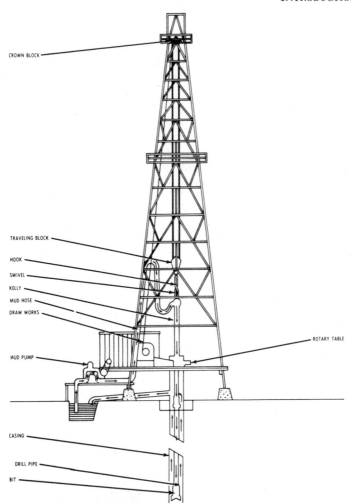

CROWN BLOCK

TRAVELING BLOCK

HOOK

SWIVEL

KELLY

MUD HOSE

DRAW WORKS

ROTARY TABLE

MUD PUMP

CASING

DRILL PIPE

BIT

**Fig. 1-1.** In rotary oil-well drilling, power machinery turns a rotary table on the derrick floor. The rotary table turns the "kelly," to which the pipe drill is attached. The rotary motion is transmitted to the bit on the end of the drill pipe. Additional lengths of drill pipe are attached as the bit bores deeper. Hoisting machinery (draw works) and a block and tackle lift or lower the drill pipe. Specially prepared mud is pumped down inside the drill pipe and passes through the bit, which it cools. Forced upward outside the drill pipe (arrows), the mud carries cuttings to the surface and helps seal the walls of the hole until steel casings can be set in place.

9

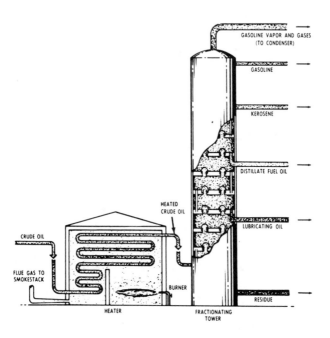

**Fig. 1-2. Fractional distillation of crude oil.**

The primary products of petroleum are then drawn off through pipes from the various trays. The entire fractionating process continues constantly. The products drawn off include the distillate fuel oils and kerosene that we are interested in for our particular portion of the heating industry. These fuels are now piped, trucked, and barged to various storage centers throughout the nation and are ultimately consumed to produce the requirements of heat and energy.

## Fuel Oil Grades

The ultimate end products of the fractionating tower process are classified into different grades of fuel oil, each with a different and specific heat and/or energy use. The information contained in Table 1-1 outlines data important to the serviceman concerning the various grades of fuel oil.

## Table 1-1. Fuel Oil Grades and Uses

| Grade | Description | Heating Value Btu per gallon | Approximate Gravity API | Use of Heating Range | Approximate Weight (lb. per gal.) | Flash Point (Minimum °F) | Pour Point (Maximum °F) |
|---|---|---|---|---|---|---|---|
| No. 1 | A distillate oil intended for vaporizing in pot-type burners and other burners requiring this grade. | 132,900 to 137,000 | 38–45 | Vaporizing equipment | 6.95 | 100 or legal | 0 |
| No. 2 | A distillate oil for general-purpose domestic heating for use in burners not requiring No. 1. | 135,800 to 141,800 | 30–40 | Domestic heating equipment | 7.29 | 100 or legal | 20 |
| No. 3 | Preheating is not usually required for handling or burning. | 143,100 to 148,100 | 20–28 | Industrial heating power | 7.78 | 130 or legal | 20 |
| No. 4 | (Light) preheating may be required for handling, depending on climate and equipment. | 146,800 to 150,000 | 17–22 | Industrial heating power | 7.94 | 130 or legal | |
| No. 5 | (Heavy) preheating required for burning; in cold climates, heating may be required for handling. | 149,400 to 152,000 | 14–18 | Industrial heating power | 8.08 | 130 or legal | |
| No. 6 | Preheating required for burning and handling. | 151,300 to 155,900 | 8–15 | Industrial heating power | 8.44 | 150 | |

## Fuel Oil Terms

The language and terms of different industries vary. The fuel oil industry has a set of terms all its own.

Baume—A scale that indicates the weight of oil per unit volume at 60°F.

Viscosity—A technical indication of the readiness with which an oil may be sprayed. In tests, the number of seconds required for a specific quantity of oil to drain through a standard orifice at 100°F.

Flash Point—The temperature of the oil at which a jet of flame passed near the surface of the oil will cause the oil vapors to flash.

Pour Point—The minimum temperature, in degrees Fahrenheit, at which oil will flow.

Conradson Test—A test process in which oil is burned, the readings indicating the percentage of carbon residue.

Sulfur Content—Low-sulfur fuel oil is used in heat treatment of nonferrous metals, in glass and ceramic furnaces, and for other special heating equipment. Therefore, a sulfur requirement may be specified in specific fuel oils. These may be specified as 0.5-percent for No. 1 fuel; 1.0 percent for No. 2 fuel, and no specific limit, except those specified by mutual agreements between buyer and seller, for No. 4, No. 5, and No. 6 oils.

Sediment Water—The amount of water by distillation, plus the sediment by extraction, shall not exceed 2 percent. The amount of sediment by extraction shall not exceed 0.5-percent. It is normal procedure to deduct in quantity all water and sediment in excess of 1 percent.

British Thermal Unit—A unit of heat energy, or a yardstick for measuring the amount of heat. A Btu is $\frac{1}{180}$ of the heat required to raise the temperature of one pound of water from 32°F to 212°F.

# HEAT

The point has now been reached where thought must be given to converting the petroleum product (which has itself been changed or converted from a crude oil into a fuel oil) into a usable heat product. Remember that heating oils contain approximately 85 percent carbon, 14 percent hydrogen, plus an assortment of other elements. The goal is to provide a chemical union of the oxygen in the air with the elements in the oil to support *combustion*. The end result of this process will be the production of heat energy.

To begin with, though, a brief discussion of *heat* is in order. Heat is a form of energy consisting of molecular motion in bodies. The higher the temperatures, the faster the molecular structure moves about. The lower the temperatures, the slower the movement. This molecular motion, or heat, can actually be measured by taking the *temperature* of the body involved. Standard temperatures (weather, human, etc.) are measured by *thermometers*, while very high temperatures are measured with a *pyrometer*. When an individual's or the weather's temperature is taken, we are measuring the condition of a body on which its power of communicating or receiving heat from other bodies depends.

A thermometer or pyrometer works on the principle of expansion or contraction of certain substances or metals due to the action of heat. A chemical inside a thermometer expands and contracts when exposed to varying amounts of heat. The expansion and contraction movement is accurately gauged so that the motion is charted and translated into degrees Fahrenheit or Centigrade. Other heat-measuring devices work on the theory of the relative expansion of two dissimilar metals or on the thermocouple principle. No matter what the operating principle, however, there are certain fixed points on thermometers or pyrometers that indicate established high and low temperatures. For example, the freezing point of water is indicated by a mark of 32°F above zero, while the boiling point is noted at 212°F above zero, and 180°F above the freezing mark. The gauge marks in between or above and below these set points are relative to the particular unit being measured for temperature.

## Heat Classifications

There are two classifications of heat. The first is *sensible heat*, which may best be indicated by the sense of feeling. It is measured by a thermometer. A person's hand held next to a hot radiator and reacting to its warmth is an example of sensible heat. The heat necessary to cause a change of state in the body is known as *latent heat*. Converting water into steam is an example of latent heat in action.

Heat is transferred from one body or surface to another in three ways—by radiation, conduction, and convection. Heat from burning fuel passes to the metal to be heated by *radiation;* through the metal by *conduction* and transferred to water contacting it by *convection*.

## Heat Measurement

In order to measure heat, certain rules have been established by heating engineers. Some of these rules have everyday applications for the oil burner serviceman. Others should be read and stored for future use. The Btu is an example of one of the rules that is in constant field use. The Btu (British Thermal Unit) is a measure of heat energy, a yardstick for measuring the quantity of heat capable of being produced by a given quantity of a given product. Technically, a Btu is $\frac{1}{180}$ part of the heat required to raise the temperature of one pound of water from 32°F to 212°F. A gallon of fuel oil has an established Btu value. A room has a certain Btu heat loss value. A furnace may be rated on its Btu output.

*Specific heat* measurement is another rule. This is the ratio of the quantity of heat required to raise the temperature of any given substance one degree Fahrenheit to the quantity of heat required to raise the temperature of the same weight of water from 62°F to 63°F.

Overcoming resistance through a certain distance, by the expenditure of energy, is known as *work*. Work is measured technically by a standard unit called the foot-pound. The *foot-pound* is the amount of work accomplished in raising one pound one foot, or in overcoming a pressure of one pound through a distance of one foot. The foot-pound, or *unit of work*, relates to the Btu in that 1 Btu equals 777.52 ft.-lb. of work.

# COMBUSTION

As discussed earlier, the final goal of combustion is a chemical union of the oxygen in the air with the elements in the oil (hydrogen and carbon). The end result of this process is the production of heat energy. A complete understanding of combustion is a prerequisite to oil burner servicing. It is necessary for the service mechanic to understand combustion in order to properly adjust oil heating equipment and correct difficulties that may arise.

Combustion is rapid oxidation. Oxidation is the combining with oxygen, or subject to the action of oxygen by means of an oxidizing agent. Oxygen is found in the air we breathe. Almost 21 percent of the air by volume and approximately 23 percent by weight is made up of oxygen. It is a prime supporter of combustion. Carbon and hydrogen, the two principle elements of fuel oil, have an affinity for oxygen. When they unite, heat is produced. Fuel oil also contains about 1.5 percent nitrogen by volume. A considerable amount of the heat developed by combustion is used up in raising the temperature of the nitrogen. That portion of this heat not extracted usefully afterward is a dead loss. Nitrogen also sets a low limit to the temperature that can be reached by combustion in the air. The burner serviceman should know that by cutting down the excess air admitted to the oil burner, nitrogen heat loss can be reduced.

During the combustion process, the carbon content of the fuel oil (approximately 85 percent) unites with the oxygen in the air and forms carbon dioxide and/or carbon monoxide. The hydrogen content of the oil (approximately 14 percent) unites with the oxygen and forms water.

The ultimate service goal is to have as complete a combustion process as possible. This is when the combustible (fuel oil) unites with the greatest possible amount of oxygen. Incomplete combustion occurs when the combustible (fuel oil) does not unite with the greatest possible amount of oxygen. Incomplete combustion can be caused by an insufficient supply of air. A lack of oxygen during the combustion process will cause the formation of carbon monoxide instead of carbon dioxide. An oversupply

15

(excess) of air, on the other hand, will dilute the combustion gases and cool the burner or furnace.

In order for each and every particle of carbon and hydrogen in the fuel oil to meet and react favorably with the oxygen of the air, it is necessary for the fuel oil to be broken up into fine particles. These particles form a fog or fine spray, which must be correctly mixed with the proper amount of air. Once this air is mixed with the *atomized oil*, and the entire mixture is raised to the proper temperature, combustion takes place. See Fig. 1-3.

**Fig. 1-3. Combustion flame.**

During the process of combustion, one part of carbon unites with two parts of oxygen to produce carbon dioxide. Each time one pound of carbon is burned, 14,544 Btu of heat are liberated. *Carbon dioxide* ($CO_2$) is recognized by service people as the end product of *complete* combustion. Should the fuel oil be raised to the correct temperature for combustion but not supplied with the proper amount of oxygen, carbon monoxide will be produced, and only 4480 Btu of heat liberated. *Carbon monoxide (CO) is recognized by service people as the end product of incomplete* combustion.

When the combustion process takes place, a number of other things occur. The complex molecules of the fuel oil "crack." They break down into smaller and simpler molecules. Free carbon is liberated. If the proper amount of air has been thoroughly mixed with the oil, and the temperature of the flame is correct, the free carbon burns completely. If the mixture is not correct, only some of the carbon burns, and the rest remains as soot on the inner walls of the combustion chamber.

## Flame Color

A correctly adjusted oil burner flame will have an orange-colored flame body with small red tips. These tips will be slightly cloudy. On one end of the *flame scale*, a red, smoky flame is an indication of a lack of air. A white, almost dazzling flame is an indication of a great amount of excess air. This subject is discussed in more detail later.

## Combustion Area

It is necessary to maintain both a high flame temperature and a minimum of excess air for the best possible combustion. This combustion process can best be accommodated in a combustion area specifically designed for the purpose. A combustion chamber or firebox made of refractory material absorbs and reflects the heat back into the flame. This increases the flame temperature as well as the air turbulence within the combustion area. Increasing the flame temperature through reflected heat increases the speed of combustion and ultimately the fullest "burning" of all fuel particles within the combustion area. It is important that the fuel oil flame be sized correctly. It must be large enough to fill the combustion chamber completely, yet not so large that the flame impinges or strikes the chamber walls. Fig. 1-4 shows a serviceman checking the combustion area and flame in an oil-fired furnace.

The serviceman should remember that incompletely burned fuel particles allowed to escape from the combustion chamber area cool rapidly and will not react with the oxygen. These

Fig. 1-4. Viewing the combustion process.

unburned or partially burned oil particles will escape up the chimney and be a complete loss.

## SUMMARY

There are over 300 refineries turning out about 8 million barrels of oil daily in the United States, with approximately a quarter of a million different oil companies involved in distributing the various products produced as a result of the refining. The word petroleum comes from the Latin words *petro* (meaning rock) and *oleum* (meaning oil). The petroleum contains about 85 percent carbon and 14 percent hydrogen. The first process of petroleum refining is called *distillation*.

Heat is a form of energy consisting of molecular motion in bodies. The higher the temperature, the faster the molecular structure moves about. The lower the temperature, the slower the movement. There are two classifications of heat: *sensible* heat and *latent* heat. Heat is transferred from one body or surface to another in three ways—by radiation, conduction, and convection.

One way to measure heat is by the Btu (British Thermal Unit). A Btu is $\frac{1}{180}$ part of the heat required to raise the temperature of one pound of water from 32°F to 212°F. One gallon of fuel oil has an established Btu value. A room has a certain Btu heat loss.

Specific heat is another way of measuring heat. This is the ratio of the quantity of heat required to raise the temperature of any given substance one degree Fahrenheit to the quantity of heat required to raise the temperature of the same weight of water from 62°F to 63°F.

For proper combustion, it is necessary to maintain both a high flame temperature and a minimum of excess air for the best possible operation. A combustion chamber made of refractory or specially treated metal material absorbs and reflects the heat back into the flame. It is important that the fuel oil flame be sized correctly. It must be large enough to fill the combustion chamber completely, yet not so large that the flame strikes the chamber walls. Incompletely burned fuel particles allowed to escape from the combustion chamber area cool rapidly and will not react with oxygen. The unburned particles will escape up the chimney and be completely lost.

## REVIEW QUESTIONS

1. What is the percentage of carbon and hydrogen in petroleum?
2. What is the first process of petroleum refining called?
3. What is todays's process of refining called?
4. What is that portion of oil not vaporized in the fractionation process called?
5. What is reflux?
6. What are the two basic ways to measure heat?
7. How many grades of fuel oil are produced?

8. What is the heating value in Btu per gallon of No. 2 fuel oil?
9. In what three ways is heat transferred from body to body?
10. Define viscosity.
11. What two instruments are used to measure temperature?
12. Define combustion.
13. What is the purpose in constructing the firebox in the combustion chamber of refractory material?
14. Define flash point.
15. What is sulfur content?

# CHAPTER 2

# Heating Systems

Heating systems began with the open fire. The next step was the addition of a duct or chimney to carry the products of combustion out of the dwelling. The fireplace was the next refinement. A grate was developed so that the fire could do double duty by providing warmth and a place to cook. The process of "mechanical" evolution added the stove to man's list of heating accomplishments. Time passed, and new demands and developments brought forth the warm-air furnace, the gravity hot-water heating system, and the steam heating system. Once again, human ingenuity was put to work, and these systems were further refined until today we have forced warm air, circulating hot water, and a variety of refinements of the old steam system.

In the beginning, wood was the principal fuel supply. Then coal replaced wood. Oil and gas have since been added to the list of fuels used to keep us warm. At the start, people hunted for the wood themselves, tossing logs into the fire as needs demanded. Today, the fuel is delivered automatically. People merely turn up a room thermostat, and their heating demands are satisfied.

The function of any heating system, whether it be an ancient wood fireplace or the most modern oil heating equipment on the market, is to supply each room of the house or building with heat, when and as required, and in the amount necessary for comfort.

All of today's modern systems incorporate a number of elements that are basic to each unit. Each has a combustion area in which to prepare and burn the fuel, a vehicle (either air or water) for transmitting the heated product of combustion, and piping to move the heated products of combustion to the residence or building. In addition, each system also has a method (radiators, registers, etc.) for carrying the heated water or air products directly into the individual rooms and devices (controls) for controlling the amount and flow of heat.

# TYPES OF OIL HEATING SYSTEMS

There are three specific types of heating systems, each with a number of variations within its design.

## Hot-Water (Wet-Heat) Systems

Water is used as the transfer medium in a hot-water system. It is heated in a boiler, transported through piping to the individual rooms of the house or building, and provides warmth through radiators directly into the rooms. These systems are further subdivided into two general circulation methods. The first type is the gravity system, which depends on the lighter hot water rising and the colder return water falling to create a circulation through the system. The second type is the forced circulation system that operates with a pump driving or pulling the heated water through the system. An *aquastat*, shown on the boiler in Fig. 2-1, automatically maintains the correct boiler water temperature in the hot-water system. A basement installation of a hot-water system is illustrated in Fig. 2-2 and a cutaway view is shown in Fig. 2-3. Circulators for hot-water systems are shown in Figs. 2-4, 2-5, and 2-6.

Courtesy Burnham

**Fig. 2-1. A hot-water boiler showing circulator and oil burner attached to heating unit.**

## Steam (Wet-Heat) Systems

Water is also used as the medium for a steam system, which includes vapor, vacuum, and steam under pressure units. The steam system operates with water at about the three-quarter level in a boiler. The water is heated by the combustion process with the balance of the system, including pipes and radiation, filled with air.The combustion process brings the boiler water to the

Fig. 2-2. A basement installation of a hot-water or hydronic boiler.

boiling point, and steam is created. The steam produces pressure in the boiler, pipes, and radiation. It "drives" the air out through the piping and out the radiators. Air valves (Fig. 2-7) on the individual radiators permit the air to escape. As the air moves out of the radiators, the steam under pressure moves in, heating them in the process. When the steam cools off, it condenses and flows back through the pipes to the boiler to be heated and used once again. The variations of the steam system (vacuum, vapor, pressure) depend on specific types of piping and valving. A *pressure-trol* automatically maintains the correct boiler steam pressure in these systems.

It might be well here to mention a few basic facts about steam. Steam is "invisible water vapor." Very often, the service mechanic will see a white cloud issuing from the boiler safety valve. This is not steam but a fog of tiny liquid particles formed by condensation and called condensate. Steam changes into this white cloud when it is exposed to a temperature lower than that corresponding to its pressure. Home heating systems use pressures ranging from a few ounces for the so-called vapor systems

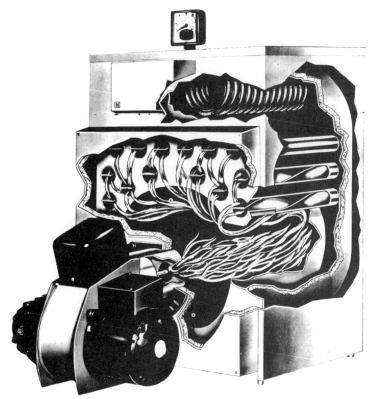

Courtesy Axeman-Anderson Co.

**Fig. 2-3. Cutaway view of oil-fired hot-water boiler showing combustion flame flow.**

to a few pounds for the ordinary steam heating systems. A typical oil-fired steam boiler is shown in Fig. 2-8.

## Hot-Air Systems

Hot-air systems include the gravity type, which depends on the principle of heated air rising to provide room warmth, and the forced warm-air type, which mechanically moves the warmed air through ductwork and out individual room registers. There are many refinements included in these systems. All depend on metalwork (ducts and registers) to transport the warm air to the

**Fig. 2-4. A circulator or booster pump used with hydronic or hot-water systems.**

living quarters. An *airstat* automatically maintains the correct furnace air temperature. The combustion process takes place in a cast-iron or steel body surrounded by a large metal outer jacket. The air in this jacket reacts to the combustion process taking place in the cast-iron or steel body by heating up. The heated air either rises through the duct work, or is moved mechanically by fans to the living areas of the residence. Figs. 2-9, 2-10, and 2-11 show a cutaway view of a forced warm-air furnace used for residential heating.

## BOILER-FURNACE SIZING

A large number of charts and graphs could be presented at this point for the serviceman to use in order to determine boiler-

Fig. 2-5. Circulator or booster pump for hydronic system. Note arrow on pump face indicating direction of water flow.

Fig. 2-6. Cutaway showing working parts of a circulator.

27

**Fig. 2-7. An air-vent valve used for steam or hot-water systems. The device prohibits air from becoming trapped within the radiation.**

furnace heat loads. These charts would, for example, indicate that a boiler with so many sections has an output of so many square feet of radiation. They might state that a furnace with a grate area of X number of square feet has a certain Btu output. It is much the better part of wisdom, however, to suggest that the service mechanic purchase a good boiler-rating handbook in order to determine the exact output of the equipment he is working with. Every unit he works with will present a different calculation problem. The use of a boiler-furnace rating handbook is quick and accurate. There are a great many heating units of all ages in the field today—far too many to suggest a general "rule of thumb" as guidance. It might also be good service sense for the mechanic to write directly to the manufacturer of equipment he finds in his area. The manufacturer will supply spec sheets on his new equipment and data on his older units.

The serviceman should know that boilers and furnaces are manufactured of either steel or cast iron and that they come either in sections (sectional boilers) or are constructed in one- or two-piece units—combustion area and heating area.

Courtesy Burnham

Fig. 2-8. Oil-fired steam boiler. Note water-gauge glass on right-hand side of unit.

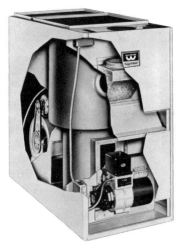

Courtesy Williamson Company

Fig. 2-9. Cutaway view of oil-fired forced warm-air furnace.

29

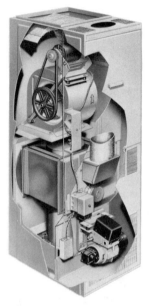

Fig. 2-10. Oil-fired downflow forced warm-air furnace showing belt-driven blower. A "cooling" or air-conditioning unit can be added on to this equipment.

Courtesy Lennox Industries

Fig. 2-11. Oil-fired "upflow" forced warm-air furnace showing direct-drive blower motor. A "cooling" or air-conditioning unit can be added on to this equipment.

Courtesy Lennox Industries

Finally, most of the equipment on the market today is adaptable to automatic firing (oil, coal, etc.). Much of the older heating equipment was not designed for automatic firing. It may be "converted," but a great deal of heat loss and inefficiency must be expected. Check boiler-rating books, consult with boiler-furnace manufacturers, and use your judgment before converting an old, obviously obsolete heating system.

It is also sound service practice to see that low-water safety controls (Figs. 2-12, 2-13, and 2-14) are installed on all wet-heat boilers (steam or hot water). These devices automatically turn the oil burner off before a dangerous "low-water condition" exists in the steam or hot-water boiler. Low-water controls operate on a float and switch principal. The unit's switch remains ·in an *on* position only as long as the float is raised by boiler water in the float chamber. When this water level lowers, the float drops and deactivates the switch. The switch disconnects the power to the oil burner and turns it off.

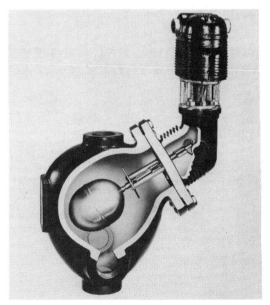

Courtesy A.Y. McDonnell Corp.

**Fig. 2-12. Low-water cutoff control.**

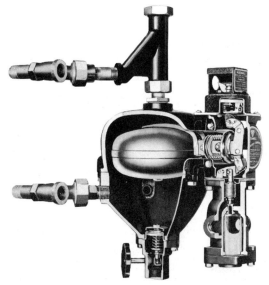

**Fig. 2-13. Cutaway view of a low-water cutoff control.**

## COMBINATION FUEL HEATING SYSTEMS— AUXILIARY/ALTERNATIVE HEAT SOURCES

Among the heating industry innovations designed to combat high energy costs are combination oil/wood-coal furnaces and boilers and "add on" wood-coal auxiliary heating units.

The first system, a multifuel unit, is engineered to allow for either automatic switch-over to the backup fuel of choice or dual fuel operation. The "add on" unit, burning wood or coal, is installed alongside the existing residential oil-fired heating system.

Dual fuel units utilize the system's oil burner not only to provide boiler or furnace combustion but to ignite the wood or coal and to control the combustion rate of these fuels. Multifuel units can also provide the homeowner with the option of burning one fuel or another independently. If, for example, a low-cost supply of wood is available, home temperatures can be maintained with this fuel. Should the homeowner leave the residence for a span of

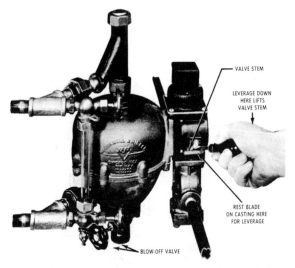

VALVE STEM

LEVERAGE DOWN
HERE LIFTS
VALVE STEM

REST BLADE
ON CASTING HERE
FOR LEVERAGE

BLOW-OFF VALVE

Courtesy A.Y. McDonnell Corp.

**Fig. 2-14. Low-water cutoff control showing the blow-off valve for internal cleaning and the method of cleaning dirt, obstructions, etc., from the valve seat.**

time and not be available to feed wood into the combustion chamber of the heating unit, a simple changeover permits oil firing.

Dual fuel furnaces and boilers come with two independent combustion chambers. The combustion area for wood firing is usually designed large enough to permit burning of big logs. The chambers generally require filling once every 12 hours. Many systems also provide grates for the boilers or furnaces should the homeowner want to burn coal as an alternative fuel. The important point about dual fuel units is that the owner of the residence has complete control of the fuel used.

"Add on" coal or wood systems are generally connected directly into the existing furnace or boiler and supply auxiliary warm air or hot water to the oil-fired installation. A system of piping and controls regulates the quantity of heat produced by both the main and auxiliary "add on" unit.

Multifuel units can be completely automatic except for providing the wood or coal supply to the combustion area. See Figs. 2-15 and 2-16.

**Fig. 2-15.** A combination oil-fired/wood-fired boiler designed for energy economy.

## Tankless Coil

The tankless coil (Fig. 2-17) is another unit available in both hot-water and steam heating systems. Composed of long lengths of tightly wound copper piping, this device is immersed in the water of the boiler's body. Hot water, created by the operating boiler, flows around the coil, which contains a water flow from the residence's main water system. This water, in turn, heats up

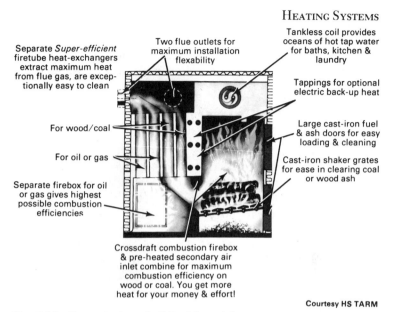

Separate *Super-efficient* firetube heat-exchangers extract maximum heat from flue gas, are exceptionally easy to clean

Two flue outlets for maximum installation flexability

Tankless coil provides oceans of hot tap water for baths, kitchen & laundry

Tappings for optional electric back-up heat

For wood/coal

For oil or gas

Large cast-iron fuel & ash doors for easy loading & cleaning

Cast-iron shaker grates for ease in clearing coal or wood ash

Separate firebox for oil or gas gives highest possible combustion efficiencies

Crossdraft combustion firebox & pre-heated secondary air inlet combine for maximum combustion efficiency on wood or coal. You get more heat for your money & effort!

Courtesy HS TARM

**Fig. 2-16. Cutaway view of oil-fired/wood-fired boiler.**

Courtesy R.W. Beckett Corporation

**Fig. 2-17. Oil-fired hot-water boiler showing tankless coil for production of domestic hot water.**

35

and supplies the home with heated domestic hot water. The beauty of this system is that it operates without a hot-water storage tank, and the hot water developed is instantaneous.

## SUMMARY

All of today's modern heating systems incorporate elements such as combustion areas, piping, and controls that are basic to each unit. There are three basic types of oil heating systems: hot water, steam, and hot air. Modern forced hot-water systems depend on circulators to move the warmed products of combustion through the piping and radiation.

Boilers and furnaces are manufactured in either steel or cast iron and are generally constructed in two pieces: combustion area and heating area. Much of the older equipment was not designed for automatic firing. It may be converted, but a great deal of heat loss and inefficiency must be expected.

## REVIEW QUESTIONS

1. Name the three basic types of oil heating systems.
2. What is the purpose of the aquastat?
3. What equipment is used to maintain correct boiler steam pressure?
4. What is an airstat?
5. Can coal furnaces be converted satisfactorily to automatic oil-fired units? Explain the advantages or disadvantages.
6. In a forced warm-air furnace, the heated air is moved through the system and ducts by what method?
7. Steam systems operate with water to about the ¾ level in the boiler. Why?

# CHAPTER 3

# Combustion

The flames of oil burner combustion require a guiding hand to direct the resulting heat toward a full, useful, and effective peak. The combustion chamber is an engineered unit designed of brick, refractory, steel, or specialized material and placed by the heating contractor within the lower ashpit or combustion area of the boiler or furnace.

## COMBUSTION CHAMBERS

The operation of an oil burner can be no better than the performance of the combustion chamber. The benefits of this efficiently engineered unit are derived by homeowner and service mechanic alike. Lower operating costs, longer equipment life, fewer service calls, and the knowledge that one has done a workmanlike job well serve as the guiding spark toward top-notch combustion chamber installation.

The combustion chamber protects boiler-furnace surfaces from the high temperatures of combustion and prevents the oil burner flame from striking the relatively colder heating surfaces of the boiler. An oil-fired furnace operates at peak efficiency when fitted with a combustion chamber that swiftly reaches the high temperatures required for complete combustion. When oil is burned in the proper type of chamber, the wall surfaces actually reflect heat back into the flame, increasing the flame temperature, thus making for more complete and efficient combustion.

A well-constructed combustion chamber acts as a muffler to deaden the roaring sounds of combustion present in most units. All in all, the correct combustion chamber is a sound investment in relation to customers, service, and performance.

## Types of Combustion Chambers

There are many types of combustion chambers available for field service use. Each has its specific or multipurpose application. Their uses are governed by cost, installation ease, and the individual contractor's skills, preferences, and whims.

**Precast Refractory Combustion Chambers**—Precast refractory combustion chambers come in premolded sections that are assembled inside the ashpit or lower combustion area of the furnace or boiler. These chambers are composed of a number of pieces (two or more, according to the job size) and very often are specific for a special brand of boiler or furnace. These precast units are always sized for a specified gallons-per-hour firing rate, with a minimum and maximum rate governing the installation. For special boiler or furnace models, consult with the combustion chamber manufacturer for exact replacements. Various sizes and shapes of precast combustion chambers are shown in Figs. 3-1 through 3-7.

**Insulating Refractory Firebricks**—Firebricks are soft, lightweight, highly insulating, refractory units measuring, in most cases, 9 in. long × 2½ in. thick and 4 in. wide. These bricks allow the installer to custom-fit almost any job, for they may be cut, trimmed, whittled, or sawed to any shape of combustion area.

**Fig. 3-1. A large precast combustion chamber.**

Refractory bricks are matched by temperature to the gallon-per-hour firing rate for the specific job. Each manufacturer has his own specific numerical designation for purchasing, but as a rule of thumb the following schedule may be used:

Up to and including 4 gal. per hour—2000°F firebrick.
Up to and including 6 gal. per hour—2300°F firebrick.
Up to and including 30 gal. per hour—2600°F–3000°F firebrick.

**Preformed Stainless Steel Combustion Chambers**—This type of combustion chamber is often found preinstalled in boilers or furnaces, but they may also be purchased by the service mechanic for field installation. Lighter in weight than their refractory counterparts, and unbreakable during shipment, these fireboxes require free air space rather than backfill after installation.

These combustion chambers are purchased in the same way that precast refractory combustion chambers are, but closer contact must be made with the manufacturing supplier because the units must be sized to fit. These boxes will *not* fit every conversion installation, and they cannot be whittled into shape. Thus, greater measuring, estimating, and purchasing care must be exercised in the initial portion of the job.

Fig. 3-2. A square precast combustion chamber.

**On-the-Job Refractory Material**—Because of combustion area design, certain installations might not lend themselves to any of the previous firebox materials. For these "special" furnaces or boilers, an on-the-job refractory material is available with which a molded firebox may be poured—actually forming a poured-in-place combustion chamber. A form is set up within the ashpit or combustion area, and into this form, preworked and premixed refractory material is poured and allowed to set. When dry, the forms are removed and the cast refractory combustion chamber remains.

This refractory material, like firebrick or the precast combustion chamber, is purchased on the basis of the gallon-per-hour firing rate of the completed combustion chamber, and on the basis of the ability of the material to withstand the temperatures of combustion.

**Cerafelt**—Fresh from the experimental platforms of rockets and space missiles comes one of the newer materials, known commercially as *cerafelt*. Many furnaces with steel combustion chambers use a lining of this material to protect the steel firebox

40

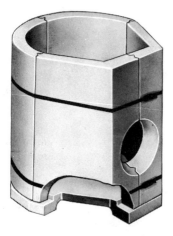

Fig. 3-3. A pear-shaped combustion chamber.

Fig. 3-4. A round combustion chamber.

41

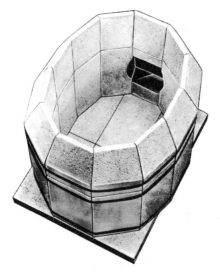

**Fig. 3-5. An oval combustion chamber.**

and deaden combustion noises. Installation and replacement of the material is easy and fast.

The oil burner must first be removed from its firing position on the boiler or furnace. Next, the front plate of the steel combustion chamber is taken out of the combustion area (if it is of the removable type). All old material is then cleaned out of the firebox.

The new combustion chamber material can now be installed in the combustion chamber. Some boiler and furnace manufacturers have the material cut to size to fit their various installations. Other chambers require that the cerafelt be cut to size specifically for the job.

Here is how the job is installed. The side walls are put into place first. The top edges of the combustion material are slid up and under any metal clips or corbel material at the top of the metal chamber. The back wall of material is put into place using the same top-holding technique. Next, the floor of combustion material is placed in the metal chamber. If the front metal piece has been removed, the combustion material is fitted to this sec-

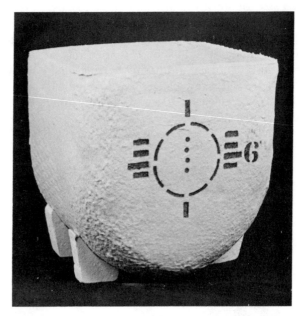

**Fig. 3-6. Precast combustion chamber for wet-base boilers.**

tion before replacing. If the front is not removable, the combustion material is placed in this area the same way as it was on the side and back walls. However, the floor material should be put in place after all wall areas are up. If required, cut out a properly sized hole for the oil burner.

Finally, all the combustion material is painted with the liquid hardener that accompanies the individual combustion chamber kit or material. Reassemble the oil burner to the boiler or furnace using new gaskets or asbestos cement around the burner opening. Connect any piping and electrical wiring that was disconnected. Test-fire the oil burner and make sure that the unit is properly adjusted.

## Combustion Chamber Size

There are a number of methods used to arrive at the correct gallon-per-hour (GPH) firing rate and matching combustion chamber size for any given installation. This sizing step is equally as important to a good combustion chamber as proper choice of materials or careful workmanlike attention to design details. Too large or too small a combustion chamber may waste fuel, produce combustion noises, and permit troublesome carbon formations. Here are but a few calculating methods. Experience will guide the service mechanic to a choice of the most adaptable one for the particular job.

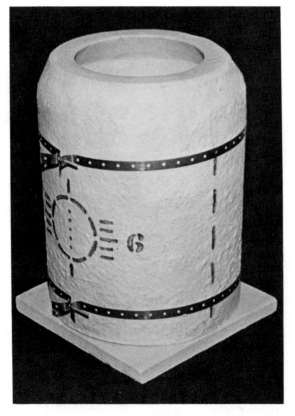

Fig. 3-7. Precast combustion chamber with corbel at top.

44

## Method No. 1

1. Total up the Btu heat loss of each room or the Btu output of each radiator, baseboard strip, convector, or register in the house.

2. Add to this total figure an allowance, as noted below, for piping pickup and loss and duct loss figure:

   Forced warm-air units—(large) 15%; (small) 20%
   Forced hot-water units—(large) 20%; (small) 30%
   Gravity hot-water units—(large) 30%; (small) 40%

3. Divide this total figure by 100,000 (this represents the Btu per gallons at 73% efficiency). The resulting figure will be the gallon-per-hour firing rate and matching firebox size.
   *Example:*
   Total house Btu heat loss—70,000 Btu. Forced hot-water unit (small)—add 30% for pickup and loss—21,000 Btu. Total house Btu heat loss *plus* pickup and loss figure: 91,000 Btu.
   Divide 91,000 by 100,000 to obtain a .91 gallon-per-hour (GPH) firing rate. This rate can now be matched to the correct firebox size from information in Table 3-1.

## Method No. 2

1. Total up the Btu heat loss of each room or the Btu output of each radiator, baseboard strip, convector, or register in the house.

2a. For forced hot-water systems, divide the total Btu heat loss by 75,000. The resulting figure will be the gallons-per-hour (GPH) firing rate and matching firebox size for the job (see Table 3-1).

2b. For forced warm-air systems, divide the total Btu heat loss by 75,000. The resulting figure will be the gallons-per-hour (GPH) firing rate and matching combustion chamber size for the job (see Table 3-1).

2c. For steam systems:

## Table 3-1. Combustion Chamber Specifications

| Gallons Per Hour | Rectangular | | | Round | | Nozzle Height from Chamber Floor |
|---|---|---|---|---|---|---|
| | Width | Length | Height | Diameter | Height | |
| .75 | 8 | 9 | 14 | 9½ | 14 | 6 |
| 1.00 | 9½ | 10 | 14 | 11 | 14 | 6 |
| 1.25 | 10 | 12 | 14 | 12½ | 14 | 6 |
| 1.35 | 11 | 12 | 16 | 13 | 16 | 7 |
| 1.50 | 11 | 13 | 16 | 13½ | 16 | 7 |
| 1.65 | 12 | 13 | 16 | 14 | 16 | 7 |
| 1.75 | 12 | 14 | 16 | 14½ | 16 | 7 |
| 2.00 | 13 | 15 | 16 | 15½ | 16 | 7 |
| 2.25 | 13 | 16 | 16 | 16½ | 16 | 8 |
| 2.50 | 14 | 17 | 17 | 17½ | 17 | 8 |
| 3.00 | 15 | 19 | 18 | 19 | 18 | 8 |
| 3.50 | 16 | 20 | 18 | 20½ | 18 | 8 |
| 4.00 | 18 | 21 | 18 | 22 | 18 | 9 |
| 5.00 | 19 | 24 | 19 | 24 | 19 | 9 |
| 6.00 | 21 | 26 | 20 | 27 | 20 | 10 |
| 7.00 | 23 | 28 | 21 | 29 | 21 | 11 |
| 8.00 | 25 | 30 | 22 | 31 | 22 | 12 |
| 9.00 | 26 | 32 | 22 | 33 | 22 | 13 |
| 10.00 | 27 | 34 | 22 | 35 | 22 | 13 |

(i) Figure 1 gallon per hour for each 200 sq. ft. of standing radiation or measured heat loss and ⅓ gallon per hour for each additional 100 sq. ft. (of measured heat loss).

(ii) Figure 1 gallon per hour for each 48,000 Btu of measured heat loss or standing radiation and ⅓ gallon per hour for each additional 16,000 Btu (of measured heat loss).

No matter what style of combustion chamber is chosen, three installation principles should be followed for a well-done "seal of self-approval" job.

1. Choose the correct size chamber—not excessively underfired nor excessively overfired—but fired just right for the installation.
2. Buy from a reputable company, using the finest possible materials.
3. Install the firebox according to the manufacturer's specs, instructions, or combustion chamber guide.

4. The engineers at Monogram Products Co., Philadelphia, Pennsylvania, suggest the following guidelines for maximum combustion chamber efficiency. They recommend designing combustion chambers for definite firing rates. A hearth area of between 80 and 95 sq. in. per gallon per hour is recommended. If hearth or internal firebox area is less than 80 sq. in. per gallon per hour, the combustion chamber will be punished; its life will be reduced and flame impingement may occur. In instances where less than 80 sq. in. per gallon per hour *must be used*, it is necessary to design a lower combustion chamber. Hearth areas of more than 95 sq. in. per gallon per hour will result in relatively cool chamber wall temperatures (less than 180°F) and a $CO_2$ of less than 10 percent.

After the correct gallon-per-hour (GPH) firing rate has been established, the next step is to design the combustion chamber to this proper firing size. The information in Table 3-1 is given for your convenience. Consult manufacturer's spec sheets where possible.

Typical measurement points for various combustion chambers are shown in Fig. 3-8.

## Firebox Installation

**Preinstallation**—Before installing any firebox, no matter what style, type, or size, the following preinstallation procedures should be followed. This holds true whether the job is a new, a conversion, or a replacement installation. A little preparation will go a long way toward making the job easier, quicker, cleaner, and better. See Fig. 3-9.

*Step 1.* Remove the boiler or furnace stovepipe and clean completely before replacing.

*Step 2.* Clean the chimney completely, including the breeching area.

*Step 3.* Clean all boiler flue passages, side walls, etc. It is much easier to do any job in a clean work area.

*Step 4.* Remove all dampers and other obstructions to the free flow of combustion gases.

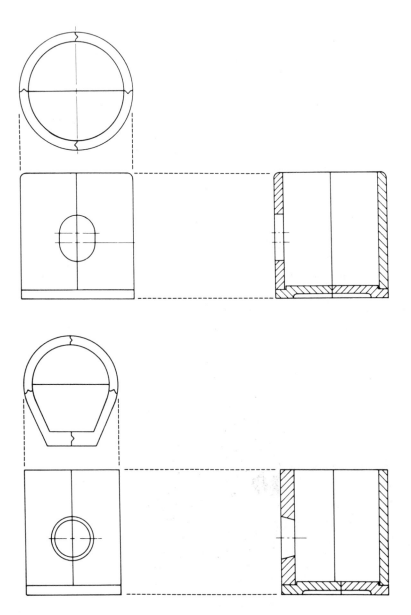

Fig. 3-8. Typical measurement points

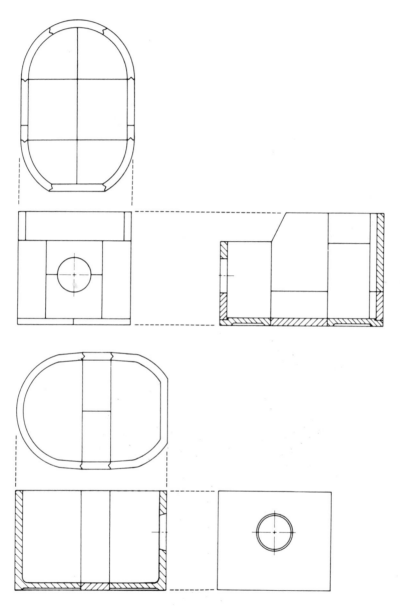

for various combustion chambers.

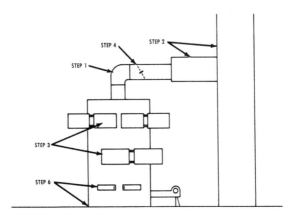

**Fig. 3-9. Preinstallation checkpoints.**

*Step 5.* Remove ashpit doors, ashpit door frames, grates, and grate-bearing surfaces, if any. Removal of these items will facilitate installation and permit the largest possible construction area.

*Step 6.* Seal all boiler joints, sections, cleanout doors, and the boiler base area with furnace cement to close off air leaks.

**Installation Techniques**—Precast refractory, stainless-steel, and other preformed and partially formed fireboxes arrive on the job with instructions or are so designed that they may be set up outside the boiler or furnace combustion area prior to installation. This "outside setting up" gives the workman a good idea of the installation method, for it is fairly repetitious to rebuild the same box within the combustion area. Firebrick combustion chamber design and installation, on the other hand, does not follow the same pattern for each job. Therefore, a definite step-by-step procedure for simplicity of installation must be followed.

*Step 1.* Lay the bricks in place within the combustion area, extending them under the front, side, and back walls of the designed firebox (For a firing rate of up to 7 GPH, use 2½-in. brick—for a firing rate of over 7 GPH, use 4-in. or 5 in. brick.)

*Step 2.* Build up the front, back, and side walls in progressive layers, following the same "stagger" method used by bricklayers. For small and medium fireboxes, the walls need be only 2½ in. thick, while 4½ in. would be best suited to larger installations. Remember to leave a measured opening in the front wall for the oiler burner tube.

*Step 3.* Build up the front wall area even with the metal boiler or furnace surfaces using firebrick cut to size. Finish off this area with asbestos cement.

*Step 4.* Backfill the area between the firebox walls and the boiler surfaces with mica pellets, tamping them down well during the pouring process. Do not use sand, old broken bricks, or other old material.

*Step 5.* Insert the oil burner tube into the firebox and fill any open spaces with bits of firebrick cut to size. Fill in any remaining spaces with asbestos cement. Make sure that the gun tube, when set in place, is about ½ in. forward of the brick face.

*Step 6.* Always use a good grade of refractory mortar between each brick joint. Corbel or build "step" overhangs on the back wall where possible. Corbelling is a form of baffling of the brickwork at the rear wall of the combustion chamber. A target wall is formed for the flame to rebound off of in order to prevent short-circuiting. On certain conversion installations, it may also be necessary to *baffle* the job in order to cope with poor construction, or where the flue passes are almost directly in line with the combustion chamber. Use a combustion testing instrument when you baffle a boiler. Make sure not to overbaffle. Retarder spirals, firebricks, and special devices purchased at equipment supply houses are used for baffling projects. These devices are usually placed in boiler uptake sections to "short-circuit" the direct flow of combustion heat from the firebox directly to the chimney. When the firebox is completed, operate the burner for a few minutes and then allow it to remain idle for a while. Repeat this process a number of times before placing the burner in regular operation.

## Troubleshooting

The combustion chamber is the heart of the entire oil burner unit, and as such it affects and is affected by many component parts. These parts, such as fuel pumps, nozzles, and draft conditions, must also be reckoned with in a troubleshooting program. See the troubleshooting chart at the end of this chapter.

# CHIMNEYS

Oil heating equipment that is supplied with the correct fuel and is properly designed for efficient combustion requires, in most cases*, a means of disposing of certain portions of the combustion process. This means is generally an integral part of the house or building, and is the common chimney. It is in the chimney that, through the action of the hot gases of combustion, a draft is created. Draft is simply a current of air in motion. The heated air of combustion expands, becomes lighter, and rises up the chimney. The colder, heavier, outside air fills in the void, and motion results. Provided that certain conditions are *just right,* the draft motion is automatic and troublefree. However, service problems begin to arise when these conditions are not perfect. These conditions include:

1. Improper construction of the chimney.
2. Chimney leakage.
3. Chimney obstructions.
4. Air deflecting surfaces: higher roofs, trees, etc.
5. Inadequate ventilation in the boiler room.
6. Broken chimney tiles.
7. Fireplace short-circuiting the chimney system.
8. Another heating unit incorrectly connected to the same chimney.
9. Chimney too small.
10. Incorrect composition of flue gases.

---

*Oil heating equipment such as certain space heaters can function without a connected chimney.

11. Restricted chimney opening.
12. Insufficient thickness of brick on outside of chimney.

It is vital that all the conditions listed, as well as those illustrated in Fig. 3-10, be checked and corrected for good draft and equipment operation.

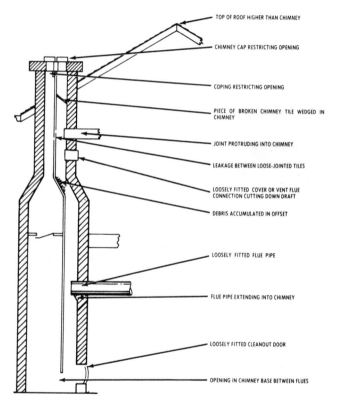

Fig. 3-10. Chimney defects.

One of the first areas to check is the chimney size in relation to the particular installation. Each manufacturer has his own particular specifications, but Tables 3-2, 3-3, and 3-4 will provide guidance if no others are available.

## Table 3-2. Gross Boiler Output in Relation to Chimney Size

| Gross Boiler Output | Rectangular Tile | Round Tile | Minimum Height |
|---|---|---|---|
| 144,000 | 8½″ × 8½″ | 8″ | 26 |
| 235,000 | 8½″ × 13″ | 10″ | 30 |
| 374,000 | 13″ × 13″ | 12″ | 35 |
| 516,000 | 13″ × 18″ | | 40 |
| 612,000 | | 15″ | 45 |
| 768,000 | 18″ × 18″ | | 50 |
| 960,000 | 20″ × 20″ | 18″ | 55 |

## Table 3-3. Gallons Per Hour in Relation to Chimney Size

| Gallons Per Hour | Rectangular Tile | Round Tile | Minimum Height |
|---|---|---|---|
| .75– 1.75 | 8″ ×12″ | 9″ | 28 |
| 1.75– 3.00 | 12″ × 12″ | 10″ | 28 |
| 3.00– 4.00 | 12″ × 12″ | 10″ | 30 |
| 4.00– 6.00 | 12″ × 16″ | 12″ | 35 |
| 6.00– 9.00 | 16″ × 16″ | 14″ | 35 |
| 9.00–12.00 | 16″ × 20″ | 16″ | 40 |
| 12.00–16.00 | 20″ × 20″ | 18″ | 45 |
| 16.00–21.00 | 20″ × 24″ | 20″ | 45 |

## Table 3-4. Altitude as It Relates to Chimney Height

| Height Above Level (feet) | Ratio Increase In Diameter | Ratio Increase In Height |
|---|---|---|
| 0 | 1.00 | 1.00 |
| 1000 | 1.015 | 1.08 |
| 1000 | 1.03 | 1.17 |
| 4000 | 1.06 | 1.36 |
| 6000 | 1.10 | 1.58 |
| 8000 | 1.13 | 1.84 |

# DRAFT

There are two types of draft. One is *natural,* such as that created by normal chimney and combustion action, while the other is mechanical, or *forced* by a motor-drive fan. Natural draft is subject to wide fluctuations caused by weather, the chimney, and the condition of the particular heating installation. It is important that the draft on the job be kept as constant as possible. The volume of fuel delivered by the nozzle, as will be noted later, is constant. It is necessary that the volume of air mixed with this fuel be kept constant too. In order to maintain draft consistency, a *draft regulator* (Figs. 3-11 and 3-12) should be installed.

Courtesy Field, Division of Heico, Inc.

**Fig. 3-11. Heating unit draft control installed on flue pipe.**

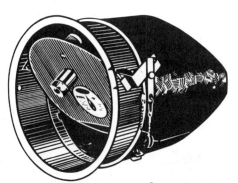

Courtesy Field, Division of Heico, Inc.

**Fig. 3-12. Heating unit draft control showing gate/regulator in operation. Unit regulates updraft and opens outward to relieve reverse draft pressure.**

This device automatically removes the fluctuations found on most installations. The regulator is adjusted so that the unit will have a draft of not less than .02 in. in the combustion chamber with the oil burner running.

It is of the utmost importance to install the draft regulator in the correct location. Fig. 3-13 illustrates the best locations as well as poor or incorrect locations.

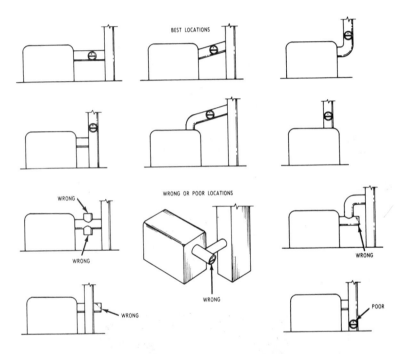

Fig. 3-13. Positioning a draft regulator.

Downdrafts are to be avoided to prevent inefficient operation and to prevent fumes from being blown back into the furnace area. A chimney hood or cap (Fig. 3-14) can be used in certain installations to minimize downdrafts caused by nearby roofs or high trees. Also available are prefabricated chimneys (Figs. 3-15 and 3-16), which are being used more and more. These prebuilt units are usually equipped with a cap.

56

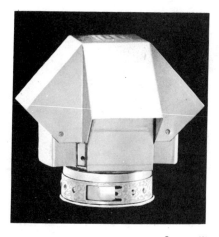

Courtesy Wm. Wallace Company

Fig. 3-14. A typical chimney cap.

## FLUE DAMPER AND BURNER AIR-CONTROL DEVICES

It is an established fact that warm air, which weighs less than cold air, rises. After a period of oil burner operation, the air mixture in the combustion chamber and in the boiler or furnace becomes heated. It flows through the heating system, out the flue pipe, and up the chimney. The speed with which the heated air moves depends on the draft generated by the residence's chimney and other factors detailed elsewhere in this book. This in turn depends on external factors such as climate, wind, temperature, and location. As the heated air moves out of the combustion/furnace-boiler areas, it draws in cooler air from the surrounding cellar. This inflow or replacement of cool air cools down the metal body of the furnace or boiler and with it the water or air within the heating system. The end result is waste because on the very next call for heat, it will take additional time (and fuel) to warm up the cooled down furnace-boiler parts and the interior products that convey the heat through the entire residence.

Manufacturers have come up with a number of solutions to this

57

**Fig. 3-15. Chimney draft inducer designed to create an adequate draft.**

problem. They have devised motor-operated flue damper controls. As soon as a residence ceases its demand for heat and the oil burner shuts down, an electronic signal is sent to a motor-drive device located on the flue pipe. This mechanism closes a damper inside the flue pipe, cutting off the flow of air up the chimney from the combustion chamber and warm-hot surfaces of the boiler or furnace. Once this flow or draw is cut off, there is no longer a call for fresh, cool air, which would instantly lower the temperature of the internal heating system parts. The metal boiler-furnace body and the internal fluid or air remain warm longer. The mechanized flue dampers are designed to be "failsafe." If the electricity should go off during operation or some other problem develop, the flue damper will either not allow the oil burner to turn on upon a demand for heat or will automatically go into an "open" position.

Other manufacturers have developed built-in burner airflow-control mechanisms for their oil burners. There are a number of different designs. Some are made specifically for the individual oil burner, and some may be fitted to units currently operating in the field. One company, for example, has a simple metal gate

**Fig. 3-16. A prefabricated chimney with cap.**

damper built in and ahead of the burner fan air supply system. When the oil burner operates, the fan blows its air supply, and the gate damper swings open from the air pressure. After the oil burner completes its cycle and the blower turns off, the gate closes and the flow of air through the system is cut off. Still another oil burner firm has a centrifugal shutter positioned inside the housing, ahead of the air supplying fan. In the *off* position, the shutter completely seals off the blower air supply opening. When the oil burner starts up, centrifugal force spins the shutter, and it opens wide, allowing the blower air to flow through the housing to the combustion area. When the burner shuts off, the shutter closes down and cuts off all airflow through the boiler or furnace.

Both of these internal draft control units require minimal maintenance. It is possible for a part to stick or wear out after a long period of use, however; and both types can be replaced simply. In an emergency, both devices can be forced into an open position, and the oil burner can function normally until a new unit is put into place.

# COMBUSTION TESTING

The techniques used to achieve high combustion efficiency rest with the proper use of modern test instruments. A complete understanding of the reasoning, the methods, and the interpretation of results attained during these tests is absolutely necessary for proper adjustment and the most effective operation of modern oil heating equipment.

The aim of "total combustion testing" is to accurately measure the $CO_2$ content, the temperature and degree of smoke present in the flue gases, and the intensity of the draft. Assemble these figures according to the accompanying rules and instructions. Make the necessary changes and settings according to tried and tested techniques outlined later in the book. The results obtained will be the most perfect combustion obtainable with any given equipment. The combustion testing techniques outlined here are applicable to any oil heating equipment.

Four instruments are used in combustion testing: the *draft gauge*, the $CO_2$ indicator, the *stack thermometer*, and the *smoke tester*. They are shown in Figs. 3-17 and 3-18.

## Draft Gauge

Draft is most important to any oil burner operation. Figures indicate that, although draft is actually not used as a scale of combustion efficiency, it is very important to efficient unit operation.

When an oil burner is in operation, combustion gases are produced. These gases (400°F and up) are hot, expandable, and weigh less per cubic foot of volume than colder surrounding air masses. As a result, the hot, lighter gases are pushed into a flow up the chimney by the pressures of relatively colder and heavier outside air volumes. As soon as the combustion gases are formed, therefore, a temperature difference and an expansion process occur, followed by a general replacement of air volumes and subsequent motion of air called *draft*. A *draft gauge* (Fig. 3-19) is used to measure the intensity of this flow, either up or down the smoke pipe into the combustion area.

Draft, which is the movement of these gases, may be retarded

Courtesy United Technologies Bacharach

**Fig. 3-17. Combustion test instruments.**

by a leaking or poorly constructed chimney, or by improper openings for other equipment. The pull of a chimney may be governed by its relative height, as can its ability to handle specific volumes by its cross-sectional area.

**How to Use**—The following is the proper procedure to follow to measure draft:

1. Place the gauge on any convenient level surface near the boiler or furnace for ease of interpretation. (This is for units requiring leveling before use.)
2. Adjust the draft gauge to zero. (See the manufacturer's instructions.)
3. Drill a ¼-in. hole in both the smoke pipe and the fire door.
4. Allow the boiler or furnace to operate for a while before starting the test procedure.

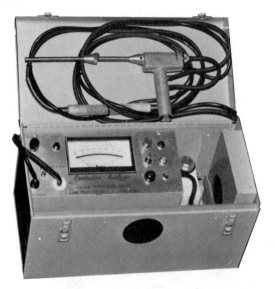

Fig. 3-18. Combination combustion analyzer kit tests heating unit's oxygen, temperature, and smoke output all at one time.

Fig. 3-19. A draft gauge.

5. Insert the sensing end of the draft gauge into the test holes. See Fig. 3-20. Read the draft gauge results.

**Interpreting Results**—Two important readings are indicators of draft conditions. The first is the overfire reading and the second is the chimney draft reading.

A poor or low draft condition will find the boiler or furnace operating with a possible back pressure, boiler pulsation, odors, noise, loose soot, and an overall reduction in oil burner capacity and efficiency. In order to maintain a constant and correct draft reading, it is suggested that an automatic draft regulator be installed on the job. This regulator should be "instrument set" to the correct draft reading for the particular job.

An *overfire draft reading* of not less than .02 in. of water may be considered sufficient to develop and maintain proper combustion.

## $CO_2$ Indicator

The key to any successful oil burner "physical" is the $CO_2$ test of the flue gas. A $CO_2$ (carbon dioxide) indicating instrument (Fig. 3-21) draws up a sample of the combustion gases. If the results are low, it is an indication that the fuel has not burned completely and that adjustments are required. Although the $CO_2$ indicator should be used in conjunction with all of the other combustion testing devices, a special comparative analysis chart using the stack temperature and $CO_2$ content is used to chart an oil burner's operational efficiency.

Courtesy United Technologies Bacharach

**Fig. 3-20. Checking draft with a gauge.**

**Fig. 3-21. A CO₂ tester.**

**How to Use**—Six easy steps must be taken to ensure an accurate $CO_2$ test.

1. Drill a ¼-in. hole in the smokestack. The hole must be directly in the path of the hot gases, no more than 12 in. from the boiler breeching, and away from the draft regulator. Another test hole of the same size should be made in the fire door of the boiler or furnace.

2. The $CO_2$ indicator must be adjusted to *zero* on its scale before use. The best way to accomplish this is to place the instrument on a level surface so that the scale may be accurately set at the proper mark. When the tester has been carried in the service truck during cool weather, allow time for the indicator fluid to warm up before use.

3. Turn the oil burner on and allow it to run before starting the test.

4. Insert the metal sampling tube into the hole drilled in the smokestack. The rubber cap end is placed on the top (plunger valve) of the $CO_2$ instrument, and the valve is held in a depressed position. This is shown in Fig. 3-22. The tester's rubber bulb is next squeezed 18 times in succession. On the 18th squeeze, the depressed plunger valve is released before releasing the squeeze bulb.

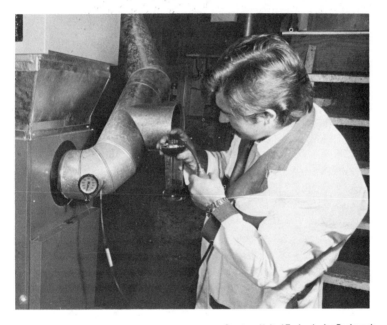

Fig. 3-22. Checking flue gases with a $CO_2$ tester.

5. The indicating instrument is now turned over twice, permitting the test fluid to run back and forth, and forcing it to absorb the gas sample. This turnover motion is the same action one might make with an hour-glass or egg timer. The indicator glass is next held at a 45°angle to permit the test

fluid to drain completely down from all parts of the instrument. This motion helps ensure an accurate reading.

6. The indicator is placed or held in an upright, level position, and the test liquid is read on the scale in percent of $CO_2$.

The six steps outlined above are now repeated, but this time using the hole drilled in the fire door. For the fire-door test to be completely accurate, an extra-long metal sampling tube must be connected in place on the short one. The longer tube will eliminate the possibility of the test picking up stray or inaccurate samples around the door or from the area not in the combustion zone of the boiler. Run through the above series of tests several times to assure accurate readings.

**Interpreting Results**—The highest possible $CO_2$ reading should always be the goal (with satisfactory smoke ratings considered). When simple adjustments are possible, $CO_2$ of about 10 percent (No. 2 smoke) may be considered satisfactory during an efficiency check. If major adjustments must be made, the following rules may be used:

*Where the net flue-gas temperatures are less than 400°F, a $CO_2$ reading of as low as 8% may be considered satisfactory. Where the net flue gases are over 500°F, a $CO_2$, reading of at least 9% to 10% should be the target.*

A low $CO_2$ reading is an indication of one or more of the following conditions. Check for and correct the condition if possible.

1. High draft.
2. Excess air.
3. Air leakage.
4. Incorrect or defective firebox.
5. Poor fuel-oil atomization.
6. Worn, plugged, or incorrect nozzle.
7. Furnace or boiler has air leaks.
8. Incorrect air-handling parts.
9. Draft regulator improperly installed or sticking.
10. Oil pressure incorrectly set.

If too great a difference occurs between the tests run in the smokestack and at the fire door, an air leak or other unsatisfactory combustion condition exists in the boiler or furnace.

## Stack Thermometer

The modern oil burner serviceman, armed with a stack thermometer, can take the temperature of a furnace or a boiler just as the doctor does of a patient. Any abnormal reading indicates that something is amiss and requires attention.

A *stack thermometer* is an instrument used in the heating industry to determine the condition of the heating industry patient. It is used in conjunction with other heating efficiency tools to diagnose and solve afflictions of the combustion process.

The stack thermometer comes in a number of styles and varieties. Some units are designed somewhat like the common fever thermometers—long and thin, but protected by a metal jacket. Others have a round recording dial (Fig. 3-23) with a sensing stem for insertion into the flue pipe area. They record temperatures from about 200°F to 1000°F, with special variations on special order.

**How to Use**—A stack thermometer is used as follows:

1. Drill a ¼ in. hole in the smoke pipe or use the one previously drilled for other test instruments. This hole should

Fig. 3-23. A stack thermometer.

be about 12 in. from the boiler breeching, directly in the path of the hot gases, and away from the draft regulator.

2. Turn the oil burner on and allow it to operate a few minutes before beginning the test.

3. Insert the thermometer stem or sensing mechanism into the test hole. See Fig. 3-24. If it is of the clip-holding type, use the clip to secure it to the smokestack.

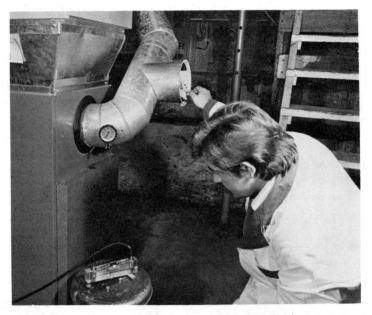

Courtesy United Technologies Bacharach

Fig. 3-24. Checking flue temperature with a stack thermometer.

4. Read the stack thermometer, noting the temperature recorded on the dial when the mercury or pointer has become constant and ceases to rise.

5. For a final determination of the true stack temperature, subtract the basement air temperature from the stack reading; e.g., stack reading 700°F, basement temperature 60°F. The reading is then 700°F − 60°F = 640°F.

Interpreting Results—As a rule of thumb, stack temperature readings over the following figures may be considered higher than normal. The higher readings are cause for special concern and adjustment. Consult the manufacturer's spec sheets for individual units.

Conversion units—600°F to 700°F
Packaged units—400°F to 500°F

A high stack temperature may indicate any of the following conditions. These should be immediately checked and remedied if the target is peak efficiency.

1. Excessive draft through boiler.
2. Dirty, carbonized boiler heating surfaces.
3. Lack of sufficient boiler baffling.
4. Undersized boiler.
5. Poor combustion chamber.
6. Large flue passages.
7. Boiler overfired.
8. Boiler not suited to automatic firing.
9. Improper adjustment of draft regulator.

Make sure before using the stack thermometer that the stem is straight and not bent—a bent tube might indicate a defective unit. Be sure that the indicating pointer rests on the *No Reading* area before starting the test.

## Smoke Tester

A *smoke tester* and the smoke scale indicator (Fig. 3-25) that accompanies each tester can give the service mechanic an indication of the smoke content of any installation. Combustion smoke has long been recognized as an indication of wasteful, incomplete, and inefficient operation. It goes hand in hand with soot formations. A soot buildup on the heating surfaces will not only mean waste (e.g., ⅛ in. of soot may reduce heat absorption by as much as 10 percent), but can also be the cause of a great number of other service difficulties.

The objective of this test is to measure the smoke content of an oil heating installation, and then in conjunction with other combustion test results, to set the burner operation according to read-ings on an indicated smoke scale that accompanies the smoke test instrument. The scale that is always used with the smoke test instrument consists of a unit containing 10 color-graded spots. Each spot is color coded from 0 (pure white) to 9 (the darkest smoke obtainable on a completely defective installation).

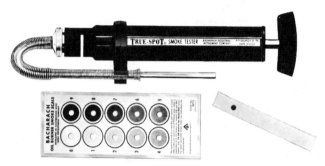

Courtesy United Technologies Bacharach

**Fig. 3-25. A smoke tester.**

**How to Use**—The proper procedure for using the smoke tester is as follows:

1. With the oil burner running, insert the sampling tube end of the tester into a ¼-in. hole drilled into the boiler flue outlet.
2. Place a clean piece of standard-grade filter paper into the "holding slot" of the instrument.
3. Pull the smoke tester handle through 10 full pump strokes (Fig. 3-26), holding for several seconds between each pump stroke.
4. Remove sample filter paper from the instrument holding slot.
5. Compare with the smoke scale indicator, matching the sample with the closest color on the smoke scale.
6. During cold weather, warm the smoke test pump to room temperature before using.

**Interpreting Results**—Here is what the smoke scale indicator numbers will illustrate about the unit's performance:

70

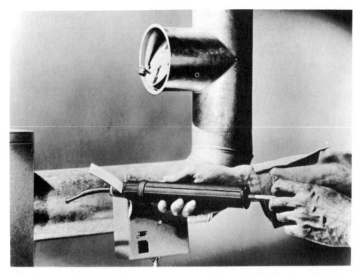

**Fig. 3-26. Checking flue gas smoke with a smoke tester.**

1. *Smoke Scale Reading 1.* Excellent. Little if any sooting of furnace or boiler surfaces.
2. *Smoke Scale Reading 2.* Good. May be slight sooting of furnace or boiler, but little if any increase in flue-gas temperature.
3. *Smoke Scale Reading 3.* Fair. Substantial sooting with some types of furnace and boilers, but rarely will require cleaning more than once a year.
4. *Smoke Scale Reading 4.* Poor. This is a borderline smoke. Some units may soot only moderately, but others may soot rapidly.
5. *Smoke Scale Reading 5.* Very poor. Heavy sooting in all cases. May require cleaning several times during the heating season.

The following is a checklist of the prime causes of smoky combustion. When a poor smoke scale reading is obtained during a combustion test, go over these pointers and attempt to eliminate the trouble spots. Remember that while a lack of smoke may

71

always indicate clean combustion, it does not necessarily mean completely efficient combustion. All tests must receive equal consideration. Soot checklist:

1. Improper fan delivery.
2. Insufficient draft.
3. Poor fuel supply.
4. Oil pump not functioning properly.
5. Nozzle defective.
6. Air leaks in boiler.
7. Poor burner oil supply.
8. Firebox defective.
9. Draft regulator out of adjustment.
10. Improper burner air-handling parts.

## Calculating Efficiency

The graph in Fig. 3-27 shows the efficiency at various $CO_2$ and stack temperature readings. Enter the $CO_2$ reading, using the figures at the extreme right-hand side of the graph. Enter the temperature readings, using the vertical figures at the top or bottom of the graph. Read the percent efficiency where these two points intersect, using the percentage scale at the extreme left-hand side of the graph.

# COMBUSTION CHAMBER TROUBLES

*Symptom and Possible Cause*          *Possible Remedy*

### Carbon Formation in Combustion Chamber

1. Wrong nozzle spray pattern.
2. Wrong nozzle angle.

1. Change to correct nozzle.

2. Change to nozzle with correct angle.

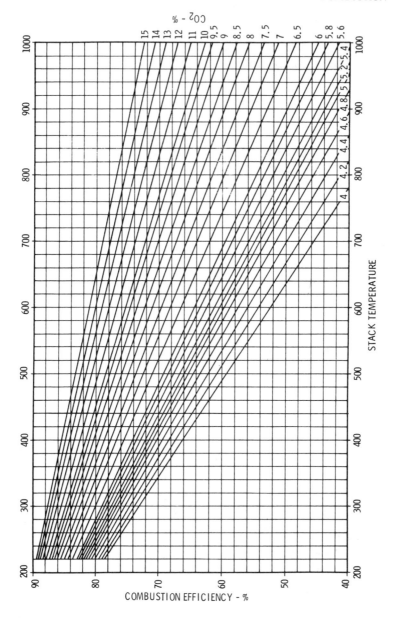

Fig. 3-27. Combustion efficiency.

*Symptom and Possible Cause*    *Possible Remedy*

## Carbon Forming on Back Walls of Combustion Chamber

1. Defective or crumbling firebox.

1. Repair or install new firebox.

## Carbon Forming on Side Walls and/or Floor of Combustion Chamber

1. Firebox undersized for GPH firing rate.

1. Change to correct-size nozzle.

## Firebox Collapsing or Falling Apart

1. Incorrect temperature brick used for job.

1. Replace with brick matched to the GPH firing rate.

## Firebox Floor Deteriorating and Walls Falling In

1. Poor grade of refractory material.

1. Replace with name brand product.

## Firebox Walls Splitting

1. Water in contact with firebox.

1. Remove source of water or provide proper drainage.

## Bricks Loosening or Shifting or Backfill Spilling into Firebox

1. Sections installed incorrectly.
2. Brickwork laid up incorrectly.

1. Check service manual instructions.
2. Check service manual for proper bricking method.

74

*Symptom and Possible Cause*     *Possible Remedy*

## Smoky Flame in Firebox

1. Nozzle too large for firebox.

1. Replace with correct-size nozzle.

## Smoke from Sighting Door or Around Cleanout Door

1. Wrong spray pattern.

2. Brick or carbon chunk in front of nozzle.
3. Firebox too small for heating requirements.

1. Replace nozzle with one having correct pattern.
2. Clean out and repair as necessary.
3. Replace with correct size.

## Noisy Flame

1. Firebox undersized for existing firing rate.
2. Chamber not built correctly.
3. Nozzle pattern not matched to firebox shape.
4. Wrong type of firebrick used.

1. Replace nozzle with correct size.
2. Consult service manual and rebuild correctly.
3. Change to nozzle with correct pattern.

4. Check service manual and rebuild with correct material.

## Low CO$_2$ Reading

1. Incorrectly sized firebox.

2. Incorrectly designed firebox.
3. Defective firebox.

1. Consult manufacturer's specs and rebuild.
2. Check service manual and rebuild correctly.
3. Rebuild.

## High Stack Temperature

1. Incorrectly designed firebox.

1. Check service manual and rebuild correctly.

*Symptom and Possible Cause*        *Possible Remedy*

**High Stack Temperature Cont.**

2. Defective firebox.
3. Incorrectly sized firebox.

2. Rebuild.
3. Check service manual and rebuild.

**Firing Tube Assembly Deteriorates Rapidly; Electrodes Carbonize Frequently; Nozzle Carbonizes and Plugs Up Rapidly; Blast Tube Burns Out; Electrode Holders Melt; Electrode Wires or Insulation Burn or Melt at Nozzle End**

1. Gun tube of the oil burner projecting too far into combustion chamber.

1. Repair or replace defective parts and reset tube about ½ in. inside face of chamber.

**Acrid Odor from Firebox Area**

1. Excessive air being admitted.
2. Brick or carbon in front of nozzle.

1. Adjust for correct air mixture.
2. Remove obstruction and repair if necessary.

**Oil-Fume Odor from Firebox Area**

1. Flame too large for firebox.
2. Improper draft.

1. Replace nozzle with one of correct GPH rating.
2. Check chimney for leaks or downdraft. Correct as necessary.

# SUMMARY

The operation of an oil furnace can be no better than the performance of the combustion chamber. When oil is burned in the proper type of chamber, the wall surface actually reflects heat back into the flame, increasing the flame temperature, making a more complete and efficient combustion.

There are many kinds of combustion chambers available for field service use. Their uses are governed by cost, installation ease, and preference. Combustion chambers are also designed to meet various degrees of temperature.

Chimneys are used not only to dispose of harmful gases but also to ensure efficient combustion. There are two types of draft; one is natural and the other is forced. Draft should be kept as constant as possible, and in order to maintain this consistency a draft regulator should be installed. There is a relation between the chimney size and the gross output of the boiler or the gallons-per-hour (GPH) firing rate of the oil burner.

The aim of total combustion testing is accurately measuring the $CO_2$ content, the temperature of the flue gases and the amount of smoke present in the flue. An overfire draft reading of not less then 0.2 in. of water may be considered sufficient to develop and maintain proper combustion.

# REVIEW QUESTIONS

1. Name the four instruments used in combustion testing.
2. What governs the type of combustion chamber used?
3. Explain why combustion chamber size is important and how you determine proper size.
4. What three installation principles should be followed when assembling a combustion chamber?
5. Why will a tight form-fitted firebox act as a muffler for the sound of combustion?
6. Why does good combustion require a high-temperature flame?
7. What happens to combustion when a chimney is not constructed properly?

8. Name the two types of draft and explain their operation.
9. Can a leaking chimney be a detriment to combustion, and if so, why?
10. Explain the use of a draft gauge.
11. Explain why an air leak in the boiler or furnace can be the cause of smoky combustion.
12. The smoke tester gives the service mechanic an indication of what?
13. Conversion units should have a stack temperature range of how many degrees?
14. What indicator is used to determine temperature and draft conditions of a heating unit?
15. Where should the stack thermometer be placed to get an accurate reading during combustion testing?

# CHAPTER 4

# Oil Burners

There are a great many oil burners both on the market and operating in the field today. Some are brand new, and some are well over a quarter of a century old. Hundreds of firms manufacture oil burner equipment, and hundreds more purchase component parts and assemble the units.

It should be noted at the start of this discussion that the term "oil burner" is neither correct nor descriptive of the mechanical equipment used to burn fuel oil in the combustion process. An oil burner only *prepares* the fuel oil for combustion. The actual burning or combustion process takes place in the combustion chamber or firebox area. The oil burner component parts (fuel pump, nozzle, etc.) spray or break up the fuel into tiny globules, mix air with these globules in the proper proportion, turbulate this mixture, and ignite the fuel for combustion. The term oil burner, however, is in such common use in the field and in technical books that it *must* be used in reference works.

# CLASSIFICATION

Generally, oil burners fall into four distinct classifications: *high-pressure oil burners, low-pressure oil burners, vaporizing oil burners,* and *rotary oil burners.*

Of all the classifications, the *high-pressure oil burner* is by far the most dominant in the field today. Therefore, a majority of the service discussions that follow deal with this type of unit. Admittedly, in certain areas where burner sales dealerships have been particularly active, other burner classifications may be more dominant. Nevertheless, surveys and figures indicate that high-pressure oil burner information is required most. Figs. 4-1, 4-2, and 4-3 show typical high-pressure units.

The basic operating principles of the four oil burner classifications are as follows:

The *high-pressure oil burner,* as mentioned, is the most dominant in the field today. Many of its components are also used in

Courtesy R. W. Beckett Corp.

**Fig. 4-1. Typical high-pressure gun-type oil burner enclosure in place.**

Fig. 4-2. Oil burner with flame-retention head. Burner body is flange mounted to boiler or furnace.

the operation of burners in other classifications. The individual components are covered later in this chapter. These discussions include service, installation, and descriptions of the units. Among these units are nozzles, fuel pumps, transformers, ignition assemblies, motors, fans, and controls. Fig. 4-4 shows the assembly of high-pressure oil burners. Figs. 4-5 and 4-6 show a residential high-pressure oil burner with adjustable flame retention head and its component parts.

The *low-pressure oil burner* uses a low-pressure oil pump and mixes air and oil within the nozzle itself. The mixture is sprayed in vapor form through an opening many times larger than the opening in a standard high-pressure oil-burner nozzle. Combustion takes place within the firebox area. The low-pressure oil burner (Fig. 4-7) looks a great deal like the high-pressure model. It uses a similar framework and ignition system, but the fuel pump and nozzle system differ completely.

Courtesy Sun-Ray Burner Co.

**Fig. 4-3. High-pressure oil burner.**

The *vaporizing oil burner* operates on the principle of a change of state of the liquid fuel oil into a gas for the combustion process. The fuel oil passes from the storage supply to the retort (combustion area) of the vaporizer. The oil flow is measured and metered before it is supplied to the vaporizer. Oil flows into the burner and is distributed over the base of the burner "floor," and is ignited. The fresh oil is heated and the vaporization process takes place. Oil vapors rise in the burner, combining with air which enters through air ports on the burner's body. These ports, or body perforations, are of a given size and properly spaced. The vapor-fuel mixture continues to rise and absorb more air until the correct quantity of air has combined with the mixture. At this point, the combustion process is functioning completely.

The *rotary oil burner* depends on a rotating element within the

**Fig. 4-4. High-pressure oil burner assembly.**

unit to generate the necessary centrifugal force to project the fuel oil onto furnace-wall flame rings. The fuel is fed into the burner under low pressure, spun off the rotating element, and ignited to produce combustion. The flame spreads around the track of the flame ring, vaporizing and igniting unburned oil in the area. Gradually, the entire ring is burning around the furnace wall. The burning fuel oil mixes with the air from a fan in the unit to complete combustion.

The oil burner classifications listed above have a number of field applications. Most are used in residential heating work. However, rotary and high-pressure equipment also has commercial and industrial application. These specific applications are discussed later.

## OIL BURNER HOUSINGS

The foundation or bulwark of any oil burner, no matter what its type, is the housing to which all component parts are to be

Courtesy Wayne Home Equipment Co.

**Fig. 4-5. Residential high-pressure oil burner showing adjustable flame-retention head.**

attached. Two standard manufacturing methods are used to produce these housings. One is by casting and the other by molding or stamping out the individual items. The first of these, the *cast housing*, is generally a one-piece unit, while the second, the *stamped housing*, is assembled from a number of individualized and form-fitted parts. The size and design of the finished product depends on the manufacturer and the ultimate output rating (gallons per hour—GPH) of the burner. All units are, of course, attractively painted and decorated to match the component parts. A number of metals are used in the manufacturing process with the one-piece cast-iron unit relatively heavy compared, for example, to an aluminum die-cut housing.

Courtesy Wayne Home Equipment Co.

**Fig. 4-6. Oil burner component parts.**

## Sections

There are a number of basic sections to the oil burner housing.

1. The main body onto which is attached the pump, motor, fan, and transformer.
2. The air or draft tube, purchasable in different lengths to fit varying installation situations. The draft tube is about 4 or 5 in. in diameter and supports the oil firing line, nozzle, and electrode assembly. At the end of the draft tube is a turbulator, or set of vanes, slightly spiral in their formation. As the air is pushed down the tube by the burner fan, these vanes give it a swirling motion before it strikes the oil spray. This is intended to provide a more complete mixing of air and oil and will result in improved combustion.

85

**Fig. 4-7. Low-pressure oil burner.**

3. The base, an adjustable item upon which the entire assembled oil burner will sit. The adjustable base allows the installer to raise or lower the oil burner, matching the boiler firing area opening with the midpoint or nozzle of the oil burner. Some oil burner housings do not require a base as they are designed to be attached directly to the boiler or furnace body.

4. All oil burner units have the manufacturer's name tag prominently displayed on the burner housing. The tag generally lists the manufacturer's name and address, the oil burner model number and the approval stamp of the Underwriter's Laboratories (UL).

5. All oil burner housings are engineered to provide all of the necessary air required for combustion. These are designed in the form of openings in some portion of the casting. A positive control of the quantity of air admitted is further governed by adjustable flappers, lens-type air diaphragms, or rotating plates that fit over the air housing opening. It is important that these adjustable items be positive and secure

so that once the unit is adjusted properly, through the use of combustion testing instruments, etc., it will remain adjusted. In certain types of installations (gas stations, workshops, etc.) it is much more satisfactory to draw the air supply from outside the furnace room. The inside air may contain fumes or harmful dust. In these cases, a hood is fitted over the air intake housing of the oil burner, and air is piped or drawn directly from outside through a simple metal duct piping arrangement.

Certain manufacturers have designed their oil burner housings to be completely interchangeable. Either side of the basic housing may be used for the pump, motor, or transformer. The changeover is accomplished by moving a few bolts and making minor frame adjustments. Never "air starve" an oil burner installation. Provide a plentiful source of fresh air to the boiler room.

## DRIVE COUPLINGS

In order for the oil burner motor to perform its basic function—motive power—a means of driving or coupling the parts must be provided. The oil burner drive coupling performs this function by securely and quietly joining the motor shafts and fuel pump shaft.

Drive couplings are available in different lengths and styles and may be purchased in increments starting from overall sizes of about 2 in. For service use, the couplings can be obtained in kits containing an easy-to-carry assortment of lengths, styles, and shaft bushings. There are many varieties of couplings on the market. Some units permit on-the-job sizing, while others require the purchase of correct lengths in order to adequately couple the motor and pump shafts. Typical couplings are shown in Figs. 4-8 and 4-9.

### Types

The drive coupling consists of three sections: the blower hub, or motor-shaft, section; the intermediate, or flexible, section; and the pump-shaft section.

## GD—Gear Grip Couplings
(three-piece construction)

## 1-R Mini-Pump Couplings
(one-piece construction)

## NF—Nylon Flange
(three-piece construction)

Courtesy Guardian Industries, Inc.

**Fig. 4-8. Various shapes and sizes of drive couplings.**

Courtesy Pioneer Products

Fig. 4-9. Drive couplings indicating assortment of lengths, thicknesses, and shaft sizes available.

The type of coupling placed between the motor shaft and pump shaft is completely dependent on the type of hub on the blower-wheel assembly. If a splined-hub blower wheel is used on the oil burner unit, then a splined-hub coupling must be used. If a regular, short, plain-hub assembly is used on the blower unit, then a regular setscrew coupling may be used. If a jaw-type blower hub is used on the unit, then the coupling must be replaced with a jaw-type coupling. In an extreme emergency, and this is rather an unusual situation, the entire blower assembly may be replaced and an available matching coupling can be substituted.

The middle, or intermediate, sections of the drive couplings are manufactured of fine-grade braided rubber or other special material. The two connecting, or outside, coupling sections are made of plastic, aluminum, or other suitable metal.

A good drive coupling must perform certain basic functions.

1. It must maintain an absolute and perfect alignment between the motor and pump shafts.
2. It must prevent the transfer or amplification of motor or pump sounds through the oil burner housing.
3. It must be strong and long lasting, and not be affected by the constant starting and stopping of the burner unit.

## Connecting the Coupling

The pump side of the drive coupling is provided with a diameter opening suitable for either a Sunstrand ($7/16$ in.) shaft or a Webster ($5/16$ in.) shaft. Special shaft bushings permit the used of different diameter couplings with different shaft sizes. The blower or motor side of the drive coupling is connected as previously described.

The fuel pump drive coupling is securely attached to the fuel pump and the blower-motor shaft with a cup-pointed allen screw on each of the connecting sections. These screws are tightened, using keys that provide the correct and necessary leverage for work within the tiny confines of the blower blades or tight motor quarters.

# FANS OR BLOWERS

The oil burner blower or fan draws air into the burner housing through the controlled intake opening provided on the unit's housing. During operation, it forces air down the draft tube, past the electrode assembly, through the turbulator, and on into the firebox area. Here it provides the necessary air for combustion.

The blower wheel is measured both at its diameter and its width, the combination of the two providing knowledge about the ultimate blower output. It is also necessary to know the size for installation within the walls of the oil burner housing.

The blower is always mounted on the motor shaft. The drive coupling is then affixed to either the blower hub or an extension of the motor shaft. The rotation of the blower is determined by holding the unit with the hub facing you. The direction of the *blower vanes* will now indicate the rotation of the unit (see Figs. 4-10 and 4-11).

Courtesy Herco Oil Burner Corp.

**Fig. 4-10. Burner showing fan in housing.**

Courtesy Revcor, Inc.

**Fig. 4-11. Typical oil burner fans.**

## Servicing

Little if any attention is required by the oil burner blower unit. It is necessary to keep the vanes clean, for an excessive dirt accumulation may reduce the output of air. It is also important that the blower body does not touch the oil burner housing walls. If it rubs or touches, the balance of the fan unit may be critically distorted. If, for any reason, a blower needs replacing, replace it with an identically sized unit or consult the manufacturer for the correct-sized unit. The inside bore of most blower wheels for oil burners is ½ in., but other bores are available on special order. Table 4-1 gives a sample list of fan sizes, which are available for

### Table 4-1. Blower Fan Sizes for Oil Burners

| Diameter | Width | Diameter | Width |
|----------|-------|----------|-------|
| $4^3/_4''$ | $2^7/_8''$ | $6^5/_{16}''$ | $2^{15}/_{32}''$ |
| $5^1/_4''$ | $2^1/_{16}''$ | $6^5/_{16}''$ | $3^7/_{16}''$ |
| $4^3/_4''$ | $3^1/_2''$ | $6^5/_{16}''$ | $2^7/_8''$ |
| $5^1/_4''$ | $2^{29}/_{32}''$ | $7^5/_{16}''$ | $3^{11}/_{32}''$ |
| $5^1/_4''$ | $3^1/_2''$ | $6^5/_{16}''$ | $2^1/_{16}''$ |
| $5^1/_4''$ | $2^1/_2''$ | $6^5/_{16}''$ | $3^{25}/_{32}''$ |

clockwise (CW) or counterclockwise (CCW) rotation—looking at the open end of the fan.

## COUPLING AND BLOWER TROUBLES

*Symptom and Possible Cause*          *Possible Remedy*

### Oil Burner Off (On Safety)

1. Coupling slipping.            1. Retighten securely.
2. Coupling incorrectly          2. Replace.
   sized.
3. Blower wheel slipping on       3. Retighten.
   shaft.

### Unit Noisy

1. Fan rubbing against           1. Realign blower unit.
   housing.
2. Coupling not secure.          2. Retighten.

### Unit Noisy—Not Operating

1. Coupling broken.              1. Replace coupling.

### Installation Blowing Fuses

1. Jammed motor, pump, or        1. Correct problem.
   coupling.

92

| Symptom and Possible Cause | Possible Remedy |
|---|---|

**Uncontrollable Excess Air**

1. Fan possibly oversized.

1. Check spec sheets and replace.

**Smoky Flame**

1. Possibly undersized fan.

1. Check spec sheets and replace.

2. Dirty vanes in blower unit.

2. Clean vanes thoroughly.

## OIL BURNER NOZZLES

Many centuries ago an anonymous writer penned this thought: "For want of a nail, a shoe was lost; for want of a shoe, a horse was lost; for want of a horse, a man was lost; for want of a man, a battle was lost." For want of a simple nail, an entire battle was lost.

The finest oil burner, modern boiler, furnace, or engineering plant would, in truth, be lost if it were not for today's modern, "precisioneered" oil burner nozzle. This unit, small in total size compared to the rest of the heating plant, plays a tremendous part in the overall combustion efficiency, operation, and control.

To begin with, the oil burner nozzle will permit only a specific amount of oil to be delivered into the furnace/boiler combustion area; this is known as the gallons-per-hour (GPH) delivery rate. This rate may be changed (within certain restrictions) by replacing one nozzle with another, as there are approximately 45 different GPH nozzle sizes available, ranging from $\frac{1}{2}$ to 100 GPH.

The oil burner nozzle must be capable of "atomizing," or breaking the fuel into a spray of small droplets. This is done in order that the fuel can be as completely consumed as possible by the combustion process which follows. This "atomized" oil must also reach the combustion area in a pattern suitable to the particular burner design, firebox area, and engineered air pattern. The nozzle bears the responsibility for directing those droplets of oil to the combustion area in a constant, unchanging pattern, quantity, and spray.

The oil burner nozzle is a precisely engineered unit gauged to feed a specified amount of fuel oil, in an atomized or droplet state, into the combustion area at a given pattern, angle, and spray design. Fig. 4-12 shows typical nozzles.

Courtesy Delavan Manufacturing Co. / Wm. Steinen Manufacturing Co. / Monarch Manufacturing Works, Inc.

Fig. 4-12. Oil burner nozzles.

## Operation

There is one vital prerequisite to understanding the operation of an oil burner nozzle, and this is an awareness of its construction. A nozzle consists of, first, a stainless-steel tip or body with a highly polished reflective surface. The reflective quality acts as a possible preventive to "gumming up" or "baking on" of the fuel oil passing through the unit during the combustion process. Certain nozzle manufacturers use a brass body and a stainless steel orifice or metering hole. They claim the brass body will conduct the radiant heat of combustion away from the nozzle and back to the adapter where the heat can be picked up by the air passing over it during burner operation, while the orifice of stainless steel will resist wear. This tip has an orifice through which oil passes from the swirl chamber, after preparation within the nozzle. See Fig. 4-13.

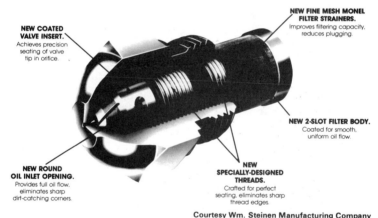

**NEW FINE MESH MONEL FILTER STRAINERS.**
Improves filtering capacity, reduces plugging.

**NEW COATED VALVE INSERT.**
Achieves precision seating of valve tip in orifice.

**NEW 2-SLOT FILTER BODY.**
Coated for smooth, uniform oil flow.

**NEW ROUND OIL INLET OPENING.**
Provides full oil flow, eliminates sharp dirt-catching corners.

**NEW SPECIALLY-DESIGNED THREADS.**
Crafted for perfect seating, eliminates sharp thread edges.

Courtesy Wm. Steinen Manufacturing Company

**Fig. 4-13. Oil burner nozzle, cutaway view.**

What is the internal nozzle like? Mated with a taper-to-taper fit in the internal unit is the nozzle stem. This stem is composed of a set of finely engineered tangential slots through which oil must pass in order to reach the swirl chamber where the oil is swirled or rotated at a high velocity. This "swirl chamber" is a small, predetermined space between the nose of the stem and the inside of the tip where the orifice of the nozzle is located. The nozzle, then, is composed of a tip with its orifice, a stem with tangential slots, and a strainer. It should be mentioned here that some strainers are part and parcel of the nozzle unit, while others might be considered as a component part.

The pressurized oil first enters the rear of the nozzle through a fine-mesh or porous bronze strainer, which is usually part of all nozzle units under 5 GPH. The reasoning behind this 5 GPH strainer designation is that, over this rate, the slots and the orifice of the larger nozzles are of sufficient size to permit passage of any normal fuel impurities. The oil travels through the slots of the valve body and swirl chamber at a high velocity and emerges from the front orifice in a cone-shaped spray pattern. The design of the swirl chamber and orifice regulates the spray angle, while the size of the orifice and the slots of the valve body control the rate flow of the nozzle. For this reason, one should not attempt to mix nozzle components by exchanging the inner parts of one unit with parts from another.

### Choosing the Correct Nozzle

Three factors affect the correct nozzle choice for any installation. These are a hollow or solid spray pattern, the angle of spray, and the gallon-per-hour (GPH) firing rate. The oil burner manufacturer's specification sheet should be conscientiously heeded at all times, for its engineering department conducts bench and field tests to determine the types of nozzles most adaptable to specific burners. If the spec sheets are not available to you, your own field testing, basic understanding of nozzle operation, and common sense will stand you in good stead, provided you guide yourself sight-wise, test-wise, and buy-wise in your nozzle choice. The proper *alignment of nozzles in the air tubes* of the oil burners and recommended *specific distances from end cones to nozzle tips* must be checked with the manufacturer's spec sheets. If this information does not come with the oil burner or is unavailable at time of service, call or write to the burner company and it will supply this data.

**Hollow-Cone Nozzles**—A hollow (H), or hollow-cone, nozzle produces a spray with a heavy concentration of "atomized" oil droplets on the outer edge of the flowing cone pattern, with only a minor quantity of droplet fuel in the central section (see Figs. 4-14 and 4-15). A hollow-cone nozzle is generally suggested when the air pattern of a particular oil burner is also hollow. This is true

Courtesy Monarch Manufacturing Works, Inc.

**Fig. 4-14. Spray patterns of different types of nozzles.**

Courtesy Delavan Manufacturing Co.

**Fig. 4-15. Hollow-cone nozzle spray.**

of most "static head" burners, which produce the so-called sun-flower, sun-flame type of flame. It is most important to remember one basic fact. The main objective is to burn the oil completely. In order to accomplish this, oil and air must mate so that each and every droplet of oil is surrounded with enough oxygen to complete the combustion process. It follows, there-fore, that if the air pattern of a particular burner has little or no air going down the center, then a hollow-cone spray will be to the best air-mating advantage. Often, on small gallonage units, a hollow spray is chosen for its quieter operation, spray stability, and especially for its "antipulsation" capabilities. Remember, all nozzles should be "fire-tested" on the particular job and, if found effective, used. Many manufacturers designate a specific spray pattern, either hollow or solid, or a combination of both, for their oil burners. Always abide by their recommendations.

**Solid-Cone Nozzles**—A solid (S), or solid-cone, nozzle permits a uniform concentration of "atomized" oil across the entire flowing spray pattern. The spray of droplet oil is evenly distributed across the entire spray pattern, as shown in Figs. 4-14 and 4-16.

Courtesy Delavan Manufacturing Co.

**Fig. 4-16. Solid-cone nozzle spray.**

Solid-spray nozzles should be used when the air pattern of the burner is such that a considerable amount of air is sent down through the center of the air cone. The main objective, just as with hollow-spray nozzles, is to successfully blend the oil and air for the highest possible combustion efficiency. There are, in fact, many turbulator types of burners on the market that deliver a solid air pattern and where a solid spray might greatly increase their combustion efficiency. Some authorities in the field claim that solid-spray nozzles provide smoother and more positive ignition in the higher gallonage areas. It bears repeating at this point that a solid-spray nozzle may be used on any job where "fire testing" proves it more effective in terms of combustion, or where the manufacturer's spec sheets call for this specific spray.

## Firing Rates

The oil burner nozzle GPH is chosen on the basis of the rating of the boiler or furnace, the house or building heat loss, the oil burner's capacity, and the restrictions imposed by the combustion area on a particular job.

A basic step in properly engineering an oil heat installation is to choose the proper firing rate for the boiler or furnace. If the unit is either under or overfired, the unit will run for excessively long periods or will burn with too high a stack temperature. Both conditions are inefficient. If one were to choose the wrong firing rate, it follows that the combustion chamber would also be incorrectly sized.

The following schedule for arriving at the correct gallon-per-hour firing rate has been recommended by one of the large nozzle and firebox manufacturers:

1. *New package units.* Information usually appears on the nameplate of the unit. If the plate is not in place, consult the spec sheets, manufacturer's representative, or boiler-rating handbooks.
2. *For boilers with a net steam rating of up to 1000 sq. ft.* Divide the catalog rating by 300 to establish the GPH firing rate.
3. *For boilers with a net steam rating of between 1000 and 3000 sq. ft.* Divide the catalog or known rating by 350 to establish the GPH firing rate.
4. *For boilers with a new steam rating of over 4000 sq. ft.* Divide the catalog or known rating by 400 to establish the GPH firing rate.
5. *For gravity warm-air furnaces (formerly coal-burning units).* For every 2 sq. ft. of grate area, fire 1 gal. of oil per hour.

6. *For forced warm-air furnaces.* Consult spec sheets, manufacturer's representative, or nameplate on furnace.

7. *For hot-water systems.* Use the net steam rating of the boiler from known or catalog sources. To arrive at the GPH firing rate, use the above formulas (1 through 4).

Once the correct GPH rate for the specific boiler or furnace has been determined, the next step is to choose a combustion chamber size. Table 4-2 can be used as a guide. Consult the nozzle, firebox, and boiler manufacturer's spec sheets whenever possible.

### Table 4-2. Combustion Chamber Specifications

| Nozzle Size GPH | Combustion Chamber Size | | Nozzle Height from Floor | Square Feet of Steam Radiation |
|---|---|---|---|---|
| | Square | Round | | |
| .75 | 8" × 9" | 9½" | 5" | 270 |
| 1.00 | 9" × 9" | 10⅛" | 5" | 300 |
| 1.35 | 10½" × 10½" | 11¾" | 5" | 405 |
| 1.50 | 11" × 11" | 12⅜" | 5" | 450 |
| 2.00 | 12⅝" × 12⅝" | 14¼" | 6" | 600 |
| 2.50 | 14¼" × 14¼" | 16" | 6½" | 750 |
| 3.00 | 15½" × 15½" | 17½" | 7" | 900 |
| 4.00 | 19" × 19" | 21½" | 8" | 1200 |
| 5.00 | 21¼" × 21¼" | | 9" | 1500 |
| 6.00 | 24½" × 24¼" | | 10" | 1800 |
| 7.00 | 26½" × 26½" | | 11" | 2100 |
| 10.00 | 31¾" × 31¾" | | 14" | 3000 |

Remember that the information in Table 4-2 and the formulas are only a guide. In selecting a particular nozzle for a special job, a specific burner, etc., the serviceman will note in comparing the rule-of-thumb guides, charts, etc., certain deviations in the recommended GPH rates and combustion chamber sizes. It is therefore wise not only to be guided by specific manufacturer's recommendations but also by the supreme criterion—what works best on the job.

### Fuel Pump Pressure

The normal operating pressure of a fuel pump is 100 psi (pounds per square inch). A nozzle stamped and marked with a particular GPH rate is gauged to this pressure setting. While changes in fuel pump operating pressure will not greatly affect the angle of spray from the nozzle, lowering or raising the pump pressure will change the GPH capacity. See Figs. 4-17 and 4-18. For example, a 2.00 GPH nozzle will operate as a 2.45 GPH unit if the fuel pump pressure is increased from 100 psi to 150 psi. It will deliver only 1.75 GPH, however, if the fuel pump pressure is lowered to 75 psi. The formula for arriving at such variations is available, but the information in Table 4-3 is recommended for on-the-spot conversion.

## Spray-Angle Selection

Our objective is to select the correct combustion chamber for the job and then to fill the firebox completely, yet comfortably

Fig. 4-17. Oil burner spray at 10 psi.

**Fig. 4-18. Oil burner spray at 100 psi.**

correct, with a flame of the right shape, size, and heat intensity. If the GPH rate is correct, we next turn to the spray angle to complete the flame picture. First of all, the angle of spray selected for the nozzle should match the air pattern of the burner. In this way, both oil and air will match for the highest combustion efficiency.

In order to select the correct spray angle, it is best to refer to Fig. 4-19. There are six angles in which all nozzles are manufactured—30°, 45°, 60°, 70°, 80°, and 90°. The correct angle may be chosen from this range for any installation. A 30° nozzle produces a spray pattern that is long and narrow, whereas a 90° nozzle produces a flame that is short and full by comparison. Between these two extremes are spray angles that offer a graduated choice to the installer to suit any job. It is wise to consult the

## Table 4-3. Nozzle Rates at Various Fuel Pump Pressures

| GPH at 100 psi | Operating Pressure of Fuel Pump (psi) | | | | |
|---|---|---|---|---|---|
| | 75 | 100 | 125 | 150 | 175 |
| .75 | — | .75 | .84 | .92 | .99 |
| 1.00 | .87 | 1.00 | 1.12 | 1.23 | 1.32 |
| 1.25 | 1.07 | 1.25 | 1.39 | 1.53 | 1.65 |
| 1.35 | 1.17 | 1.35 | 1.51 | 1.65 | 1.79 |
| 1.50 | 1.30 | 1.50 | 1.68 | 1.84 | 1.98 |
| 1.75 | 1.51 | 1.75 | 1.96 | 2.14 | 2.32 |
| 2.00 | 1.73 | 2.00 | 2.24 | 2.45 | 2.65 |
| 2.50 | 2.16 | 2.50 | 2.80 | 3.06 | 3.30 |
| 3.00 | 2.59 | 3.00 | 3.35 | 3.68 | 3.97 |
| 3.50 | 3.03 | 3.50 | 3.91 | 4.29 | 4.63 |
| 4.00 | 3.46 | 4.00 | 4.47 | 4.90 | 5.30 |
| 5.00 | 4.33 | 5.00 | 5.59 | 6.13 | 6.61 |
| 6.00 | 5.19 | 6.00 | 6.71 | 7.33 | 7.94 |
| 7.00 | 6.05 | 7.00 | 7.82 | 8.58 | 9.25 |

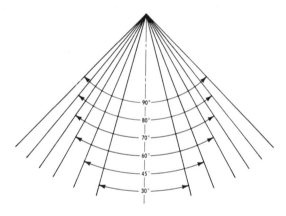

**Fig. 4-19. Spray nozzle angles.**

manufacturer's spec sheet for his recommendations on his own equipment. If these sheets are not available, field testing, understanding, and evaluation will lead you to the proper choice.

The angle of spray is not chosen to suit the shape of the firebox. Rather, it is selected to fit the air pattern of the particular burner being fired. You must "fire test" or know the pattern in advance from spec sheets in order to choose the correct spray angle. In testing, both sight observation and $CO_2$ reading are invaluable in leading you to the selection of the correct "spray path."

## How Foreign Matter Affects a Nozzle

An oil burner nozzle is vulnerable to numerous avenues of attack from dirt, sludge, gums, and other foreign matter. At the least, any of these ingredients or conditions render a nozzle's angle, spray pattern, or flow rate inaccurate.

First, fuel oil passing through a nozzle may carry in its flow foreign particles, which are easily capable of blocking the slots and metering orifice. Second, any minute foreign particles in the oil flow may be turned into clogging sludge by certain critical temperature conditions, which, in turn, are caused by firebox and draft factors. With an oil burner in operation, relatively cool oil and air flows through and around the nozzle body (cool air from the action of the oil burner fan and cool oil from the storage tank area). When the heating demand is satisfied, however, the cooling effects of the flowing oil and air are shut off, and the radiant heat of the firebox is automatically permitted to belabor the nozzle body. If the "radiant" or "back-heat" is constant and critical enough, sludge and gum particles will begin to build up and bake on within the nozzle body. The third route through which dirt may attack a nozzle is plain simple mishandling. A service mechanic who has greasy hands and dirty nozzle tools, and who carries new nozzles in any spare spot in the toolbox or in his hip pocket, starts off with a nozzle of questionable value.

## Nozzle Care

Nozzles for field service come to us from the manufacturer with three-way protection. Each is usually individually packaged in a dustproof, marked container (Fig. 4-20) and should remain in this plastic or cardboard container until ready for installation. It is wise to store these individual nozzle packages in handy "service boxes," such as shown in Fig. 4-21, often supplied at nominal cost by the manufacturer. Not only will this type of handling maintain order, but if the box is separated into the proper sizes, angles of spray, and patterns, this system can provide an exacting inventory and emergency service control at all times.

Every nozzle goes through an extensive testing program at the factory to ensure that the GPH rate, angle, and spray pattern die-stamped on its body are accurate. New nozzles are further

Fig. 4-20. Stainless-steel oil burner nozzle in container.

Courtesy Eddington Metal Specialty Co.

protected from dirt invasion with a mesh strainer, an integral part of the nozzle itself. These unit strainer screens have a mesh of 200 for nozzles firing up to 1 GPH; 120 mesh for 1.00–1.35 GPH; and 100 mesh for nozzles firing over this rate. Although additional protection is afforded by a strainer in the fuel pump itself, it is advisable in all installations to include yet another high-quality, independent oil filter in the supply line. This will provide the ultimate in protection and ensure a longer service-free nozzle life on any type of job, large or small, old or new. Fig. 4-22 illustrates some strainers found in various makes of nozzles.

## Cleaning a Nozzle

The nozzle manufacturer, plus your own field experience, will soon show you that the best way to handle a used, dirty, or troublesome nozzle is to replace it. More often than not, this will prove to be an economic practicality for both the customer and

105

Fig. 4-21. Carrying case with various-size nozzles.

Fig. 4-22. Nozzle strainers.

yourself. A new nozzle, firing the correct GPH rate and spray pattern, is far superior, both mechanically and economically, to a nozzle that is worn or incompletely cleaned. Monetary gains will show up for the customer in reduced oil consumption and superior burner operation. For the service department, the nozzle cleaning process is time consuming, unrewarding financially, and leaves an opening for customer dissatisfaction with recalls and inefficient operation.

There are occasions, however, such as emergencies, out-of-stock nozzle sizes, or unreasonable customers, which necessitate the field cleaning of a nozzle. Here is a 10-step procedure to follow for nozzle cleanup:

1. Remove the nozzle from the oil adapter line, using either a special nozzle wrench (Fig. 4-23) or the correct-size socket or box-end wrenches. Work on a clean surface at all times.

Courtesy Delavan Manufacturing Corp.

**Fig. 4-23. Nozzle removal tool.**

2. Place the removed nozzle body in the grip of the correct-size wrench, with the rear (mesh strainer side) easily accessible.

3. Unscrew the mesh strainer from the nozzle body (Fig. 4-24) and place it aside in a clean work area.

4. Use a firm, downward pressure with a screwdriver and unscrew the valve body or locknut, holding it in place from the main nozzle body.

5. Thoroughly clean all disassembled nozzle and mesh strainer

107

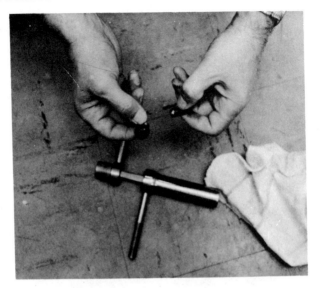

**Fig. 4-24. Disassembly of nozzle using nozzle tool.**

parts in carbon tetrachloride, a carbon solvent, or a commercial nozzle cleaner.

6. Brush the parts with a nonmetallic brush, if necessary. Never use a metal brush or a metal pick of any kind on nozzle parts. Clean the slots and swirl area with a toothpick or business card. Clean the orifice with a clean bristle or hair brush.

7. Reassemble the nozzle. Make sure that your hands and all tools used during this process are dirt-free. Tighten the locknut or valve body securely with a screwdriver before replacing the mesh strainer.

8. Flush the entire oil firing line and adapter body with a few pints of clean oil before reinstalling the newly cleaned nozzle into the brass adapter.

9. Reinstall the nozzle into the adapter. Make sure you do not cross-thread the nozzle or adapter unit. Tighten securely with the special nozzle tool or the correct-size box or socket wrenches. The nozzle body can become subject to distortion and leakage if too great a strain or torque is placed on the units during the tightening process.

10. The final test of your work is in actually firing the nozzle and judging its capacity to function. If there is any doubt as to its capabilities, do the job over until you are able to arrive at a suitable spray pattern.

## Nozzle Adapters

A nozzle is attached to the oil burner firing tube or fuel supply line by a special brass adapter. These adapters (Figs. 4-25 and 4-26) come in a variety of lengths to suit the particular make of burner or installation. One end is gauged to fit the male nozzle

Courtesy Wm. Steinen Manufacturing Co.

Fig. 4-25. Nozzle body adapters.

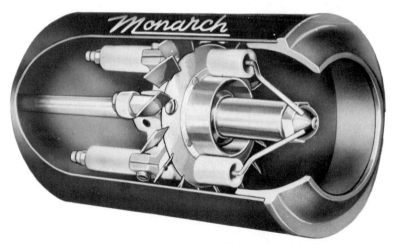

Courtesy Monarch Manufacturing Works

Fig. 4-26. Nozzle in place in air tube of oil burner. Nozzle body tightened into place on oil-delivery pipe with electrodes in igniting position.

body thread (9/16-24 threads per inch or TPI) and the other end
to fit the fuel supply line, generally ⅛, ¼, or ⅜ in. in diameter.
Adapters are also made to take two, three, and four individual
nozzle bodies at one time. See Fig. 4-27. The use of these "mul-
tinozzle" adapters often aids the unit's combustion efficiency and
increases a burner's output capacity. This is accomplished by a
finer "atomizing" of the oil droplets. It is most important that
care be given to the handling of these adapters, both in shelf
storage before use and when in actual service as part of a fuel
supply line. Damaged threads on either end will cause leaks that
can be potentially hazardous.

Fig. 4-27. Dual nozzle body.

Courtesy Wm. Steinen Manufacturing Co.

### Inspection Mirrors

Use an oil burner flame mirror when working with a nozzle-
electrode assembly. It can save you a great deal of guesswork
and wasted time. Nozzle or (combustion chamber) mirrors come
in a number of sizes and shapes, as shown in Fig. 4-28. All are
made of a high-grade reflective steel and are easy to carry and
use. Fig. 4-29 shows a serviceman using a mirror to inspect the
interior of a furnace.

## NOZZLE TROUBLES

The nozzle is part and parcel of the entire oil burner unit, and
as such it affects and is affected by many other component parts.

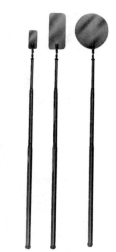

**Fig. 4-28. Nozzle flame-inspection mirrors.**

Courtesy Wm. Steinen Manufacturing Company

These parts, such as fireboxes and fuel pumps, must therefore also be reckoned with in an overall troubleshooting program.

| *Symptom and Possible Cause* | *Possible Remedy* |
|---|---|

**Dirty Nozzle**

1. Flame burns to one side of firebox.
2. Stringy-sparky flame.
3. Eye-burning acrid fumes.
4. Fire floats and burns on back wall.

1. Clean or replace nozzle.
2. Clean or replace nozzle.
3. Clean or replace nozzle.
4. Clean or replace nozzle.

**Flame Too Large**

1. Oversize nozzle.

2. Wrong nozzle pattern.

3. Pump pressure too high.

4. Incorrectly sized firebox.

1. Change to correct-size nozzle.
2. Use nozzle with correct spray pattern.
3. Adjust pump pressure (gauge).
4. Measure and rebuild firebox.

111

**Fig. 4-29.** Illustrating the use of a mirror to inspect the furnace interior.

*Symptom and Possible Cause*     *Possible Remedy*

### Flame Too Small

1. Undersized nozzle.
2. Pump pressure too low.
3. Nozzle partially clogged.
4. Wrong nozzle pattern.
5. Incorrectly sized firebox.
6. Defective pump.

1. Change to correct GPH rate nozzle.
2. Adjust pump pressure (gauge).
3. Clean or replace nozzle.
4. Use nozzle with correct spray pattern.
5. Measure and rebuild firebox.
6. Test and replace or repair.

*Symptom and Possible Cause*　　*Possible Remedy*

## Flame Too Smoky

1. Nozzle too large.
2. Wrong spray pattern.
3. Nozzle partially clogged.
4. Carbon in front of nozzle.
5. Insufficient air supply.
6. Incorrectly sized fan.
7. Poor draft condition.
8. Defective firebox.

1. Change to correct GPH rate nozzle.
2. Use nozzle with correct spray pattern.
3. Clean or replace nozzle.
4. Clean and check nozzle pattern.
5. Adjust for more air.
6. Change fan or entire burner.
7. Correct or use forced draft.
8. Rebuild firebox.

## No Flame at All

1. Nozzle completely clogged.
2. Out of oil.
3. Defective fuel pump.
4. Defective ignition (white mist).
5. Clogged filter.
6. Restricted oil suction line.
7. Broken oil suction line.
8. Fuel pump loses prime.

1. Clean or replace nozzle.
2. Secure oil supply.
3. Replace or repair pump after testing.
4. Test and correct.
5. Replace filter cartridge.
6. Clean or replace line.
7. Repair break or replace line.
8. Change to a two-pipe system.

## Flame Has Odor

1. Partially clogged nozzle.
2. Boiler or chimney blocked (soot).
3. Poor draft condition.
4. Oversupply of air.

1. Clean or replace nozzle.
2. Clean soot from blocked area.
3. Correct or use forced draft.
4. Adjust air or fan supply.

*Symptom and Possible Cause*     *Possible Remedy*

### Changeable Flame

1. Nozzle capacity greater than fuel pump output.
2. Burner motor not running at rated speed.
3. Partially clogged strainer or filter.
4. Leaking supply line.
5. Defective or leaking fuel pump.

1. Change fuel pump to next rated size.
2. Replace or repair motor.
3. Replace with new cartridge.
4. Repair suction line.
5. Repair or replace fuel pump.

### Flame Produces Large Supply of Carbon

1. Incorrect nozzle size.

2. Wrong spray pattern.

3. Wrong nozzle spray angle.
4. Flame striking back wall—carbon.
5. Flame striking side walls—carbon.
6. Flame striking floor—carbon.
7. Firebox defective— breaking up.
8. Pump cutoff defective.

9. Air trapped in oil firing line causing afterdrip.

1. Change to correct GPH rate nozzle.
2. Use nozzle with correct spray pattern.
3. Use correct-angle nozzle.

4. Correct nozzle pattern.

5. Correct nozzle pattern.

6. Correct nozzle pattern.

7. Rebuild firebox.

8. Repair or replace fuel pump.
9. Purge line of air.

### Noisy Flame

1. Nozzle too large.

2. Wrong spray pattern.

1. Change to correct GPH rate nozzle.
2. Use nozzle with correct spray pattern.

114

| *Symptom and Possible Cause* | *Possible Remedy* |
|---|---|

**Noisy Flame Cont.**

3. Incorrect nozzle angle.
4. Incorrect firebox.
5. Burner tube touching boiler base.

3. Use correct-angle nozzle.
4. Rebuild firebox.
5. Insulate by leaving space.

**Hissing or Sparking Flame**

1. Water in oil supply.
2. Partially clogged nozzle.

1. Check and remove water.
2. Clean or replace nozzle.

**Flame Remains On After Burner Shuts Off**

1. Air leak in suction line.
2. Air pocket between valve and nozzle.
3. Defective pump piston seat.
4. Strainer cover loose.
5. Loose nozzle body.

1. Repair leak.
2. Purge line of air.
3. Repair or replace pump unit.
4. Tighten cover.
5. Tighten up entire unit.

## FUEL PUMPS

The oil burner fuel pump must perform two functions. First, it must receive or draw oil from a remote storage tank located either below ground or in the basement. Second, it must deliver this oil under pressure to the burner nozzle, properly prepared for combustion. Perhaps no other single portion of an oil burner contributed and controls so great a portion of an oil heating unit's operation and efficiency.

### Single-Stage Unit

Most fuel pump manufacturers have two distinct types of pumps, one of which they designate as a single-stage unit. The

115

single-stage unit (Figs. 4-30, 4-33, and 4-34) has one set of internal gears that performs a dual duty. First, it draws oil from the storage tank, and second, it places it under pressure for proper combustion. From a dollars-and-cents standpoint, if a single-stage

Courtesy Sundstrand Corp.

Fig. 4-30. A single-stage fuel pump produced by Sundstrand.

Courtesy Sundstrand Corp.

Fig. 4-31. A two-stage fuel pump produced by Sundstrand.

unit is adaptable for the job, it is lower in cost than a two-stage unit.

Whenever the lift involved is not over 12 ft. by actual measurement, or the suction-line vacuum reading is not over 10 in., a single-stage unit is the most desirable.

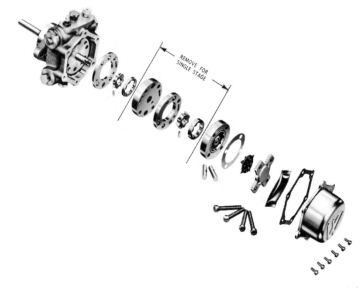

**Fig. 4-32. Internal pump parts.**

## Two-Stage Unit

A two-stage unit (Figs. 4-31, 4-35, and 4-36) has two complete sets of gears. The first set lifts the oil from the storage tank and places it in a storage area internally within the fuel pump. The other set of gears draws oil from this internal reservoir and puts it under pressure for proper combustion.

A two-stage unit must be used when the lift requirements are over 12 ft. by actual measurement, or the suction line vacuum reading is over 10 in. Fig. 4-32 shows an exploded view of a two-stage pump. A single-stage pump is identical if the indicated parts are removed.

## One-Pipe System

In the initial installation of a fuel pump, we must decide whether it is to consist of a one-pipe system (suction-supply line alone) or a two-pipe system (suction and return line).

A one-pipe system is used when the oil flow can move by gravity from the oil storage tank to the fuel pump on the oil

**Fig. 4-33. A single-stage fuel pump produced by Webster.**

burner unit. The lowest oil level in the storage tank must *always* be above the intake port of the fuel oil pump.

## Two-Pipe System

A two-pipe system is used when the fuel unit is above the lowest level in the oil storage tank. This piping system takes the excess oil drawn up by the fuel pump and sends it back to the storage tank via a return line. For example, a certain fuel pump may have a drawing capacity of 18 gal. of oil per hour. It will draw this amount from the oil storage tank. Only 2 gal. per hour of this oil is used for combustion purposes, leaving 16 gal. to be returned to the oil storage tank. This excess oil is sent back to the

**Fig. 4-34. Cutaway view of single-stage Webster fuel pump.**

storage tank for reuse through the return line of a two-pipe installation.

## Replacement Fuel Pump Units

Here is how to order replacement fuel pump units when it becomes necessary because of unit breakdown to make a part change.

1. *Check the pump's rotation.* Hold the fuel pump in your hands with the shaft pointing toward you. Read the rotation of the unit from this position, either clockwise (CW) or counterclockwise (CCW) according to the unit's direction. This direction may be determined by markings on the fuel pump or the known rotation of the oil-burner motor and fan.

2. *Nozzle port check.* In order to determine the left or right

120

Courtesy Webster Electric Co.

**Fig. 4-35. A two-stage Webster fuel pump.**

nozzle port, hold the fuel pump with the shaft pointing toward you. If the fuel pump is a left-port unit, the nozzle port into which a ⅛″ fitting is usually screwed will be on your left side. If the fuel pump is a right-port unit, the port will be on your right side.

3. *Shaft-size check.* There are two common sizes of shafts which most fuel pump manufacturers have adopted for their pumps—⁵⁄₁₆″ and ⁷⁄₁₆″. A smaller fuel pump shaft may be "bushed up" to a larger size, if an exact replacement is not available, with a special pump-shaft bushing. (Webster fuel pumps have a ⁷⁄₁₆ in. shaft—Sundstrand fuel pumps have a ⁵⁄₁₆ in. shaft.)

4. *Flange or hub installation.* Pumps must always be securely attached to the oil burner housing in order to function effectively and quietly. This is accomplished in two ways:

   a. A flange pump relies on bolts or screws that pass through the fuel pump and burner housing. Threads or nuts then tighten the pump against the burner housing for an immovable fit.

121

Fig. 4-36. Cutaway view of a two-stage Webster fuel pump.

    b. A hub fuel unit has a number of shallow depressions built into it that allow an allen screw, prebuilt into the oil burner housing, to tighten into the fuel unit hub.

If required, large-capacity fuel pumps with capacities up to 90 GPH are available for big jobs (see Figs. 4-37, 4-38, and 4-39).

## Fuel Pump Servicing

For venting, priming, or bleeding a fuel pump of air:

*When.* Anytime a fuel pump runs out of oil or is permitted to pick up a quantity of air either through a leak or break in the suction line or strainer, the pump must either be primed or purged of air.

Fig. 4-37. Big-capacity fuel oil pumps with capacities of up to 90 GPH are available for large installations.

*Why*. Air trapped in the fuel lines can cause a number of fuel pump operating difficulties. The fuel oil cannot flow through to the pump correctly until all air is purged from the lines. A service condition known as improper nozzle cutoff and a pulsating or changeable flame condition exists when air is permitted to remain in the fuel system.

*How*. In Fig. 4-40, the letter *B* shows the location of the bleeding or priming plug on many fuel pumps found in the field today. Open the plug or port, run the oil burner, and allow all air or foam to be pumped out of the unit. Continue this priming operation until all the air is removed and a clear stream of oil flows into your catch container. Replace the plug and operate the fuel pump normally. A two-pipe unit will often purge itself by just

123

**Fig 4-38. Cutaway view of a large-capacity fuel pump.**

operating the unit. In order to speed up the process, however, open the priming plug as described above.

For changing fuel pump pressure:

*When.* The operating pressure of a fuel pump should only be changed by using a pressure gauge in order to make an accurate adjustment.

*Why.* An increase or decrease in fuel pump pressure sometimes increases combustion efficiency, decreases an annoying noise level, or improves the overall efficiency of the oil burner.

*How.* The letter *A* in Fig. 4-40 shows the location of the pressure adjustment screw on many units found in the field today. Turning the screw or key counterclockwise will lower the pressure of the fuel pump. Turning the screw or key clockwise will increase the pressure.

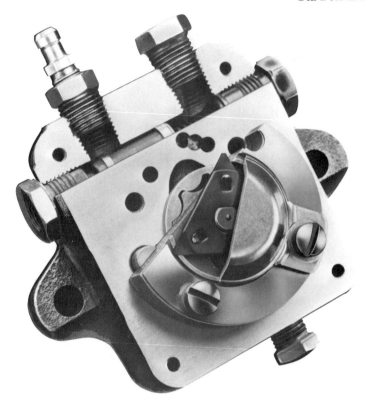

**Fig. 4-39. Interior rotary filter on this fuel pump by Webster reduces need for periodic filter cleaning.**

For cleaning a fuel pump strainer:

*When.* For a longer pump life and uninterrupted heating service, the wise serviceman cleans the internal strainer of the fuel pump on annual cleanups.

*Why.* A clogged pump strainer may be the cause of a number of service difficulties. It may cause a pulsating or changeable pressure and flame, or in severe cases can stop the flow of oil to the working parts of the fuel pump. Preventive service is easier.

*How.* See Fig. 4-40 for the location of the strainer in many fuel pumps in the field today. Remove the screws or bolts holding the

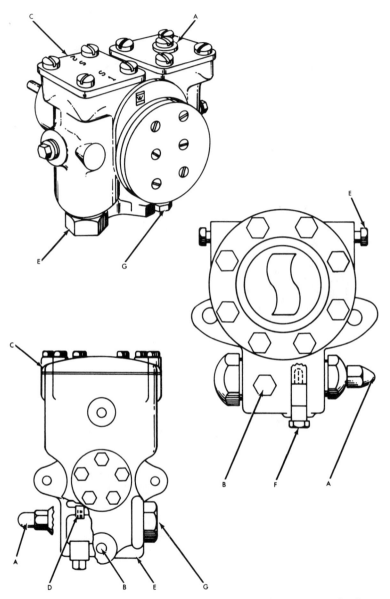

Fig. 4-40. Pictorial diagram of pump showing various parts and adjustments.

strainer in place, being careful not to damage the gasket. Remove the strainer and clean thoroughly in clean fuel oil, kerosene, or a solvent. Use a soft brush. Replace the strainer in the body of the pump after cleaning. Use a good gasket sealer on the present gasket. It may be necessary to replace the gasket. Insert the bolts into the fuel pump body and tighten up evenly and securely. Remember to turn on the fuel supply valve you turned off at the start of this job.

For servicing nozzle cutoff or afterdrip:

*When.* Very often it appears that an oil burner has an afterdrip or afterburn, even after the heating demand has been satisfied. The burner produces a small, smoky flame in the firebox, which remains a few minutes or longer after burner turnoff.

*Why.* This condition can lead to inefficiency, sooty boilers, and presents a potential "blowback" condition. Should the flame die out and the drip continue, the accumulation of oil can also cause odor and smoke when the burner starts up again.

*How.* The first step to be taken is the Pump Shut-Off Test (see the section "Pump Testing") to determine if the cause is the internal fuel pump. The following service items should also be checked:

1. The intake or suction line for air leaks.
2. A loose strainer.
3. The nozzle line for an air pocket.

For servicing a fuel pump that cannot produce a pressurized flame:

*When.* A fuel pump, due to internal pump leakage, very often cannot produce the pressure required for proper combustion (see "Pump Testing").

*Why.* In service cases of this type, either the pump will deliver no oil to the nozzle line or will deliver only an intermittent supply. This, of course, will lead to a no-flame condition or a very small flame and thus a "cold house" service call, even though the oil burner itself is functioning properly.

*How.* In an emergency, you may loosen the key or screw that controls the fuel pump pressure by turning it counterclockwise

(CCW). This will allow a quantity of oil to reach the nozzle line until a new pump or replacement part is available. For completely satisfactory service results, it is best to take the unit into the shop. This repair is usually a bench job.

For changing from a one-pipe to a two-pipe system:

*When*. If the lowest oil level in the storage tank is above the fuel pump, a one-pipe system may be used. A two-pipe system is used when the oil level in the storage tank is below the intake port of the fuel pump.

*Why*. Although either piping system may work under certain conditions, even though the intake is above or below the intake port of the fuel pump, the fuel unit becomes more readily exposed to airbound conditions when the above rules are not observed. This airbound, or loss-of-prime, condition can be the cause of a great deal of extra and needless service work.

*How*. The letter *D* in Fig. 4-40 shows the location of the conversion spots on many of the units found in the field. In Webster units (class 1800), rotation of the top cover so that the "S-2" cast on the cover lines up with the "P" cast into the pump body will change the unit to a two-pipe operation. Lining up the "S-1" on the cover with the "P" cast on the pump body will adjust the fuel pump for one-pipe operation. In a Sundstrand unit, the internal bypass plug must be inserted tightly into the fuel unit with the proper sized allen key in order to make it operative as a two-pipe system. Removing the plug and closing the bottom return line outlet will reset this Sundstrand unit for single-pipe operation.

For removing tank hum or pump noise:

*When*. Fuel pump noises are sometimes forerunners of service problems in mechanical equipment. As a potential producer of future service calls, they should be attended to as soon as possible after they are heard.

*Why*. Sounds are, to some people, simply annoying, and if for no other reason, the noisy pump should be attended to. From a mechanical standpoint, a poor coupling alignment may, in time, throw an otherwise good pump completely out of line. This can cause replacement expenses.

*How*. Check first to see that all hub or flange bolts, screws, and keys holding the fuel pump in place are securely tightened. Next, check the drive coupling to make sure the screws are tight against the pump shaft. Check closely for internal gear clicks by placing your ear against the pump housing. Make sure that the oil supply or return lines are not resting against the ceiling, against water pipes, or touching other spots where the vibration may be transmitted to living areas in the house. A tank hum or vibration transmitted through the lines by the action of the pump may be eliminated by any of several antihum devices currently on the market. These antihum units are generally placed either in the oil pump body itself or in the oil lines.

For servicing a leaky fuel pump:

*When.* Nothing can drive a customer to the competition quicker than an oil burner surrounded by an oil-soaked floor. Always service a fuel pump that has caused this condition immediately.

*Why.* An accumulation of fuel oil around the base of a heating system is a potential fire hazard. The odor is a constant reminder of a wasteful and dangerous piece of heating equipment.

*How.* Find the leak. If the problem is a fitting leak, change, tighten, or reseal the pipe, part, or fitting causing the drip. If the fuel pump is at fault, the service problem will probably be in the pump seal located around the shaft. This is generally a bench repair job. Replace the fuel unit and repair the defective one in your shop.

## Fuel Pump Testing

The serviceman will save a great deal of time by observing one simple rule when working with oil burner fuel pumps—always use your fuel pump test gauges. Do not rely on sight, smell, sound, or simple savings. Always use your test gauges, and you will be in complete control of the service situation. No guess and no mess.

For checking for vacuum or drawing power of the fuel pump:

*When.* Anytime the problem of a weak pump or a fuel pump that does not draw oil from a storage tank arises, use this test.

129

*Why.* A good fuel pump produces a vacuum reading of 25 in. on the gauge dial. A low reading indicates:

1. Leaking or broken gaskets.
2. Worn internal pump parts.
3. A defective pump.
4. Pump fittings or bolts loose or leaking.

*How.* Insert vacuum gauge in a tee-fitting near the pump or in the spare inlet opening as in Fig. 4-41. Operate the oil burner. Close off the valve between the source of the oil and the pump (always keep the furnace observation door open). Read the gauge.

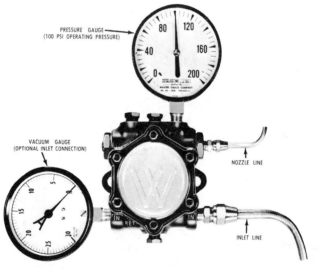

PRESSURE GAUGE
(100 PSI OPERATING PRESSURE)

VACUUM GAUGE
(OPTIONAL INLET CONNECTION)

NOZZLE LINE

INLET LINE

Courtesy Webster Electric Co.

**Fig. 4-41. Fuel pump vacuum and pressure gauge.**

For checking for restrictions in the fuel line of an outside tank:
*When.* Very often, a fuel pump will not draw oil from a fuel storage tank for reasons other than a weak pump. This pump test, which can follow the preceding vacuum test, will prove out the supply line and allied parts.

*Why.* A high vacuum reading (over 15 in.) on the gauge dial indicates:

1. Clogged filter.
2. Foot or check valve stuck.
3. Excessive lift.
4. Line blocked or kinked.
5. Frozen oil line.
6. Hand valve partially closed.
7. Undersized oil line.

*How.* Insert a vacuum gauge in a tee-fitting near the fuel pump. Operate the oil burner. Read the gauge.

For checking fuel pump nozzle pressure:
*When.* The manufacturer's recommended pressure for an operating fuel pump is 100 psi (pounds per square inch). In order to determine this figure accurately, the only foolproof method is through the use of a pressure gauge.
*Why.* A low pressure reading will indicate:

1. A defective bellows or pump piston.
2. Motor not rotating at the correct or rated speed.
3. Nozzle capacity greater than pump capacity.

A pulsating reading (needle jumps from high to low) indicates:

1. A clogged or loose strainer cover.
2. A leaky suction line.

*How.* Remove the fuel pump bleeder plug and insert the pressure gauge. Run the oil burner and read the gauge dial.
*Note.* The normal recommended pressure is 100 psi. This figure may fluctuate a bit, according to the pump, job, and particular installation.

For checking fuel pump cutoff:
*When.* If there is any indication of afterdrip or afterburn in the furnace/boiler combustion area once the heating demand of the unit has been satisfied, the cutoff of the pump should be checked.
*Why.* An afterdrip or afterburn can be the cause of inefficiency and soot accumulation, and be a potential hazard from blowbacks.

*How.* Remove the fitting from the fuel pump nozzle port and insert the pressure gauge as shown in Fig. 4-42. Run the oil burner and read the gauge. If the pressure drops to 0 psi when the unit is turned off, the cutoff is dirty, damaged, or defective.

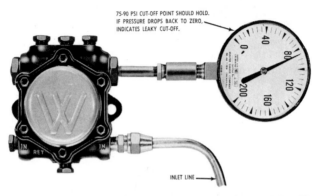

75-90 PSI CUT-OFF POINT SHOULD HOLD. IF PRESSURE DROPS BACK TO ZERO, INDICATES LEAKY CUT-OFF.

INLET LINE

Courtesy Webster Electric Co.

**Fig. 4-42. Fuel pump pressure gauge.**

## FUEL PUMP TROUBLES

The exploded views in Figs. 4-43 to 4-45 of a typical fuel pump may be used to advantage when necessary to perform service on a unit.

*Symptom and Possible Cause*

*Possible Remedy*

### No Oil Flow

1. Fuel level below suction or intake line in oil supply tank.

1. Measure oil in storage tank and fill with fuel.

2. Clogged oil strainer or filter. (High vacuum reading—see Test section)

2. Remove strainer or filter and clean thoroughly.

3. Stuffed, frozen, or restricted suction or supply

3. Replace, thaw, or clean lines.

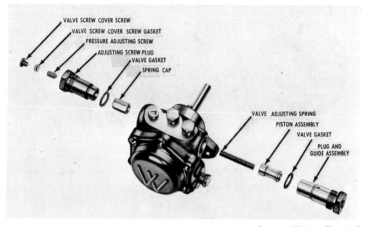

VALVE SCREW COVER SCREW
VALVE SCREW COVER SCREW GASKET
PRESSURE ADJUSTING SCREW
ADJUSTING SCREW PLUG
VALVE GASKET
SPRING CAP

VALVE ADJUSTING SPRING
PISTON ASSEMBLY
VALVE GASKET
PLUG AND
GUIDE ASSEMBLY

Courtesy Webster Electric Co.

**Fig. 4-43. Pictorial view of valves in pump.**

*Symptom and Possible Cause*     *Possible Remedy*

## No Oil Flow Cont.

lines. (High vacuum reading—see Test section)

3. Replace, thaw, or clean lines.

4. Stuck, frozen, or restricted foot or check valves. (High vacuum reading—see Test section)

4. Replace, repair, or discard defective valves.

5. Air leak in suction line.

5. Tighten and seal all pipes, fittings, and valve heads.

6. Air leak in filter cover or gasket.

6. Tighten or replace seal gasket.

7. Incorrect rotation of either motor or fuel unit.

7. Replace with correctly rotating unit.

8. Frozen fuel pump shaft.

8. Replace fuel pump unit.

9. Airbound unit—loss of prime.

9. Open gauge port plug and prime unit.

10. Two-pipe system becomes airbound.

10. Check fuel pump for missing bypass plug.

133

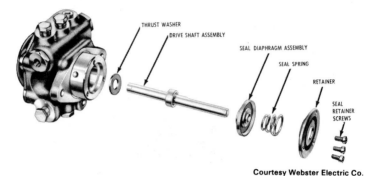

THRUST WASHER
DRIVE SHAFT ASSEMBLY
SEAL DIAPHRAGM ASSEMBLY
SEAL SPRING
RETAINER
SEAL RETAINER SCREWS

Courtesy Webster Electric Co.

**Fig. 4-44. Internal view of drive shafts and seals.**

*Symptom and Possible Cause*          *Possible Remedy*

## Oil Leaks

1. Loose plugs, fittings, or pipe.

2. Blown fuel pump seal.

1. Dope with high-grade sealer after retightening.

2. One-pipe System—Check to see if bypass plug has been left in unit. Replace unit and take to shop. Two-pipe System— Check for visible obstructions in return line. Replace unit and take to shop.

3. Leaking pressure-adjusting cap.

3. Washer missing or cap threads stripped. Replace washer or assembly.

4. Slightly leaking seal.

4. Examine seal for scratches. Replace unit and take to shop for bench work.

## Noisy Fuel Pump

1. Bad coupling alignment.

1. Loosen fuel-unit screws or bolts and readjust unit.

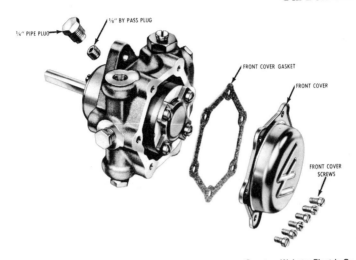

**Fig. 4-45.** Pictorial view of pump housing assembly.

*Symptom and Possible Cause*          *Possible Remedy*

### Noisy Fuel Pump Cont.

2. Tank hum on two-pipe system and on inside storage tanks.

3. Gear click of rebuilt fuel unit.

2. Add antihum devices to either fuel pump or in unit fuel lines.

3. Continue fuel pump operation for a few hours until noise ceases. If noise does not cease, replace unit.

### Fuel Pump Loses Prime

1. Weak fuel pump. (See vacuum test)

2. Incorrect type of fuel pump. (Determine by vacuum test reading or measured feet of lift)

1. Replace unit.

2. Replace single-stage unit with a two-stage unit.

135

| *Symptom and Possible Cause* | *Possible Remedy* |
|---|---|

**Fuel Pump Loses Prime Cont.**

3. Pump operating as a two-pipe system, but bypass valve not in place.

4. Lift too great for pump in use.

3. Replace bypass valve if left out. Rotate pump head if in wrong position.

4. If total measured lift is over the pump capacity or very close to it, replace with a suitable unit.

**Pulsating Pressure (changeable flame)**

1. Partially clogged strainer or filter.

2. Air leak in intake or suction line.

3. Air leak in filter gasket.

4. Air leak around fuel-pump cover.

1. Remove strainer or filter and clean.

2. Tighten all fittings, unions, and pipes and reseal with a good-grade sealing material.

3. Tighten or replace gasket.

4. Tighten all fuel pump screws evenly.

**Low Oil Pressure**

1. Defective testing gauge.

2. Electric motor not running at correct speed.

3. Nozzle capacity greater than fuel pump's output.

1. Rerun tests with a known good gauge.

2. Motor should be rated at 1725 rpm. If no test equipment is available, replace with a known good motor.

3. Replace fuel pump with correct-sized unit for job.

**High Oil Pressure**

1. Defective testing gauge.

1. Rerun tests with a known good gauge.

| Symptom and Possible Cause | Possible Remedy |
|---|---|

**High Oil Pressure Cont.**

2. Fuel-pump piston stuck.

3. Unit assembled incorrectly.

2. This is a shop job. Replace fuel pump.

3. This is a shop job. Replace fuel pump.

**Improper Nozzle Cutoff**

1. Air leak in suction or intake line.

2. Air leak between valve and nozzle.

3. Strainer cover loose.

4. Defective piston seat.

1. Tighten all fittings and pipes.

2. Run and rerun oil burner until pulsation, after-flame, and excess smoke cease.

3. Tighten and/or replace gasket.

4. This is a shop job. Take unit back to the shop and repair.

## SUMMARY

Generally, oil burners fall into four classifications: high-pressure, low-pressure, vaporizing, and rotary oil burners. The most popular of these four is the high-pressure burner.

Oil burner nozzles are precise engineered units gauged to feed a specified amount of fuel oil, in an atomized or droplet state, into the combustion area at a given pattern angle, and spray design. Many factors are considered in selecting the proper spray nozzle, but above all there are three very important considerations. They are hollow or solid-spray pattern, angle of spray, and gallon-per-hour (GPH) firing rate.

Nozzles are vulnerable to numerous attacks from dirt, sludge, gum, and other foreign matter. The best way to handle a dirty nozzle is to replace it with a new one. A new nozzle, firing the

137

correct GPH rate and spray pattern, is far superior, both mechanically and economically, to a nozzle that is worn out or incompletely cleaned.

There are two distinct types of fuel pumps: the single-stage and the two-stage. Fuel systems use the one-pipe system or the two-pipe system. The one-pipe system uses the suction-supply principle, where the two-pipe system uses a suction line and a return line. Any oversupply of oil can be returned to the supply tank through the return line.

The low-pressure oil burner mixes air and oil within the nozzle itself. The mixture is sprayed in vapor form through an opening many times larger than the opening in a standard high-pressure nozzle. The combustion takes place within the firebox area.

The vaporizing burner operates on the principle of a change of state of the liquid oil into gas. Oil is measured and metered before it is supplied to the vaporizer. Oil flows into the burner and is distributed over the base of the burner, then ignited. The fresh oil is heated and the vaporization process takes place.

The rotary oil burner depends on a rotating element within the unit to generate the necessary centrifugal force to project the oil onto the furnace wall flame rings. The flame spreads around the track of the flame ring, vaporizing and igniting unburned oil. Oil is fed into the burner under low pressure and is spun off of the rotary elements.

## When to Replace Equipment

A decision often must be made as to whether or not to replace the oil burner that is currently in use. Is it using fuel conservatively, or is it wasting it? Manufacturers recommend replacing units of older design, but the sensible decision would be based on the actual efficiency of the unit. The goal is to save energy and reduce home heating costs. After you have put a unit through an efficiency testing procedure and find that despite all adjustments, the steady efficiency rating is below 75 percent, the oil burner should be replaced. If the combustion testing develops a steady 75 percent plus, but the smoke level is greater than 2, the burner is also a candidate for replacement.

# REVIEW QUESTIONS

1. Explain why the housing is one of the most important parts of an oil burner.
2. Name the four basic types of oil burners.
3. Which of the four oil burners is most popular?
4. Why is the nozzle an important part of the combustion system?
5. Name the three very important considerations when selecting a nozzle.
6. Should a dirty nozzle be cleaned or replaced? Why?
7. What is the principal operation of the low-pressure oil burner?
8. How many basic types of fuel pumps are used? Name the types and their operation.
9. What determines the GPH of a nozzle?
10. Why is nozzle spray angle important in the combustion chamber?
11. What is the basis for selecting the proper burner nozzle?
12. Can nozzle inner parts be interchanged? Explain.
13. When should a single-stage pump be used? A two-stage pump?
14. Should a pressure gauge always be used to check the pump pressure? Why?
15. What is meant by "afterdrip" and "afterburn"?
16. What is wrong when a vacuum gauge reads too high?
17. What is the normal operation pressure of a fuel pump?
18. Explain why all leaks in the oil line should be repaired.
19. Can the operation pressure of the pump be decreased if the tank is above the oil supply line? Why?
20. In changing from a one-line to a two-line system, what should be done to the pump?

# CHAPTER 5

# Ignition Systems

Those of you who remember the famous Chicago Cubs triumvirate "Tinkers to Evers to Chance" will recall their teamwork in exciting baseball plays. Though a far cry from "home plate," an oil burner's ignition system consists of just such a triumvirate, moving along with the same coordinated motion required of top-notch big league teams.

An oil burner's ignition system consists basically of three component, hand-in-glove parts:

1. The stepup high-voltage transformer in which the standard residence electrical voltage is increased or stepped up from the 115-volt line on the primary side to approximately 10,000 volts on the secondary side. This provides us with our "spark" source.

2. A pair of ignition wires or bus bars, transporting the voltage produced by the transformer from this high-voltage source to its terminal points, the electrode assemblies.

3. An electrode assembly provides a combination of an insulated porcelain "holding and mounting surface" and steel electrode working and "gapping" areas.

We discuss the ignition transformers in this chapter and the balance of the ignition system and its components in the chapter that follows.

## HOW AN IGNITION SYSTEM WORKS

The ignition system provides the spark or light-off required to ignite the fuel oil as it enters the combustion chamber. The spark must be correctly positioned to provide immediate ignition to the prepared "atomized" fuel—it cannot be delayed, weak, or off target. If any of these or a host of other defective conditions exist, such as blowbacks, backfires, or ignition, it can result in odor, dirt, inconvenience, and possible hazard. The ignition system is called on to do its duty each time a demand for heat is made by the unit's heating system. Some units are designed so that the spark remains on for just a short period after providing initial ignition or light-off (intermittent ignition), while in other hook-ups, the spark remains in an *on* position during the entire firing cycle (constant ignition). Some manufacturers recommend the use of constant ignition in installations of over 4 GPH.

The spark is the end result of the gapping of the two properly positioned electrode tips and high-voltage electricity stepped up within an effective transformer. The spark must, of course, be strong enough to bridge the correctly set gap between the two electrodes while a column of air from the oil burner's fan blows strongly against it, enlarging even further the arc area it stretches across. It must also be so positioned that the oil spray does not hit on the electrode tips or porcelains and load these devices with a carbon formation. The points should be set in such a way that they are never closer to any other metal surface than they are to themselves, thus drawing the spark away from the preset gap.

The oil burner ignition system provides us with one of fuel oil's strongest selling implements—that of constant, automatic lighting-off of the system's heating plant. No fuss—no muss—no bother. No gas pilot to blow out. No danger and no waste of pilot fuel.

# THE TRANSFORMER

The dictionary briefly defines a transformer "as an apparatus capable of changing an electrical current from a low to a high (and vice versa) potential without changing the current energy."

The oil burner ignition transformer consists of a box-type metal unit called a body. These bodies are approximately 4½″ × 4½″ × 5½″ in size and house the active component parts of the entire unit. The primary side of the transformer is 115 volts, the secondary side totals approximately 10,000 volts. Also included are the interface eliminator, the secondary high-tension terminals, the primary wire connections, and the moisture-proof sealing and filler compound. Figs. 5-1 and 5-2 illustrate two various types of ignition transformers.

Courtesy Dongan Electric Manufacturing Co.

**Fig. 5-1. Typical oil burner ignition transformer.**

## The Interior Component Parts

The primary side (115 volts) is essentially made up of a comparatively few turns of fairly stout wire over a laminated metal core; the dual secondary side is made up of many, many equal

143

**Fig. 5-2. Oil burner ignition transformer.**

turns of finer wire, also wound around laminated metal core. The units operate on the principle of magnetic induction. The current in the primary side magnetizes the metal core, which in turn magnetizes the secondary side. The change in current and voltage from one winding to another depends on the ratio of the number of turns in each secondary side. The primary side is connected to the line or residence house voltage, and the secondary side feeds a stepped-up voltage to the attached electrodes. In addition to the windings of the primary and secondary wiring, a radio-shielding or static screen is generally built into the transformer bodies, in the form of a capacitor across the line or midpoint grounding of high-voltage wiring to the case. The entire transformer is then filled with a hard tar or waxlike compound that serves as a moisture-proofing seal for the wiring in the unit.

## Mounting Plates

In order to properly mount the transformer body onto an oil burner housing, we must attach a suitably fitting metal base plate to the transformer body unit. The mounting plates come in a variety of sizes and shapes and are designed to fit every known model oil burner casting or can be adapted to do so (see Fig. 5-3).

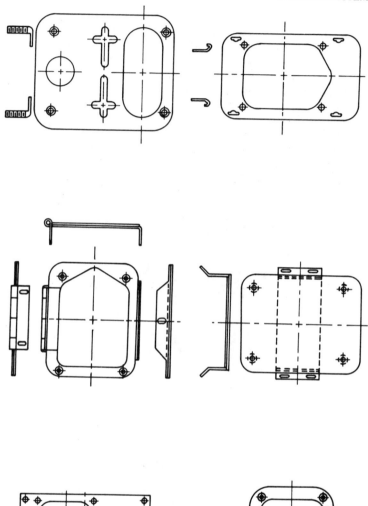

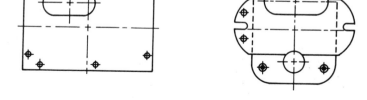

Fig. 5-3. Various types and sizes of mounting plates.

The mounting plate must not only fit the oil burner casting but should also have screw holes or adapter clips, which line up properly with duplicate mounting holes in the relatively larger and heavier transformer bodies.

## High-Tension Terminals

From the secondary terminals of the transformer comes the high-voltage necessary to produce the spark to light-off the oil burner cycle. These are known as high-tension terminals and come in a number of styles and shapes (see Fig. 5-4). To these

Courtesy Webster Electric Co.

**Fig. 5-4. High-tension transformer terminals.**

terminals are attached the wires, bus bars, spring clips, etc., which transport the voltage produced to the ultimate end points, the electrode assemblies. These units may be simple thread or knob-type terminals, spring-clips, plug-in types, or a variety of plunger or well-type models. It is most important that the connections be tight, easy to get to, and positive in their contact with the transporting wires or metal springs. These dual high-tension terminals may be situated on the ends, base, center base, etc., of the transformer bodies. In ordering or replacing a defective unit, proper care must be taken to ensure correct measurements and positioning of these high-tension terminals.

## Primary Lead Wiring

The primary transformer leads, which are hooked up directly into the residence oil burner wiring service, are housed in one section of the transformer body. This section is usually accessible through a screw or clip-on work plate on the unit's body. Additional space or knock-outs are available to secure neat electrical connections to and from the main service. In most cases, the lead wires are left long enough so that the unit may be wired into other component parts without additional wire splicing. Some transformer bodies also have built-in junction boxes with inscribed diagrams for ease of installation (see Figs. 5-5, 5-6, and 5-7).

There are two (2) wires coming from the primary side of the transformer, and these are hooked into the burner service wiring as follows:

1. *For constant-ignition installations.* Attach one wire to the white feed wire going to the No. 2 or ground terminal of the stack relay. Hook up the remaining wire to the black feed wire going to the No. 3 or motor-ignition terminal of the stack relay.
2. *For intermittent ignition (spark goes off after approximately 90 seconds).* Attach one wire to the white feed wire going to the No. 2 or ground terminal of the stack relay. Hook up the remaining wire to the red (in most cases) feed wire going to the No. 4 or ignition terminal of the stack relay.

As with many other components in the oil heating industry, the manufacturers have made constant strides toward providing universally applicable products to decrease, as much as possible, inventory and field service problems. Some manufacturers have devised universal mounting plates, each adaptable to a great

**Fig. 5-5. Transformer primary wiring and high-tension terminals.**

number of individual and different burner models, while other manufacturers have designed transformer bodies with as many as three separate sets of high-tension terminals in each transformer unit. This design, as the spec sheet of the manufacturer points out, will allow one transformer, when combined with a universal mounting base, to take the place of twelve individual transformer styles.

Most transformers are guaranteed for a period of 12 months by the manufacturer with some extending the period to 18 and 24 months. This guarantee covers only the replacement of the manufacturer's product under usual operating conditions, and excluding "abnormal" stress, improper application, or excessive moisture. It does not cover a serviceman's installation or mail-back for guarantee, postage, and handling costs.

Courtesy Dongan Electric Co.

**Fig. 5-6. Transformer body showing primary lead wires and high-voltage terminals.**

## Ordering Replacement Transformers

When it becomes necessary to order or replace an existing transformer, it is best to mark down the pertinent facts, figures, and sizes on paper for complete accuracy.

1. Note, first, the size of the mounting base (width and length) and the position of the oil burner casting and mounting holes.

2. Mark down the position of the high-tension terminals (end terminals, base terminals, center base terminals) in the transformer body, measuring for correct distance if necessary.

3. Determine the style of high-tension terminals (screw type, plug type, springs, etc.).

4. Make sure of the secondary output of the individual transformer you are working with (e.g., 8000, 10,000, 14,000 volts) for replacement purposes.

5. Make sure of the primary of the individual transformer you are working with (e.g., 115–230 volts) for replacement.

149

Fig. 5-7. Transformer body showing high-voltage leads connected.

6. Mark down the transformer body size (width, length, depth) if the replacement area you are working with is compact or specially designed.

7. Purchase a standard brand product. Do not look for bargains. As you will note in the section dealing with rebuilding transformers that follows, many shortcuts in production methods materially affect the useful life of transformer equipment.

## Rebuilding Defective Transformers

Transformer units can be rebuilt when they become defective or are too weak to be considered useful for satisfactory operation. This can be especially helpful when an identical replacement part is requested or required. There are, however, certain points that should be checked on a rebuilt unit. First, make sure that the rebuilding firm is reputable and not a fly-by-night outfit. Then assure yourself that the rebuilt unit you are purchasing can pass the following 10-step checkup program:

1. Are the high-tension insulating terminals replaced if cracked, crazed, or carbonized?
2. Is an interference eliminator installed on each rebuilt transformer?
3. Is the primary coil tested and replaced unless perfect and in good-as-new condition?
4. Are the secondary coils mated identically for correct output?
5. Can the secondary coils stand up under additional high-voltage loads?
6. Are the secondary coils tested and replaced unless as good as new?
7. Are the interior electrical shunts adjusted for correct amperage?
8. Is the compound refiller a new charge or old used material?
9. Is the transformer outer case just cleaned off or spray painted for maximum customer satisfaction?
10. Will the rebuilt transformer develop and hold a spark of at least ¾ in. instantly, and without faltering?

If the rebuilt unit can pass the above checkup program, you have purchased and placed a satisfactory transformer into field service duty.

## Radio Interference

Occasionally, radio interference can be the cause of nuisance service calls. These may be caused by an ungrounded transformer body, absence in the unit of a built-in radio-shielding device preinstalled during manufacture, or high-frequency waves being transmitted directly from the high-voltage cables, electrode assembly, and spark gap. The situation is caused by these high-frequency waves, generated by the spark gap, traveling from this area to the secondary coils, being transmitted to the primary coil and house electric service. In modern transformer units, copper barriers are placed between the primary and secondary coils and attached to the core. Such barriers, grounded to the transformer core, collect the high-frequency impulses sent back through the unit by the gap and dissipate them to the ground.

If a field transformer gives static or radio interference difficulties, there are a number of solutions. These can vary from the replacement of any obviously cheap or defective transformer units to the other extreme of repairing the existing bodies through the installation of an external radio-interference eliminator placed directly across the line. Another solution is to securely ground the transformer unit, with a piece of wire, to a water pipe or other suitable ground. Resetting the spark gap and replacing leaking high-tension wires will usually clear up the interference if it comes from the above sources. At times this problem may be a bit stubborn, but persistence and good equipment will ultimately win out.

## Transformer Testing

Don't waste time with weak or defective transformers. A poor unit can only be troublesome, time-consuming, and temperamental in its operation. Test each transformer, and when there is any question as to its effectiveness, replace it immediately for safety's sake.

You may purchase available commercial transformer testers or there are a number of methods to field-test a transformer unit.

**Preliminary to Testing**—Disconnect the motor terminal lead at the relay (Terminal No. 3-Intermittent Ignition) or the motor lead wires in the oil burner junction box (Constant Ignition). In carrying out this operation, no oil should be permitted to flow during the test. Open up the back or access plate of the oil burner so that the high-tension terminals are exposed to working view. Turn the unit on during the test. Turn if off immediately following the completion of the unit test. Use one of the following test methods:

**Method 1**—Using an insulated handle screwdriver, touch the high-tension terminals with one end of the driver while shorting out the upper end of the tool against the burner frame or housing. Slowly draw the upper part of the tool away from the frame, continuing to hold the point of the screwdriver on the high-tension terminals. Note the length of the spark that can be drawn out during this operation. A strong, unfaltering spark of at least 3/4 in. is indicative of a good transformer—anything less than this is subject to immediate replacement.

Method 2—Go through the preliminary steps outlined above. Hold a *neon test lamp* about ½ to ¾ of an inch from the secondary or high-tension terminals of the transformer. The bulb should glow strongly if the unit is to be considered satisfactory. If there is a weak glow, or the lamp does not light at all, change the transformer.

Method 3—Repeat the preliminary steps outlined above. Plug in a known "good" set of high-tension transformer lead wires into the transformer terminals. Hold these about ¼ in. apart and slowly separate to approximately ¾ of an inch. The spark should continue to unfalteringly gap or jump the full wide area if the transformer is to be considered effective—anything less is subject to immediate replacement.

## TRANSFORMER TROUBLES

*Symptom and Possible Cause*

*Possible Remedy*

### Poor, Ineffective, or No Ignition

1. Defective terminals.

1. High-tension terminals may be loose, cracked, crazed, or oil-soaked. Repair or replace as necessary.

### Spasmodic or No Ignition

1. Contacts in ignition relay not being made.
2. Wire to No. 4 terminal loose or broken.
3. Wire to No. 2 terminal loose or broken.

1. Clean contacts or replace relay as necessary.
2. Tighten connection or repair broken wire.
3. Tighten connection or repair broken wire.

153

| *Symptom and Possible Cause* | *Possible Remedy* |
|---|---|

## No Ignition

1. Loose primary connections on transformer.

2. Weak or defective transformer.

3. Moisture in transformer case.

4. Abnormal stress on transformer.

5. Bus bars or spring clips not seating or making proper contact.

6. Wire leads loose, disconnected, or broken.

7. Transformer installed incorrectly.

---

1. Tighten connection.

2. Replace unit.

3. Place transformer in oven and bake dry or replace with new unit.

4. Loosen and retighten all fasteners holding transformer in place. If this does not remove stress, determine cause and correct it.

5. Repair, relocate, or replace spring clips or bus bars until proper contact is made.

6. Check all leads and tighten, reconnect, or repair as necessary.

7. Install correctly.

## HIGH-VOLTAGE IGNITION TRANSPORTATION

In order to effectively move the high voltage produced in the ignition system to its ultimate end point, the electrode assembly, a safe means of voltage transportation must be provided. The three major choices that present themselves are ignition cable, bus bars, and spring clips. Each has its special advantage, adaptations, and special oil burner model and make uses.

# IGNITION CABLE

Ignition cable, in most instances, is made of a heavy-gauge, stranded-copper conducting wire. These wires are marked and stamped to indicate the voltage they are safely capable of transporting to and from given points in the ignition system. The cable, UL or Underwriter's approved, is completely insulated with a polyethylene jacket or is vinyl coated on its outer sides (see Fig. 5-8). The combination not only ensures an excellent conduction of the high voltages but also provides insulation against dampness and ensures transmission around, over, or under any other conducting surface. The flexible ignition wire permits easy bending, handling, and installation on any oil burner housing situation. In addition, the wire may be cut to any desired length for either new or replacement work.

To ensure a positive contact between the insulated cable and both the electrode assembly and the transformer, terminal or attachment ends in many different shapes and forms are provided. These terminals are securely attached to both ends of the ignition cable through the use of a "crimping tool," solderless twist-on connectors or specially designed adapters that lend themselves to quick and easy hook-ups.

The cable, of course, has potential disadvantages, such as drying out, aging, heat injuries, and cracking. However, the use of modern materials and protective coverings have cut these problems to a minimum.

# BUS BARS

Bus bars are manufactured in countless varieties, shapes, and lengths, and usually are specific for definite models or makes of oil burners. Unlike ignition cable, these one-piece units are a completely uninsulated strip of conducting metal. Once manufactured and bent into the required shape at the factory, they generally remain so formed for the balance of their functioning life, if left undisturbed. One end of the metal bus bar is threaded or left completely blank. This end is screwed or pressed into the

155

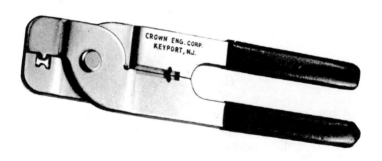

Fig. 5-8. Ignition cable and crimping tool.

electrode assembly and the transformer body, with sufficient space provided from other conducting surfaces along all points of its transporting pathway. The advantages are obvious. Dampness, dryness, cracking, heat, and aging cannot mar bus bars. On the other hand, they are not easily adaptable to changeover in unit-rebuilding situations.

## Spring Clips

The spring clip is, as its name implies, made up of a spring-type adapter that provides positive contact between the electrode assembly and the transfer body. The "springiness" of these specialized units takes the place of regular screw or clip-on adapters found in other ignition transporting mediums, with the pressure of the springs often substituting for these connectors.

Spring clips are designed specifically for individual burner models and are usually not interchangeable without a great deal of part adaption. Like the bus bar, spring clips are completely uninsulated, especially designed and preformed at the factory. The advantages and disadvantages of their use in the ignition transporting assembly parallel those of the previously discussed bus-bar units.

Because of the great variety in styles, types, and sizes, it would obviously be difficult to "service-stock" the latter two types of ignition transporters, although they definitely do possess certain outstanding advantages. Generally, most service departments appear to prefer to use "roll" ignition wire, and to stock a variety of adapters in regular everyday service.

# IGNITION TERMINALS

There are a multitude of ignition terminal styles and shapes, as illustrated in Figs. 5-9 through 5-12. Some of these require special "crimping" tools for secure attachment to ignition wires, while others are simply hand assembled through specially constructed

| | | | |
|---|---|---|---|
| IT200<br>CAGE | IT201<br>SPRING | IT202<br>RING | IT202-H<br>HOOK |
| IT203<br>SPLIT RING | IT204<br>ANGLE CAGE | IT204-L<br>RIGHT ANGLE CAGE | IT205<br>ANGLE SPRING |
| IT206<br>STUD FERRULE | IT207-6 (6-32)<br>IT207-8 (8-32)<br>IT207-10 (10-32)<br>HEX BASE STUD | IT207-6X(6-32) THRU<br>SPECIAL HEX BASE STUD | IT207-10X (10-32)<br>LONG HEX BASE STUD |
| IT208-4 (4-40)<br>IT208-6 (6-32)<br>IT208-10 (10-32)<br>HOLLOW THRD. STUD | IT209<br>EYELET | IT210<br>FERRULE/FERRULE | SIT210<br>SOLDERLESS BASE STUD |

Courtesy Crown Engineering Corp.

**Fig. 5-9. Ignition terminals.**

Fig. 5-10. Ignition terminals.

159

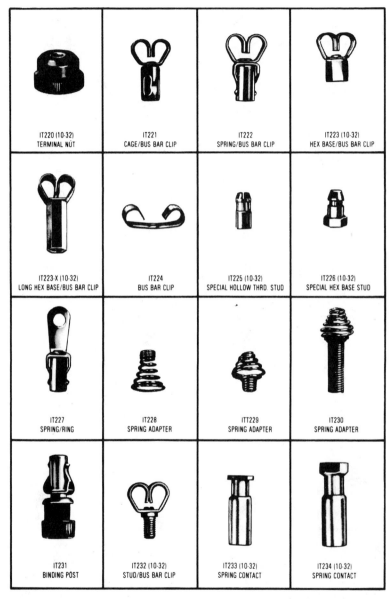

Courtesy Crown Engineering Corp.

**Fig. 5-11. Ignition terminals.**

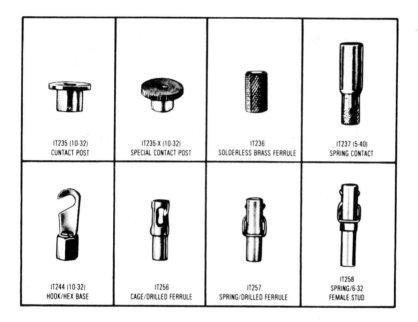

| IT235 (10-32)<br>CONTACT POST | IT235-X (10-32)<br>SPECIAL CONTACT POST | IT236<br>SOLDERLESS BRASS FERRULE | IT237 (5-40)<br>SPRING CONTACT |
| IT244 (10-32)<br>HOOK/HEX BASE | IT256<br>CAGE/DRILLED FERRULE | IT257<br>SPRING/DRILLED FERRULE | IT258<br>SPRING/6-32<br>FEMALE STUD |

Courtesy Crown Engineering Corp.

**Fig. 5-12. Ignition terminals.**

"pin-screw-twist contacts." The units can be purchased in lengths from ¼ to 1 in. to suit any particular ignition wire requirement.

The ignition terminal installation process follows a rather general pattern regardless of the style used. The following method is standard procedure: Strip back and clear off about ³⁄₁₆ in. of insulation from a correctly sized piece of ignition cable. This will expose the strands of conducting wire. The strands are then firmly seated in the proper side of the terminal with the cleaned wire ends passing through a small manufactured "hole" in the terminal body. The entire unit is then "crimped" or "hand assembled" securely for positive electrical contact.

Ignition terminals are usually purchased in containers of 50 pieces per unit, but some manufacturers are turning to smaller packaging groups in order to permit variety stocking. Although there are numerous styles of ignition terminals, practically all fall into four categories.

### Ring

The ring terminal slips over the transformer or electrode assembly stud, and a screw or nut is used to hold it securely in place on these ignition units.

### Stud

The stud terminal, designed in the form of a male plug, is pushed into the female or receptacle end of the transformer or electrode assembly unit.

### Cage

The cage terminal, one of the most popular in service work, simply slips onto the transformer or electrode assembly with stud and cage providing positive electrical contact. The terminals are preformed at the factory to provide maximum contact.

### Spring Snap

The spring-snap terminal shares service popularity with the cage, and functions in the same manner. This unit is factory-designed so that the spring metal holds it securely in place on the transformer or electrode assembly stud once the unit is snapped into place.

## ELECTRODE ASSEMBLY

In previous sections of this chapter and the chapter on transformers, we have covered the source of the spark and reviewed the major high-voltage transporting mediums available, such as ignition wires and bus bars. We now arrive at the end point, the area in which the ultimate spark is actually put through its paces—the "light-off" area.

The electrode assembly is a team of precisely engineered parts in which a spark, resulting from a combination of two properly positioned, "gapped" electrode tips, and high voltages, produced in an effective stepup transformer, join together to produce a "light-off." This arc of electricity ignites the prepared oil being pumped into the unit's combustion area. The flames of combustion result.

An electrode consists of two parts: the insulator, or porcelain; and the metal electrode rod, or tip. The insulator or porcelain section is a round or square piece of glazed or unglazed ceramic, carefully made and fired under the finest possible conditions and workmanship. These insulators, made in two major external diameters ($7/16$ in. and $9/16$ in.), service almost all oil burner manufacturers' requirements (see Fig. 5-13). Each porcelain is so designed and engineered that its coefficient of thermal expansion matches that of other electrode parts for maximum stability and strength. The insulators come in a number of lengths. They may either be ordered in the required individual sizes (4 in. to 30 in. in length) or be cut to size on the job with a special tool. The porcelains serve a dual function. They securely hold or position internally the electrode rods and tips; at the same time, they serve as insulators, protecting the metal rod passing through them from surrounding metal surfaces. These metal bodies might be the main assembly holder itself or any other section of the oil burner housing through which the high-voltage electricity passes. Each porcelain is center-bored to receive the metal electrode rods, with $3/32$ in. and $1/8$ in. serving as standard internal diameters.

The electrode rod or tip is made of a low-resistance high-nickel-alloy steel, carefully milled at both ends of the rod for top-grade performance. The tip, or front end, is usually rounded to provide a steady, even, high-voltage arc. The butt, or rear section, is carefully threaded to receive one of the many previously discussed ignition connecting terminals. Each rod, a short way back from the front tip area, has a lug precisely attached during manufacture which ensures permanence and stability when the rod is tightened into the porcelain body.

## COMPLETE ELECTRODE ASSEMBLY

A complete electrode assembly consists of a pair of porcelain insulators and electrode rods properly affixed with ignition terminals connected to each individual unit as shown in Fig. 5-14.

A set of transporting high-voltage wires or bus bars of the

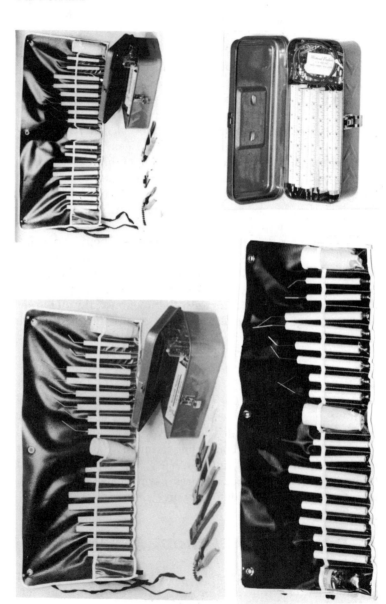

Fig. 5-13. Various types and

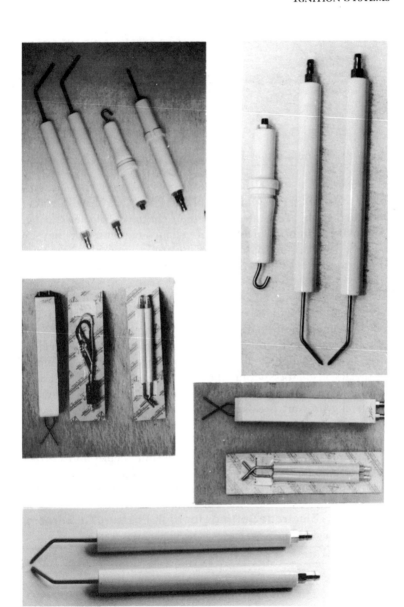

Courtesy Westwood Products

shapes of oil burner electrodes.

165

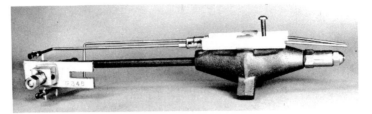

**Fig. 5-14. Electrode assembly.**

correct length to reach the transformer is also part of the assembly, as is a holder in which all of the above parts are securely mounted for insertion and ultimate use in the oil burner casting. There are a number of other miscellaneous items that may be classified as part and parcel of an electrode assembly. These are the various cable supports and protective bushings inserted into the electrode holder.

The cable supports serve merely to guide the high-voltage wires neatly back to the transformer, along the firing tube, without touching any of the internal parts of the burner. The protective bushings serve a dual purpose. First, they allow the serviceman to interchange small ($\frac{7}{16}$ in.) and large ($\frac{9}{16}$ in.) diameter porcelain insulators within the electrode holder unit. Second, they protect the delicate porcelain bodies against screw or tightening-pressure breakage. The bushings distribute more evenly and safely the pressure effects of tightening within the electrode holder.

The oil burner electrode holders permit secure and correct mounting of the porcelain bodies and electrode rods within an established framework (see Table 5-1), allowing the serviceman

**Table 5-1. Electrode Settings for High-Pressure Oil Burners**

(unless otherwise specified by burner manufacturer)

| Nozzle GPH | A | B | C |
|---|---|---|---|
| 45° (.75–4.00) | $\frac{1}{8}$" to $\frac{3}{16}$" | $\frac{1}{2}$" | $\frac{1}{4}$" |
| 60° (.75–4.00) | $\frac{1}{8}$" to $\frac{3}{16}$" | $\frac{5}{8}$" | $\frac{1}{4}$" |
| 70° (.75–4.00) | $\frac{1}{8}$" to $\frac{3}{16}$" | $\frac{5}{8}$" | $\frac{1}{8}$" |
| 80° (.75–4.00) | $\frac{1}{8}$" to $\frac{3}{16}$" | $\frac{5}{8}$" | $\frac{1}{8}$" |
| 90° (.75–4.00) | $\frac{1}{8}$" to $\frac{3}{16}$" | $\frac{5}{8}$" | 0" |

to set and maintain a constant distance and degree from other metal objects (see Table 5-2).

Above 4.00 GPH it may be advisable to increase dimension C by ⅛ in. to ensure smoother starting. For adjustment guide, see Fig. 5-15.

### Table 5-2. Insulator Spacing

| Secondary Voltage of Ignition Transformer | Minimum Surface Distance Over Insulator (inches) |
|---|---|
| Not More Than 6000 volts | 1 inch |
| Not More Than 10,000 volts | 1½ inches |
| Not More Than 15,000 volts | 2 inches |

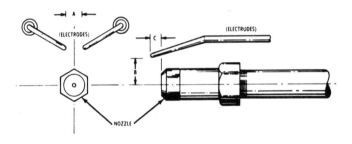

**Fig. 5-15. Electrode tip adjustment.**

Recommended spacing over surface of an insulator between any part of the electrode and the nearest grounded metal parts are given in Table 5-2.

Let us refer back for a moment to earlier sections of this chapter where it was pointed out that "the assemblies must be so positioned that the oil-spray pattern does not hit on the electrode tips, and that these points should be set in such a way that they are never closer to any other metal surface than they are to themselves."

Listed in Table 5-1 are a number of suggested electrode settings arranged according to nozzle angle and gallon-per-hour rate. This table is just a guide. It is recommended that you consult your oil burner manufacturer's spec sheets whenever possible.

## ELECTRODE TOOL

In reading over Tables 5-1 and 5-2, you will notice that certain electrode distances and spacing are set forth. Very often it becomes necessary, in order to obtain these settings, to bend or manipulate the electrode rods. This must be a very gentle effort on the part of the serviceman because it is easy to snap or crack the porcelain during this operation. Special tools, known as electrode benders, are available at supply houses and may be useful for this particular operation. The tool is designed especially to give proper bending leverage with maximum porcelain safety.

## CLEANING AND MAINTAINING ELECTRODES

From the descriptions in previous paragraphs of electrode assemblies and porcelain insulators, it should be obvious that these insulators must be treated with the utmost respect. They should never be dropped, packed loosely in a service kit, or otherwise manhandled. Porcelains should be packed, preferably in workable pairs, in containers protected completely from anything that might damage the ceramic bodies.

In the field, electrode units should be cloth wiped and cleaned in solvent during the annual burner checkup. If there are any signs of lines, crazing, or cracking, replace them immediately to ensure continuous trouble-free operation.

## TESTING ELECTRODE ASSEMBLIES

If you have any suspicion of ignition difficulties and you have already ruled out the high-voltage transformer as a cause of the problem, it is imperative that you thoroughly test out the entire electrode assembly. These units can be tricky, and often only top-grade service work will sleuth out the troublemaker.

Begin your testing procedure by removing the entire firing assembly from the burner housing, and cleaning it thoroughly (see Figs. 5-16 and 5-17). Disconnect or turn off the oil supply

**Fig. 5-16. Electrode assembly installed in oil burner unit.**

source. Lay the assembly on a newspaper or a clean section of the floor next to the oil burner, and begin your testing program:

1. Reconnect the ignition wires to the burner transformer and turn on the oil burner. Look for any high-voltage leaks or areas where the spark appears to jump from either the wires or porcelains, other than at the electrode tips. If such a leak develops, the defective porcelains or cable should be changed.

2. With the unit's electricity turned off, disconnect one of the high-tension ignition wires from the electrodes. Make sure that the wire is leakproof and sound before attempting this test. Hold the wire in your hand and electrically reactivate the unit. Keeping it close to the assembly, run the wire up

169

**Fig. 5-17. Electrode assembly removed from oil burner unit.**

and down the length of each porcelain and the opposite cable. If a spark gap appears at any point on either of the porcelains or the insulated wire, except at the metal connections, the insulator or cable should be changed. Repeat this test using the other ignition cable.

3. Reconnect the cable as in test number one, and electrically activate the unit. When a spark forms at the electrode tops, blow strongly against it watching closely for any leaks to develop either in the ignition cable or porcelain areas. The more the spark is separated from the electrode points, the greater is the chance of potential leakage showing up.

Don't waste time with defective porcelains or ignition cables. Replace these units immediately for completely safe operation. This portion of the equipment is very reasonable in price and can spell the difference between a happy or unhappy customer.

# ELECTRODE-ASSEMBLY TROUBLES

*Symptom and Possible Cause*          *Possible Remedy*

### High-Voltage Leakage

1. Oil-soaked or crazed porcelains.
2. Porcelain broken.

3. Oil-soaked, broken, or incorrectly assembled terminals.
4. Broken or scraped high-voltage cable.

1. Replace electrode assembly.
2. Replace electrode assembly using care in the tightening process.
3. Replace terminals or assemble correctly.
4. Replace and position to prevent abrasion by fan or other moving parts.

### No Arc

1. Electrode gap set incorrectly.
2. Carbon or oil-soaked tips.

3. Bus bar or spring clip broken, bent out of shape, or incorrectly installed.
4. Terminals crimped or connected incorrectly.
5. Electrode assembly loose, permitting electrode to turn.
6. Electrodes shorting against burner housing.

7. Defective transformer.
8. Loose relay wires.
9. Broken relay terminal.
10. Loose wiring in unit.

1. Reset gap to proper specs.
2. Clean thoroughly or replace assembly if necessary.
3. Replace, repair, or correctly install.

4. Replace and connect correctly.
5. Align and tighten assembly.

6. Install correct size or type of holder for the burner casting.
7. Repair or replace.
8. Repair as necessary.
9. Repair or replace.
10. Repair as necessary.

## SUMMARY

The ignition system provides spark to ignite the fuel oil that enters the combustion chamber. There are basically two types of ignition: intermittent and constant. Spark is developed across the electrode tips from the stepup transformer.

Most manufacturers have devised a universal mounting plate adaptable to many individual and different burner models. This eliminates the need to stock various makes of transformers. Secondary high voltage totals approximately 10,000 volts, which is fed to the burner electrodes. The entire transformer is encased in a hard tar or wax-like compound that serves as a moisture-proofing seal.

Ignition cable is made of heavy-gauge stranded copper wire. This cable is flexible, permitting easy bending for any installation. Various ignition terminal connectors are used that require a special crimping tool for a secure attachment.

The electrode consists of two parts: the porcelain insulator and the metal electrode rod or tip. The porcelain serves as a holder to position internally the electrode rod and tip. It also serves as an insulator, protecting the metal rod when passing through surrounding metal surfaces. The electrode rod is made from a low-resistance high-nickel-alloy steel, carefully milled at both ends for top-grade performance.

## REVIEW QUESTIONS

1. What function does the transformer perform?
2. Explain constant ignition.
3. Explain intermittent ignition.
4. A ¾-in. unfaltering spark is a good indication of what?
5. What are the two major parts of an electrode unit?
6. What should be considered when selecting a replacement transformer?
7. Explain the principles of the electrode and its operation.
8. What can be done to eliminate radio interference from ignition system?

9. What type of material is used to make the electrode firing tip?
10. What type of wire is used in the high-voltage portion of the ignition system?

CHAPTER 6

# Electrical Wiring and Control

This chapter contains wiring diagrams of motors, relays, and thermostats that cover almost every automatic oil heating installation.

The diagrams are general in nature with application to controls manufactured by almost any company in the field. The diagrams listed are specific for *constant-ignition* oil burner circuit installations. An electrical wiring diagram indicating connections for *intermittent-ignition,* as applied to all units, is also listed.

Specific electrical wiring hookups are outlined where necessary so that the coverage is comprehensive enough to meet most any field-service-installation problem.

Remember to observe all local electrical regulations. Always select top-quality products for your installation. Do a neat, workmanlike job no matter how large or small the project may be. Always install a fused switch box between the oil burner unit and the main electrical house supply. Use emergency switches in your installation. Place these devices in a spot convenient for both the homeowner and the service mechanic. Do not locate an oil burner switch in a position where it can be mistaken for a basement light switch. If possible, use a brightly marked cover plate, indicating that the switch controls the oil burner.

### Operational Sequence (Fig. 6-1)

A thermostat senses the need for heat in the room and turns *on* the stack switch, which closes the low-voltage circuit across the terminals of the stack switch. The stack switch, when turned *on* by the thermostat, starts the oil burner, provided the stack has cooled sufficiently to return the helix-operated contacts to the starting position. The oil burner runs until the thermostat is satisfied and turns *off* the stack switch. This action opens the low-voltage circuit across the stack-switch terminals. If either the boiler pressure or water temperature reaches its preset high point, the safety limiting controls (pressuretrol or aquastat) will turn *off* the entire system, regardless of whether the thermostat is calling for heat.

### Controls Used in System

*Gravity steam.* Thermostat—steam-limit control—stack switch—optional clock thermostat.

*Gravity hot water.* Thermostat—hot-water limit—stack switch—optional clock thermostat.

## STEAM SYSTEM WITH TANK-TYPE DOMESTIC HOT-WATER HEATER

### Operational Sequence (Fig. 6-2)

A thermostat senses the need for heat in the room and turns *on* the stack switch, which closes the low-voltage circuit across the

## STEAM OR GRAVITY HOT-WATER SYSTEM

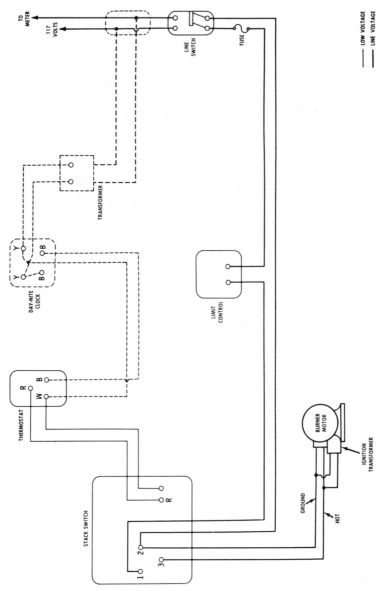

Fig. 6-1. Electrical circuit for oil-burning hot-water system.

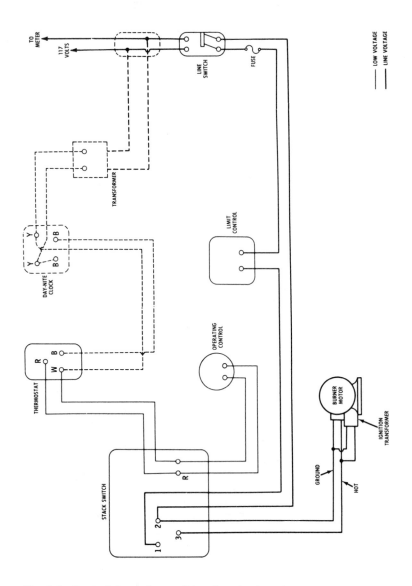

**Fig. 6-2.** Control circuit for an oil-burning steam system.

terminals of the stack switch. The operating control used to maintain summer-winter domestic hot water can also sense a drop in water temperature and turn *on* the stack switch, which closes the low-voltage terminals of the stack switch. The oil burner will run until the thermostat is satisfied and turns *off* the stack switch. This opens the low-voltage circuit across the terminals of the stack switch. The domestic hot-water temperature can also reach the cutoff setting of the operation control, turning *off* the stack switch. If the boiler pressure reaches its preset high point at any time, the safety-limit control will turn the entire system *off*.

### Controls Used in System

Thermostat—steam-limit control—stack switch—operating control—optional clock thermostat.

# FORCED-CIRCULATION HOT-WATER SYSTEM

### Operational Sequence (Fig. 6-3)

A thermostat senses the need for heat in the room and turns *on* the relay, closing the low-voltage circuit across the terminals of the relay. The relay, when turned on by the thermostat, starts the circulator and also turns *on* the stack switch. The line voltage circuit is closed to the circulator and the low-voltage circuit is closed across the terminals of the stack relay. When the stack switch is turned on by the relay, the oil burner starts, providing the stack has cooled and returned the helix-operated contacts to the starting position. The oil burner runs until the thermostat is satisfied and turns *off* the relay, stopping the circulator. This breaks the low-voltage pilot circuit to the stack switch, which stops the oil burner. If the boiler temperature reaches its preset high point at any time, the limit control will turn *off* the stack switch, stopping the oil burner.

179

## FORCED-CIRCULATION HOT-WATER SYSTEM

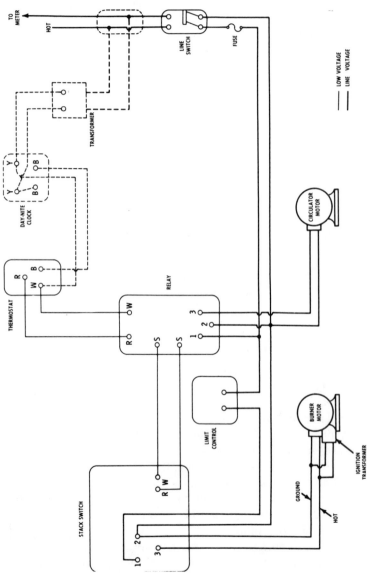

Fig. 6-3. Control circuit for an oil-burning forced-circulation hot-water system.

## Controls Used in System

Thermostat—limit control—stack switch—relay—optional clock thermostat.

# FORCED-CIRCULATION HOT-WATER SYSTEM WITH TANK-TYPE DOMESTIC HOT-WATER HEATER

## Operational Sequence (Fig. 6-4)

A thermostat senses the need for heat in the room and turns *on* the relay, closing the low-voltage circuit across the terminals of the relay. The relay, when turned on by the thermostat, starts the circulator and also turns on the stack switch. This closes the line voltage circuit to the circulator and the low-voltage circuit across the terminals of the stack switch. The stack switch, when turned *on* either by the relay or the operating immersion control, starts the oil burner if the stack has cooled and returned the helix-operated contacts to the starting position. The oil burner runs until the thermostat is satisfied. The thermostat then turns *off* the relay which stops the circulator and simultaneously breaks the low-voltage circuit across the terminals of the stack switch, stopping the oil burner.

If the boiler water temperature reaches its preset high point at any time, the limit control will turn *off* the stack switch, stopping the oil burner. In addition to the preceding sequence of operation, when the operating immersion control used to maintain summer-winter domestic hot water senses a drop in the boiler water temperature, it turns *on* the stack switch as required. It breaks the low-voltage circuit across the relay terminals when the water temperature reaches its cutout setting. This operation does not affect the unit's hot-water circulator.

## Controls Used in System

Thermostat—combination limit control and operating control—relay—stack switch—optional clock thermostat.

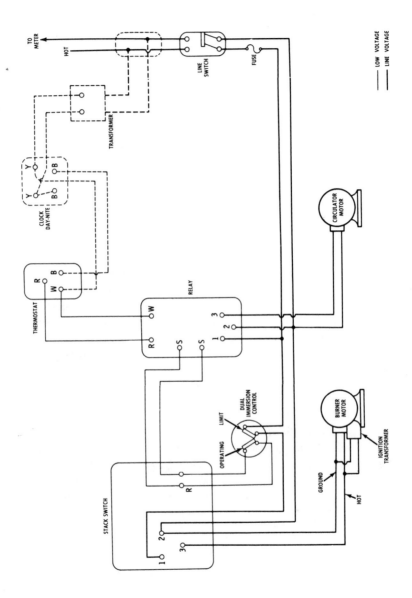

**Fig. 6-4.** Oil-burning forced-circulation water heater circuit.

# FORCED-CIRCULATION HOT-WATER SYSTEM WITH TANKLESS DOMESTIC HOT-WATER HEATER

## Operational Sequence (Fig. 6-5)

A thermostat senses the need for heat in the room and turns *on* the relay, closing the low-voltage circuit across the terminals of the relay. The relay, when turned *on* by the thermostat turns *on* the circulator if the low-limit immersion circulator control is turned *on*. The relay also turns *on* the stack switch, closing the line voltage circuit through the limit control to the circulator, and the low-voltage circuit across the terminals of the stack switch.

The stack switch, when turned *on* by the relay or the operating immersion control, starts the oil burner if the stack has cooled and returned the helix-operated contacts to the starting position. The oil burner runs until the boiler water temperature reaches its preset high point causing the limit immersion control to turn *off* the stack switch, stopping the oil burner, or until the thermostat is satisfied and operates the relay, stopping the circulator and simultaneously breaking the low-voltage circuit across the terminals of the stack switch, stopping the oil burner. In addition to the above sequence of operation, the operating immersion control turns *on* the stack switch when the boiler water temperature drops below its preset lower limit. When the water temperature rises to the cutoff setting, the immersion control turns *off* the stack switch, stopping the oil burner.

*Note:* The boiler's low-limit immersion circulator control is turned *on* at all times when the boiler temperature is high enough to give hot water for circulation to the residence's radiation. Both this control and the relay must be *on* for the circulator to run. If either one turns *off*, the circulator will not run.

## Controls Used in System

Thermostat—combination limit and operating immersion control—relay—reverse-acting low-limit circulator control—stack switch—optional clock thermostat.

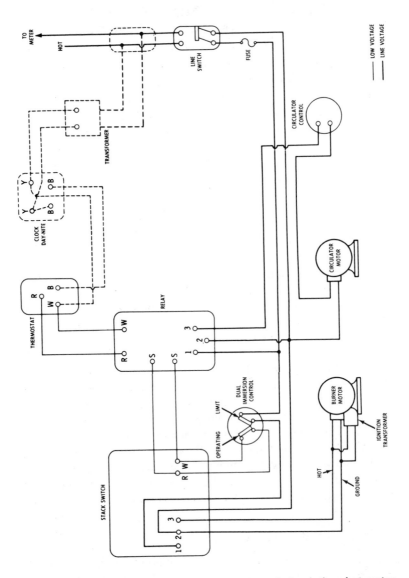

Fig. 6-5. Control circuit for oil-burning forced-circulation hot-water system.

# FORCED WARM-AIR SYSTEM

## Operational Sequence (Fig. 6-6)

A thermostat senses the need for heat in the room and turns *on* the stack switch, which closes the low-voltage circuit across the terminals of the switch. When the stack switch is turned *on* by the thermostat it starts the oil burner if the stack has cooled and returned the helix-operated contacts to the starting position. The oil burner runs until the thermostat is satisfied and turns *off* the stack switch, which opens the low-voltage circuit across the terminals to the stack switch, or until the bonnet temperature reaches its preset high point, which causes the safety-limit control (part of the fan and limit control) to turn *off* the unit.

As soon as the combustion unit increases the bonnet temperature enough to ensure that warm air will be forced out of the residence registers, the fan side of the fan and limit control starts the blower. The blower continues to function until the bonnet temperature is reduced to its cutoff setting.

## Controls Used in System

Thermostat—combination fan and limit control—stack switch—optional clock thermostat.

# GRAVITY WARM-AIR SYSTEM

## Operational Sequence (Fig. 6-7)

A thermostat senses the need for heat in the room and turns *on* the stack switch, which closes the low-voltage circuit across the terminals of the stack switch. The stack switch, when turned *on* by the thermostat, starts the oil burner if the stack has cooled and returned the helix-operated contacts to the starting position. The oil burner runs until the thermostat is satisfied and turns *off* the stack switch, or until the bonnet temperature reaches its preset high point, causing the limit control to turn *off* the entire system.

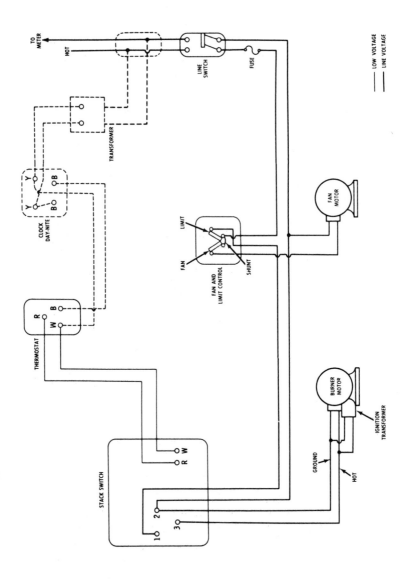

**Fig. 6-6. Circuit for an oil-burning forced warm-air unit.**

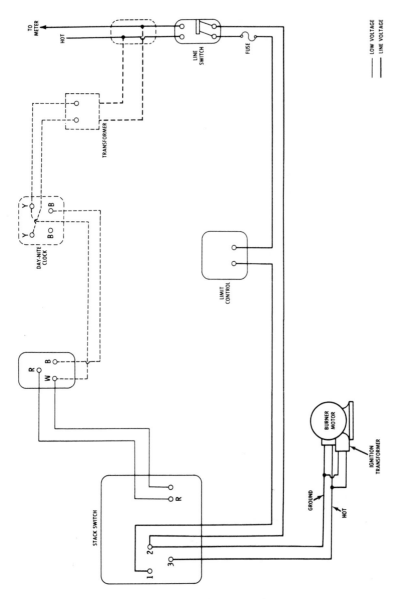

**Fig. 6-7.** Circuit for an oil-burning gravity warm-air system.

### Controls Used in System

Thermostat—limit control-stack switch—optional clock thermostat.

# ZONE CONTROL FORCED HOT-WATER SYSTEM WITH TANK-TYPE DOMESTIC HOT-WATER HEATER

### Operational Sequence (Fig. 6-8)

A thermostat senses the need for heat in a room and energizes the relay. The relay, when actuated by the thermostat, starts the circulator and starts the stack switch in operation. The stack switch, when activated by the relay or the operating immersion control, starts the oil burner if the stack has cooled and returned the helix-operated contacts to the starting position. The oil burner runs until the thermostat is satisfied. When this occurs, it turns *off* the relay, stopping the circulator and simultaneously breaking the low-voltage circuit to the stack switch; or the boiler water temperature reaches the preset high point, and the immersion limit control turns *off* the stack switch, stopping the oil burner operation.

In addition to the preceding sequence of operation, the operating immersion control, in order to maintain summer-winter domestic hot water, senses a drop in water temperature and turns *on* the stack switch. This activates the burner but not the circulator. This immersion control also turns *off* the stack switch, stopping the oil burner when the domestic hot-water temperature reaches ther cutoff setting.

### Controls Used in System

Thermostat and relay—combined limit and operating control—stack switch—optional clock thermostat—additional relays for each individual zone—additional thermostats for each individual zone.

*Note:* The electrical diagrams included in this chapter were all designed for *constant-ignition* oil burner circuit installation. For

188

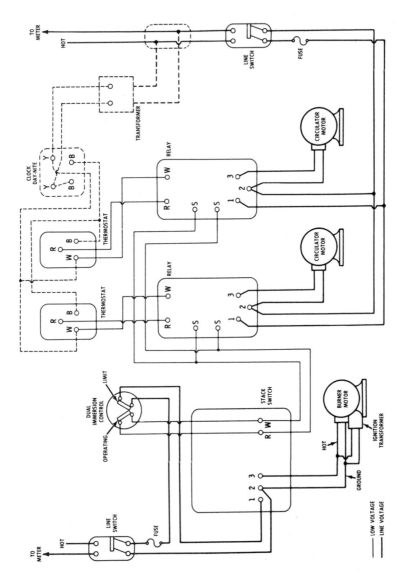

**Fig. 6-8.** Electrical circuit for an oil-burning zone-control forced hot-water system with tank-type domestic hot-water heater.

*intermittent-ignition* oil burner circuit installation, use the No. 4 terminal of the relay as indicated in Fig. 6-9.

## MOTORS

To explain the multitude of specific reasons for, and the uses of, the modern electric motor would be a waste of time and space, for all around us are examples of its primary function— motive power. Whether they be the tiny motors that power our electric shavers and household clocks or the big units operating the heavy equipment of our industries or the fractional horse-power motors that activate our oil burner units, basically their "use value" is the same—a source of power. A slight breakdown in the utility company's electrical system, for example, serves to actively demonstrate the countless labor-saving services that motors perform every second of the day. It is enough to note here, simply, that energy transmitted by the fractional horse-power motor will supply power to drive the fans and fuel pumps of our oil burner units, the blowers of our warm-air furnaces, the circulating pumps of our hot-water heating systems, and a host of other items.

Basically, an electric motor consists of seven major component parts:

1. A rigid, sturdy, steel frame in which all of the motor parts are housed. The housing, always attractively decorated, is styled to complement the overall design of most oil burner units. In addition, by virtue of their universal design, these cases are often made to be interchangeable or usable as replacement units for hundreds of different burner makes and models (see Fig. 6-10).

2. A shaft for accurate location and placement of the rotor. Onto this finely ground and perfectly balanced shaft will also be placed the ultimate outside load to be carried by the motor. These shafts come in different lengths and thick-nesses; attachment to other items is secured through cou-plings, setscrews, or similar locking devices.

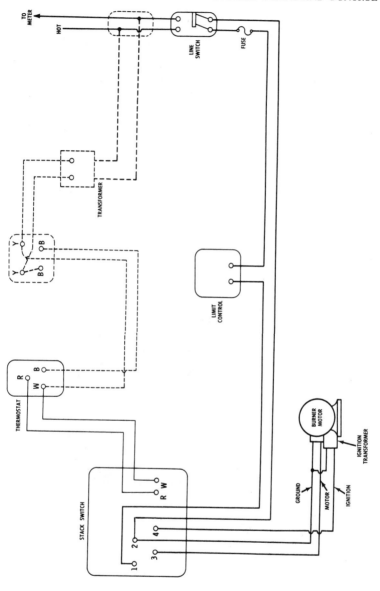

Fig. 6-9. Control circuit for intermittent-ignition oil burner.

3. An overload or *thermoguard* switch, which provides quick, dependable response to abnormal loads or possibly defective operating situations. This built-in safety factor eliminates the possibility of the motor restarting until the motor difficulty has been corrected (see Fig. 6-11).
4. The rotor, armature, or motive section of the electric motor.
5. The stator or stationary section of the electric motor.
6. Every motor contains, of course, the necessary internal and external wiring hookups. In addition, an easy-to-read, instructive wiring diagram is imprinted on some section of every unit. The motor usually comes with 20-in. attaching lead wiring as shown in Fig. 6-12. Some manufacturers even provide built-in line-cord strain relief devices. These permit up to about 35 lb. of emergency or "error pull" to be exerted on the motor leads without damage to the internal wiring. The electrical installation connections are positioned as uni-

Courtesy Marathon Electric Co.

Fig. 6-10. Standard oil burner motor looking at the shaft side.

Courtesy General Electric Co.

Fig. 6-11. Oil burner motor showing overload reset button (white button at top of motor).

formly as possible for easy service on all units. Also available are special "reversible" motors that permit instant rotational changes through a simple exchange of external wiring or quick panelboard adjustments. This feature, incidentally, can eliminate double stocking of motors, for one unit may serve for either direction of rotation.

7. The starting switch and motor-starting mechanism.

There are many important features to look for in the choice of an electrical motor. In the forefront are longevity, ease of installation, and a minimum of service. When we think of motor life expectancies, we must consider, first, the number of starts and stops the average motor makes. Are the starting mechanisms geared to handle this? Is the unit protected with an overload switch to handle emergencies? Are the motor casings, rotors, shafts—in fact, all integral parts—made to last under long operational stress and strain? Is the internal insulating material and wiring of the best grade?

It often follows that a minimum of service will be required on fine, well-assembled equipment. This logic is even further justified when a piece requiring oiling, for example, is designed with adequate self-oiling features ensuring complete lubrication of all parts. Still other mechanical "life-preserving" features are the modern metals and precision engineering that go into electric motor construction. These help to evenly dissipate the opera-

193

**Fig. 6-12. Oil burner motor showing external wire connections.**

tional heat, thus preserving the bearings and other metal parts either through elimination of "hot spots" or the conduction cooling of critical areas.

Each manufacturer does his utmost to simplify and universalize his particular branded product. Ease of mounting, speedy hookups, and reversibility are prime results of this progressive approach. Consider for a moment a compact, lightweight, reversible motor. Not only is it physically easier for the serviceman to install, but these same features reduce transportation and handling costs while cutting down stockroom area requirements. Because of its reversibility feature, this identical motor also reduces by half both shop and service-truck inventory requirements. Still another important installation feature is the versatility of mounting, which once again permits a single design to cover a multitude of oil burner makes and models.

Two additional features complement most top-grade modern

electric motors. The first is a nonerasable data, or "I.D.," plate on which all the vital statistics of the motor are stamped for reference. The second is the approval of the Underwriter's Laboratories (UL) and standardization of construction under NEMA.

## REBUILDING DEFECTIVE MOTORS

Oil burner motors can be rebuilt when they become defective. This can be especially useful when an identical replacement is requested or required for a specially mounted oil burner housing. There are, however, certain points that should be checked on a rebuilt unit. First, make sure that the rebuilding firm is reputable and not a fly-by-night outfit. Then ensure yourself that the rebuilt motor can pass the following eight-step checkup program:

1. Is the *starting winding* replaced or just peeled back to the break and then repaired? Less winding and wire than the specs require means shorter and less dependable motor life.
2. Is the *running winding* replaced or just peeled back to the break and then repaired? As above, the fewer the windings and the less the wire, the shorter the life and less effective the motor.
3. If the *starting winding* is replaced, is the running winding replaced also, and vice versa? If the motor has reached the stage requiring winding repair, it is wise to replace both windings before breakdown.
4. Is the *starting switch* replaced, or just cleaned or bent into shape? Quick, inexpensive solutions such as the above can only lead to additional breakdowns.
5. When either of the *windings* is reworked, is the number of turns complete or are they left short of turns for the sake of economy? Fewer turns than the specs require cause motors to run hotter and have a shorter life expectancy.
6. Is the *gauge of wire* used in the rewinding correct or is a smaller gauge used for economy purposes? Smaller wire than required will also cause a motor to run hotter and shorten its life expectancy.

7. Is the motor *shaft* changed or reworked to ensure a good fit? A sloppy shaft fit will cause quick motor wear and affect other burner component parts, such as the pumping unit.

8. Is the rebuilt motor's outer shell spray painted or just cleaned off? For maximum customer satisfaction and company profit, a good, like-new paint job is necessary.

## TYPES OF MOTORS

A number of different types of motors are available for service and installation use. It might be wise to review different styles and types available to service people, and their specific uses.

1. The *split-phase* motor is used for jobs that do not impose too heavy a starting load and that come up to full speed quickly. In the heating industry, the split-phase motor is used chiefly for belt-driven or direct-drive equipment where only a low starting torque (power output) is required.

2. The *capacitor-start* motor has a high starting and accelerating torque and is quite economical and quiet during its operational run. These motors may be easily recognized by the small round metal case that houses a part of the integral starting mechanism. These units are also adapted to the requirements of our industry.

3. The *shaded-pole* motor is especially adapted to direct-drive equipment and is designed to provide economical and dependable performance where a low starting torque is required. This is one of the simplest motors and is adaptable to certain control operations where reversibility is not required.

## DATA PLATES

The data plate, which is mounted externally on each motor and is shown in Fig. 6-13, was mentioned previously. This plate, with

**Fig. 6-13. Oil burner motor showing data plate.**

its information on vital statistics, might be considered the "dog tag" of the electric motor. All necessary information is permanently inscribed on it.

**The Fractional Horsepower Motor**—The word "fractional" is merely an arithmetic word denoting a part of one or, in this instance, a part of a full horsepower. Motors are rated in horsepower (hp), and in their smaller sizes, fractional horsepower. These range in size from about $\frac{1}{12}$ to $\frac{3}{4}$ hp for our particular applications. Generally, the range required for our industry use is $\frac{1}{12}$, $\frac{1}{8}$, $\frac{1}{6}$, $\frac{1}{4}$, $\frac{1}{3}$, $\frac{1}{2}$, and $\frac{3}{4}$ hp. This information is clearly marked on the data plate.

**Revolution per Minute**—The data plate expresses revolutions per minute with the initials rpm. This is the number of times the motor shaft will revolve in one minute. Most oil burner motors turn at 1725 revolutions per minute (rpm) and the fuel pump and fan output are built and geared to match this known speed.

**Voltage, Amperage, and Cycles**—Three additional and independent markings are to be found on the motor data plate and concern the electrical characteristics of the particular unit. The first, *voltage*, is marked as either 115V or 220V (volts) according to the particular wiring setup of the installation. The second, *amperage*, is the total amperage or current drawn by the motor

197

under a full load. The third electrical item, *cycles,* is generally noted on the data plate as sixty (60) for the number of electrical cycles per second.

**Model and Make**—Each manufacturer notes on the data plate the particular model and type of motor. These numbers are used for reference and replacement purposes, serving a most important function on the "I.D." of the motor.

A number of additional items, such as the name and address of the manufacturer, special code number, NEMA frame designation and allowable temperature rise of the motor during operation, complete the information on the data plate.

## MOUNTING MOTOR

Certain motors, for positioning purposes, require specific types of housings. One motor might be mounted in a cradle mount, and this cradle, in turn, designed to be secured to the burner housing. Cradle mounts come in a great number of styles and designs to fit varying installations and manufacturer model situations, with the motors fitting simply into designed holding mechanisms.

The two-hole mounted motor is designed to be attached directly to the oil burner casting through the use of two (sometimes three) ordinary screws or bolts. These units have a definite mounting seat where the face of the motor fits flush with the oil burner housing. There are a number of variations, but the principle remains the same.

To disassemble a motor from the oil burner housing, the coupling or drive shaft attachment must first be removed from the motor shaft. The electrical wiring to the oil burner motor should be completely disconnected. The mounting screws may then be released and the motor gently removed. Assembly to the oil burner housing is accomplished by reversing the above procedure, with care being given to accurate faceplate mounting and tight, even drawing-up of the attaching screws or bolts. Handle an electric motor gently, whether it is during installation or storage, repair, or transportation.

# OIL BURNER MOTOR TROUBLESHOOTING

*Symptom and Possible Cause*          *Possible Remedy*

## Motor Fails to Start

1. Low or no voltage.

2. Improper connections.

3. Open circuit.

4. Thermal overload device open.

5. Open motor capacitor. Will have same effect as open winding.

6. Defective starting switch.

7. Brush mechanism sticking (wound-rotor motor).

8. Excessive load.

1. Check power source for proper voltage. Check fuses or circuit breakers if no voltage is present.

2. Check all wiring connections with diagram supplied with motor. Correct if necessary.

3. Check all connections. If motor has starting windings, and hums when power is applied, check starting switch in motor for proper operation. Repair as necessary. If motor comes up to speed after the shaft has been spun by hand, starting winding may be open. Repair or replace motor.

4. Reset if manual type. Repair or replace if automatic type.

5. Replace capacitor.

6. Clean contacts or replace as necessary.

7. Repair or replace as necessary.

8. Check for binding of motor and fuel pump shafts. Repair as necessary.

199

| *Symptom and Possible Cause* | *Possible Remedy* |
|---|---|

**Motor Fails to Start Cont.**

9. Brushes worn or incorrectly set (wound-rotor motors).

    9. Replace brushes or adjust as required.

10. Excessive end play of motor armature.

    10. If motor will run if shaft is spun by hand, check shaft for excessive end play. Add washers on the shaft journals on the end opposite the starting switch to remove end play and permit switch contacts to close.

11. Bearings frozen.

    11. See Overheating Bearings.

**Noise in Motor**

1. Unbalanced rotor.

    1. Rebalance rotor or pulley.

2. Bent shaft.

    2. Straighten shaft or replace rotor and check for balance.

3. Loose parts.

    3. Check accessories and tighten if necessary. Make sure motor is clamped firmly to the mounting base or bracket.

4. Faulty alignment.

    4. Align motor properly with the driven elements.

5. Worn bearings.

    5. Replace bearings if necessary. See Overheated Bearings.

6. Dirt in air gap.

    6. Dismantle motor and blow out dirt with dry compressed air.

*Symptom and Possible Cause*     *Possible Remedy*

**Overheating Bearings**

1. No oil.

2. Dirty oil.

3. Oil not reaching shaft or bearings.

4. Excessive grease.

5. Belt too tight.

6. Rough bearing surface.

7. Bent shaft.
8. Shaft misaligned.
9. Excessive end thrust.

10. Excessive side pull.

1. Lubricate motor with a good grade of light mineral oil.

2. Clean out bearings and wick and reoil with clean oil.

3. Check wick or means provided to hold wick against shaft. In ring rotation, make sure ring rotates. Repair as necessary.

4. Excess grease may cause ball bearings to overheat. Remove excess grease.

5. Adjust belt tension to proper value.

6. Replace bearings. Examine shaft for damage. Replace if necessary.

7. See Noise in Motor.
8. See Noise in Motor.
9. May be caused by improper position of rotor on shaft, or by driven equipment not located properly. Repair or replace rotor if defective, or relocate driven equipment to relieve end thrust.

10. Check application of motor to driven equipment. Check and adjust alignment or belt tension as necessary.

*Symptom and Possible Cause*     *Possible Remedy*

## Motor Overheating

1. Ventilating system obstructed.

2. Motor overloaded.

3. Rotor rubbing on stator.

4. Polyphase motor operating on single phase.

1. Remove dust from motor. Check ventilating openings and remove obstructions if necessary.

2. Check driven equipment for binding. Correct as necessary. Check application by measuring watts and ampere input under normal conditions. Replace motor with large unit if necessary.

3. Check for worn bearings or bent shaft. Replace or repair as necessary.

4. Check for open fuses or circuit breakers. Replace or reset.

## Burned-Out Rotor or Stator

1. Worn bearings.

2. Moisture.

3. Acids or alkalies.

1. See Overheating Bearings.

2. Repair or replace as necessary. Remove source of moisture if possible. Extra or special varnish may be necessary on new or repaired parts.

3. Repair or replace motor with special or extra varnish on new or repaired parts. Remove source of acids or alkalies if possible.

| *Symptom and Possible Cause* | *Possible Remedy* |
|---|---|

**Burned-Out Rotor or Stator Cont.**

4. Harmful dusts.

    4. Repair or replace defective unit with one having extra or special varnish. Remove source or reduce amount of harmful dust.

5. Overload.

    5. See Motor Overheating.

**Speed Too Slow**

1. Open or high-resistance rotor joints (squirrel-cage motors).

    1. Repair rotor or rebraze in shop.

2. Overload.

    2. Reduce load or replace with larger motor.

**Speed Too High**

1. Shorted field (universal motors).

    1. Replace field or motor.

2. Short-circuiter sticking (repulsion-start motors).

    2. Clean or replace short-circuiter.

3. Underload (repulsion or universal motors).

    3. Increase load, if possible, or replace motor with one having a smaller rating.

## A SPECIAL NOTE ABOUT CONTROLS

Along with illustrations of new oil burner control equipment in the pages of this book are photographs of units that may no longer be manufactured or are older and outdated models. Residential oil burner equipment has a long life so that large numbers of these older controls are still in place and performing a satisfactory job. Many of the controls can still be obtained as rebuilt-replacement units. The editors felt it useful that readers have

203

opportunities to see and become familiar with as many different controls as possible.

# THERMOSTATS

Automatically turning the heat on or off in most modern homes is the job of the room thermostat. Perhaps this is the result of extensive advertising campaigns waged by control manufacturers using the thermostat as the focal point. Possibly it is because it is the one and only control the homeowner sees and handles daily. Whatever the reason, the thermostat represents the comfort point of modern automatic oil heating.

What does a thermostat do? Basically, it "telegraphs" electrical impulses, which start or stop the firing equipment, blowers, circulating pumps, or specialized valves when the room temperature reaches or falls below predetermined levels or settings. A drop in room temperature will cause thermostat contacts to "make" or "close." This permits current to flow through the circuit and activate the other mechanisms. A rise in room temperature to the point where it equals the setting will cause the opposite to occur. The elements will "break," and the other devices will cease operating.

Almost all thermostats, whether modern or "antique," follow a definite sequence or action. A dial or scale is set to a predetermined room temperature. This may be varied manually or mechanically (e.g., clock thermostat) or set once and left alone. The room temperatures will then activate a bimetal blade (arm or coil spring) within the thermostat. The movement of this mechanism tilts a mercury bulb, moves a set of contacts or a pair of points together, activating the thermostat and sending an electrical impulse to the spot where it will cause something to happen. Naturally, the reaction is dependent on the dial settings and room temperature conditions.

The bimetallic element used in the thermostat works in the following manner: All metals expand when heated, but the rate of expansion varies widely with different metals. Copper, for example, will expand more and faster than iron. So when a length of copper and a length or iron are placed back to back and riveted, brazed, or welded together along their entire length, and the assembly held firmly at one end, the free end will curl or bend from the unequal forces exerted by the expanding metals. The amount of "bend" will always be at a known position at any given temperature. For example, the free end will describe a wide arc when heated from 50°F to 90°F, but will return to its exact original position when the temperature goes down to 50° again. This known response to air temperatures is converted into mechanical action through gearing, direct contact, or specially designed devices. A set of electrical contacts, or mercury bulbs, are made to open, close, or move, completing or breaking circuits to control the on-off operation of the heating system.

There are three main sections of the average residential room thermostat:

1. The *mounting plate,* which provides a "hanger" for the main body and cover. This plate, made of plastic or fiber, usually has built-in screw terminals or posts for wiring connections. It also serves as a template for positioning and mounting, and must be securely attached to the wall and positioned perfectly level for accurate mounting.

2. The *main thermostat body,* which includes the bimetal element, activating mechanisms, internal and external wiring, and heater devices. In addition, temperature-setting dials, differential adjustments, and calibration screws are built into this section of the thermostat.

3. The *cover* or styled case. This section is designed to beautify and protect the main mechanisms from excessive dirt accumulations, tampering, or any reasonable physical damage. One part of the cover houses the simple room thermometer so the homeowner can keep tabs on inside temperature conditions. The entire thermostat case, in most instances, is decorated to suit the decor of the room in which it is to be installed.

Historically, the first practical room thermostats were put on the market in the very late 1800s, with basic versions of the clock thermostat appearing in the early 1900s. One wonders when we see the modernistic home and office "weather station" what the future can and will bring.

## Thermostat Types

Earlier, it was pointed out that the thermostat is the one control the homeowner has daily contact with, the one heating system device that actually "lives" in the rooms of his home. It follows, therefore, that thermostat designers would, and should, emphasize beauty and styling. At the same time, however, modern housing and heating systems demand the latest and best in equipment. The control manufacturers must therefore turn out a mechanically versatile and advanced line of thermostats to meet competitive demands. The following examples illustrate some (but not necessarily all) of the thermostat types on the market today. Each has its specific place in the heating system control lineup, or, as in one specific thermostat's style, the home cooling system.

## Heating-Cooling Thermostats

In many sections of the country, contractors and builders with an eye to the future have added summer cooling to the regular heat distributing system. To keep up with this modern trend, the manufacturers have devised thermostats capable of controlling both winter and summer comfort in one device, as shown in Figs. 6-14 through 6-17. A two-in-one unit, the heating-cooling thermostat allows the consumer to almost completely control his year-round comfort from a central point. These thermostats range in style from simple room models to decorative and home weather stations.

## Clock Thermostats

For homeowners who wish to take advantage of style plus economy and convenience, the control manufacturers have provided clock thermostats. These units automatically provide a "night setback" of room temperatures for a predetermined length of time and then return to a normal setting at a set time in the morning. Field tests have indicated that in addition to the convenience of automatic setbacks, they can also offer fuel savings. The automatic, continuous, day-in, day-out features make for ease and convenience, while night setbacks provide comfort and economy. The addition of an electric clock adds practicality to

Courtesy Honeywell, Inc.

Fig. 6-14. Chronotherm, or fuel-saving clock thermostat.

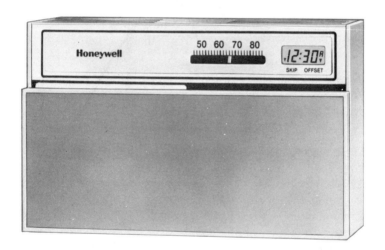

Courtesy Honeywell, Inc.

Fig. 6-15. Microelectric chronotherm, or clock thermostat, has capabilities of controlling both heating and cooling systems with programmed temperature timing.

207

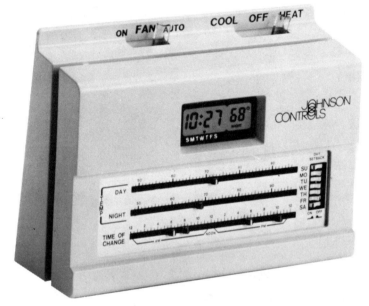

**Fig. 6-16. Automatic night/day setback clock thermostat. This control also has the capability of controlling the residence's air conditioning system.**

the unit's design, which cannot detract from the decor of any room.

## Low-Voltage Thermostats

The mainstay of the thermostat industry is the attractive low-voltage room thermostat. Each manufacturer has his own style and type, but basically its job is to accurately control temperatures. Some are round, while others are oblong or rectangular; one manufacturer uses a square motif. No matter what its style, the general makeup of the standard room thermostat permits ease of wiring, simplicity of installation, and often freedom from certain electrical codes and ordinances. To the homeowners and service company alike, the outstanding feature of the modern low-voltage room thermostat is its accurate, carefree control of comfort.

**Fig. 6-17. A residential thermostat.**

## High-Voltage Thermostats

Certain specific job characteristics require an installation of high-voltage thermostats. These units generally control a line voltage mechanism such as a hot-water circulating pump. These thermostats, once again, are modern in decor with each manufacturer attempting to design the finest from both an appearance and operational standpoint. This type of thermostat is manufactured in two basic models—the light and the heavy duty—each designed to handle a rated electrical code. All wiring to and from this device comes under local or national electrical codes, which should be strictly followed.

## Weather-Watching Thermostats

This temperature-controlling device actually operates one step ahead of prevailing outside weather. Temperature settings are automatically adjusted to compensate, practically minute by minute, for outdoor temperature changes. A section of the master thermostat is placed in a sensitive outdoor position, and when

209

temperature changes occur, it automatically transmits, changes, compensates, and adjusts the indoor thermostat for maximum occupant comfort.

## Thermostat Design

The old saying that "beauty is only skin deep" is equally true for room thermostats. We've covered beauty and design and spoken just a bit about interior thermostat mechanisms. There are several additional features, however, which all thermostats, no matter what their style, design, or manufacture, must have. The first is air circulation. A device completely blocked off with no provision for feeling air changes would be useless in controlling heating, or for that matter cooling, comfort. Check a room thermostat and note the slots that provide air circulation around the interior sensing elements.

The second feature important enough to consider when we speak of thermostat design is the ease and simplicity with which a customer may read the temperature and operate the mechanism. An attractive dial with large clear numbers will share equal space with a scale or lever a customer can easily manipulate.

Feature number three, although admittedly not a necessity at all times, is important under certain installation circumstances. Each thermostat should have a method of locking the movement of the setting dials or levers. In some units, the setting handles may be completely removed; in most other units, a screw securely locks the levers if desired. This feature discourages tampering with the setting levers by youngsters or unauthorized persons and leaving the device set at exceptionally high or low temperatures.

Our final design feature is installation simplicity, producing a unit that can be installed routinely and, in most instances, be serviced easily. This saves man-hours during installation and service-hours in the years that follow.

## Thermostat Installation

There are a series of pointers to be considered at and during installation time—a guide of do's and don'ts. If these pointers are followed, we know that they can be of help to you with your next thermostat job. To start with, a most important point is to choose the spot you feel will satisfy the potential homeowner. Do not be "bulldozed" into picking an inferior location.

Follow the rules that are tried and tested.

Install the thermostat on an inside wall, keeping it away from cold outside exposure.

Pick a location approximately 5 ft. above the floor, a spot in the "living height" of the temperature area, away from children and possible furniture damage.

Choose a spot in the living room for the thermostat installation. Place it in the room where it will get the "feel" of the house.

Locate it in an area where air circulation is good, in the natural air circulation of the room.

Avoid empty, unused rooms, outside stairwells, etc.; the unit should be mounted in a used, useful area of the home.

Mount in a convenient location, e.g., between the wall stud.

Make all electrical connections clear and secure; the best installation can be ruined by loose wires.

Follow all wiring diagrams supplied by the thermostat manufacturers; each company has its own installation plans for specific reasons.

Plug up any holes you have made in the walls behind the mounting plates; a cold draft running between the studs may completely throw off a thermostat.

Mount the unit level, especially the type using a mercury switch; a device off-level cannot function accurately.

Remember to adjust or match the heater elements in the thermostat to the current used by the stack relay or control on the furnace.

Do not mount the thermostat on an outside wall. The relatively cold outside wall areas will unbalance an otherwise correctly functioning thermostat.

Do not install a thermostat behind a door, draperies, furniture, or other obstructions. Natural air currents must be permitted to reach the sensing elements.

Do not locate next to hidden ducts or hot-water or steam pipes.

211

It is obvious that these items give off heat, which will throw a thermostat's sensing mechanisms completely out of order.

Do not place in the direct rays of the sun or in the path of fireplace flames and heat. Once again, this "false heat" can cause a thermostat to be satisfied long before the rest of the house becomes satisfactorily warm.

Do not mount in areas of every-present warm air, such as near TV sets, lamps, or radios. The units give off enough heat to disrupt the orderly functioning of the thermostat.

Do not place a thermostat in a corner. There are always the possibilities of dead-air space.

Do not install a thermostat in cold draft areas; too much cold can be just as upsetting as too much heat.

Do not mess up a wall when installing a thermostat. This control is actually the only one the homeowner sees day in and day out.

The "do's and don'ts" of thermostat installation have been covered first for a definite reason. A thermostat's physical installation is relatively simple. The important part is the foundation phase—choosing a location in the home which is acceptable to the homeowner and desirable to the service company. The customer has his idea where he would like to see the thermostat; the serviceman, on the other hand, has practical thoughts on where it should be placed. Very often a compromise is the best solution. It is important that the position finally chosen meets all of the "do and don't" qualifications listed.

For the installation of the thermostat:

1. Select a proper position in the residence for the thermostat. Let the homeowner and other contracting personnel know where it is to be.
2. Use the plastic or fiber mounting plate that comes with every thermostat as a template, and mark the position of the holding screws.
3. Drill a hole (about ½ in. in diameter) in the mounting plate location for the thermostat cable.
4. Drill a hole (first a pilot and finally a full ¾-in. to 1-in. hole) in the basement ceiling at the measured site of the upstairs thermostat location.

5. Use a stout cord with a weight at the end and drop it through the hole drilled at the mounting plate.

6. The line with the weight attached will now drop to the basement beams. Make sure the line is firmly secured upstairs.

7. Use a hook and "fish" the dropped line through the cellar beam directly into the basement area.

8. Attach the thermostat cable to the cord and pull it up and through the mounting plate in the living area of the home.

9. Leave about 6 to 8 in. of slack, cut off the excess wire, and then attach upstairs wire to the terminals of the mounting bracket.

10. Assemble the thermostat body onto the mounting brackets.

11. Put the cover in place so it does not get lost during the balance of the job.

12. Direct the downstairs thermostat wiring to its proper place in the control system. Be sure to tack all wiring securely with correctly sized and designed staples.

13. Do the entire job neatly and in a workmanlike manner.

## Calibrating a Thermostat

A thermostat is a delicate sensitive instrument and is always calibrated and checked at the factory. There are however, circumstances over which there is no control, such as rough handling, tampering, or shipment damage. The unit then may be recalibrated for accurate room temperature control if any adjustment damage is suspected. Proceed as follows:

1. Allow the thermostat, if recently installed, a sufficient amount of time (15 minutes to 2 hours, depending on the type) to get used to the room temperature.

2. Keep away from the thermostat, as even your body temperature can affect the final accurate setting. When you use tools on the thermostat, make sure that they also are at room temperature.

3. Remove the thermostat cover so that you may work on the inside area.

4. Use a low-voltage test lamp (tattle-light) for models that are

not snap-acting; otherwise your mechanical sense will serve you well.

5. Set the indicator dial to the current room temperature and lock it securely in position.

6. Now, turn the *calibration screw* slowly until the contacts *open.*

7. Next, turn the *calibration screw* slowly in the opposite direction until either (a) the test lamp lights, or (b) the contacts snap closed. The thermostat should now be in calibration.

8. Loosen the dial lockscrew so that the device may be retested.

9. Replace the cover and check the settings once again.

If the thermometer (current room temperature) and the pointer, or setting dial differ by more than 2°, the thermostat should be calibrated. Remember, however, that different makes, brands, models, etc., use different methods to accomplish the job. Use the manufacturer's spec sheets whenever possible. The entire calibration operation is most important. The homeowner often gauges the value of his entire heating system by the "accuracy" and "comfort-feel" of his thermostat. This holds true for new as well as older installations.

## The Differential

Another important built-in feature of all thermostats on the market is the *differential.* Simply stated, the differential is the *temperature degree time lapse* between the time the burner shuts off and the time it is called on to start up again, and vice versa. It matters little whether the thermostat is set at 60°F or 80°F, the differential or spread of degrees between on-off operation should remain the same. Some units do not require differential adjustments while others have provision on the thermostat. A spread of approximately 2°F may be regarded as a satisfactory figure, keeping in mind that a differential of less than 1½°F is unsuitable to comfortable operation.

A comfortable differential degree figure may be built into a thermostat, but the time lag, from the moment the thermostat calls for heat and the time this heat finally comes up, must also be reckoned with. In these minutes, a house can become uncomfortably cool (or uncomfortably warm), overshooting "set" temperature limits. In order to compensate for this "time lag," all control manufacturers have devised some sort of *preheating* device or resistor.

When the contacts or points are closed, current begins to run through a heating element or resistor in the thermostat. This will cause the resistor to become warm and heat up the inside of the thermostat case a bit faster than the heat of the room could. This "heat-up" will anticipate the thermostat's call for heat, preventing overshooting of room temperatures. Some manufacturers use interchangeable, color-coded heaters; others prefer adjustable types.

Remember that the current flowing through the thermostat must pass through the heater, and thus its resistance must be adjusted to match the current used by the primary control. If it is set (adjustable) too low or is drawing too low a current for the primary device, the thermostat will cycle too rapidly, causing short running cycles. If the dial is set too high, with no regard to matching the primary control, running time may be too long. Always consult the manufacturer's spec sheets, installation bulletins, and catalogs for the correct setting or heater designation.

## Thermometer Bulb Liquid

In order to determine how accurate the temperature settings are, the thermometer must be functioning properly. Very often, during shipment or in handling, the liquid in the thermometer bulb will separate, with part of the fluid going to the upper portion of the stem and the other part remaining in the lower bulb. One control manufacturer makes the following suggestion as a remedy for this difficulty.

Hold the control cover in an upright position in one hand, with the thermometer bulb-end down. Gently tap it against the palm of the other hand, using care not to strike the tube. This should start the liquid down toward the bulb. Continue this motion until the liquid is all united. If any part of the liquid is separated, the thermometer will not read correctly.

## Locking Devices

In addition to the build-in or built-on thermostat locking mechanisms described previously, there is often a demand for "special" or more secure locking methods. The call is usually made by landlords, or where thermostats are placed within the reach of children or vandals. To solve this difficulty, "lock boxes" have been designed to fit most styles and brands of thermostats. These items permit the individual to read the current room temperatures, but not to reset the thermostat. The lock box permits air circulation but will not permit tampering.

## Choosing the Correct Thermostat

Each installation has its own job characteristics and requires a thermostat to match the job. In Table 6-1, many of the thermostats developed by Honeywell are covered. Each manufacturer has charts covering his own equipment and its placement. Always check these charts.

## Thermostat Care

Normally, thermostats in the field today require very little maintenance. About once a year the units should be checked, using the following guide as a routine:

1. Check the thermostat accuracy in relation to the known room temperature.
2. Check the unit calibration if necessary.
3. Clean the sensing elements (contacts, bellows, mercury tube, etc.). Never use abrasives, and be gentle. A business card will do fine for points and contacts.
4. Check all terminals for tightness.
5. Make sure all connections are clean and not broken.
6. Check and recheck the thermostat operation in actual use.
7. Look over the clock and transformer mechanisms. Be sure the switchover gears are functioning properly and the step-down transformers are supplying voltage to the thermostat clock.

## Table 6-1. Thermostat Cross Reference Chart

| Voltage | Operation of Thermostat | Thermostat Identification | Limit Control | Primary Controls | Series |
|---------|-------------------------|---------------------------|---------------|------------------|--------|
| 1. Low | Two contacts make in sequence to start, and break in reverse sequence to stop. | 3-wire, low-voltage — both contacts on same side of moving blade. | Series #10 or Series #40. | Series #10 relays and protectorelays. | #10 |
| 2. Low | Spdt switching. | 3-wire, low-voltage contacts on opposite sides of moving blade. | Series #20. | Series #20 motors, valves, motor switches. | #20 |
| 3. Line | Spdt switching. | 2-wire, line-voltage mercury tube or line switch makes contact in one position. | Series #40. | Series #30 relays, controls, direct relay controls. | #40 |
| 4. None | Nonelectrical (mechanical). | Self-contained unit. | None. | None. | #50 |
| 5. Line | Spdt switching. | 3-wire, line-voltage contacts on opposite sides of moving blade. | Series #60. | Series #60 motors, Series #60 valves. | #60 |
| 6. Limited | Electronic relay senses minute voltage changes. | Resistance coil. | As required. | Series #10, #40, #80, #90 motors, valves, relays. | #70 |
| 7. Low | Spdt switching. | 2-wire, low-voltage mercury tube or switch makes contact — one position. | Series #40 or Series #10. | | |

# THERMOSTAT TROUBLES

*Symptom and Possible Cause*       *Possible Remedy*

## Thermostat Does Not Shut Off Heating System

1. Wiring shorted or defective.

2. Device jammed or locked in *on* position.

3. Contacts welded together. Mercury tube not level ("making" constantly).

4. Thermostat not wired correctly.

5. Thermostat dial set too high.

6. Wrong thermostat for the job.

7. Thermostat installed in a cold position.

8. Aquastat for the domestic hot water set too high (hot-water heating systems).

1. Remove short, or repair or replace defective equipment.

2. Remove jam or locked condition. Repair or replace unit if necessary.

3. Replace unit if contacts defective. Level unit if mercury type.

4. Rewire correctly.

5. Set dial to desired temperature.

6. Replace with a proper unit.

7. Relocate thermostat, keeping away from cold walls, drafts, etc.

8. Reset domestic hot-water aquastat in a lower temperature.

## Thermostat Does Not Turn On Heating System

1. Thermostat-body or mounting-plate screws loose.

1. Tighten all mounting screws in thermostat and mounting plate.

218

*Symptom and Possible Cause*          *Possible Remedy*

## Thermostat Does Not Turn On Heating System Cont.

2. Wiring to thermostat terminals loose, broken, or off parts.

3. Thermostat dial setting too low.

4. Thermostat wired incorrectly.

5. Low-voltage circuit or components defective.

6. Dirty contacts in thermostat.

7. Mercury tube or bellows broken.

8. Mercury tube not level (not "making").

9. Wrong thermostat for job.

10. Thermostat installed in a hot position.

11. Clock thermostat set on wrong 12-hour interval.

2. Secure all wiring under the proper screws.

3. Reset thermostat to desired temperature.

4. Rewire correctly.

5. Check all wiring and components in low-voltage circuit. Repair or replace as necessary.

6. Clean contacts with paper, business card, etc.

7. Repair or replace thermostat.

8. Level thermostat.

9. Replace with correct unit.

10. Relocate thermostat away from register, out of sun, away from radiator, etc.

11. Reset clock forward 12 hours to bring it to the correct day/night relationship.

## Heat in Room Does Not Reach Thermostat Setting

1. Heating system too small, wrong firing rate, etc.

1. Install larger furnace, increase firing rate, etc.

219

*Symptom and Possible Cause*     *Possible Remedy*

## Heat In Room Does Not Reach Thermostat Setting Cont.

2. Insufficient radiation.

3. Thermostat dial defective.
4. Thermometer reading incorrect.
5. Defective thermostat contacts or other parts.
6. Wrong thermostat for job.

2. Increase size or number of radiators, convectors, registers, etc.
3. Adjust or replace thermostat.
4. Adjust or replace thermostat.
5. Replace thermostat.

6. Replace thermostat with proper unit.

## Heating in Room Overshooting Setting Temperature

1. Adjustment dial on thermostat defective.
2. Incorrect thermometer reading.
3. Old-style thermostat.

4. Incorrect heater element or setting in thermostat.

5. Heating system oversize or radiation too great.

1. Adjust or replace thermostat.
2. Adjust or replace thermostat.
3. Replace with modern thermostat.
4. Adjust heater element or replace thermostat with one having correct heater.
5. Replace with correct-size unit or decrease radiation.

## System Short-Cycling (running for short periods only)

1. Dirty contacts in thermostat.

1. Clean contacts.

*Symptom and Possible Cause*          *Possible Remedy*

**System Short Cycling
(running for short periods
only) Cont.**

2. Incorrect heater element or setting in thermostat.

2. Adjust heater element or replace thermostat with one having correct heater.

3. Heating system oversize or radiation too great.

3. Replace with correct-size unit or decrease radiation.

4. Old-style or wrong thermostat.

4. Replace with correct modern thermostat.

**Thermostat Testing Procedure**

Disconnect the low-voltage wires at the thermostat. A defective or ineffective thermostat is indicated when:

1. The thermostat does not shut off the burner, but disconnecting the wires does shut it off.
2. The thermostat will not start the burner, but the burner starts when the wires are disconnected from the thermostat and twisted together.
3. *Short Circuiting* is indicated when disconnecting the thermostat (or domestic hot-water aquastat) completely will not stop the burner operation.

A *broken wire* is indicated when the wires which have been disconnected at the thermostat will not start the burner even when they are all twisted together. If the *wires* are *disconnected at the relay* (low voltage) and the burner continues to run, a faulty relay may be suspected.

## LIMIT CONTROLS

Why is a limit control necessary on any automatically fired heating equipment? Simply because the burner, operating in

221

either a boiler or furnace, can generate heat more rapidly than the distribution system can carry it to the rooms. And in extreme weather, the thermostat may call for more heat than the distribution system can deliver. When this occurs, the burner will continue to build up heat in a furnace or pressure in a boiler until something burns up or blows up.

Solely to prevent such accidents and damage, the limit control stops the burner when the temperature of the heating medium reaches the high setting on the control, even though the thermostat is calling for heat. The fan or circulator continues to run, and when it has carried enough heat away from the furnace or boiler (temperature drop), the limit control shifts back into a "neutral" position and permits the thermostat to again control the burner.

## Types of Limiting Controls

There are three major types of limiting controls: steam, hot water, and warm air. Each is designed to handle a specific type of system.

**Steam System Control**—A *pressuretrol,* when installed in the oil burner's electrical circuit, effectively and safety limits the operation of steam heating plants. It does this by controlling the pressure limits in the boiler. The pressuretrol is usually installed directly into a suitable fitting at the top of the boiler. It may also share a common installation space with the pressure gauge when properly "T" connected. The pressure control is usually installed *above* the water line in the boiler, and a syphon or "pigtail" connection is used to prevent the device from getting too hot and to keep "live steam" (over 15 lb.) from entering the control. In actual fieldwork, the "pigtail" tends to trap sludge and other materials that may harm the pressuretrol. An excellent service procedure during annual cleanups is to check these pigtails, as they may be partially or completely blocked, thus preventing proper functioning. Standard pressuretrols are provided with 1¼-in. male N.P.T. connections at the base for installation on the steam boiler.

A number of precautions should be observed during the installation of a pressuretrol:

1. Do not use pipe dope on the first few threads of the pres-

suretrol. This dope may get into the mechanism and impair the unit's operation.

2. Always make sure that the pipes connecting the pressuretrol to the boiler are pitched correctly. The condensate must be allowed to drain back to the boiler. Use a level for accurate installation.

3. Do not change the pressuretrol during installation by twisting or using oversize tools on the body nut. Be gentle and use correctly sized tools.

4. Always install the pressuretrol in a level position. Certain units use mercury activating tubes and must be correctly leveled for maximum accuracy.

5. Be careful. The pressuretrol is well built, but it is a delicate pressure device upon which the safe operation of the entire steam heating system may depend.

**Hot-Water System Control**—An *aquastat*, when installed in the oil burner electrical circuit, effectively and safely limits the operation of hot-water heating plants. It does this by controlling the hot-water temperature limits produced by the automatic firing device. The aquastat is screwed or clamped into or onto a heat-sensitive section of the boiler. Standard aquastats are provided with ½ to ¾-in. male N.P.T. connections for installation in the hot-water boiler.

A number of precautions should be observed during installation of an aquastat:

1. Always install the tube or well in a boiler tapping close to the top or hottest section of the boiler. If the aquastat is a "clamp-on" variety (surface type), attach it to a horizontal or vertical riser about 18 in. above the boiler.

2. Do not damage the aquastat during the installation by twisting or using oversize wrenches on the body nut. Be gentle and use the correct-size tools.

3. Install the aquastat in a level position. Certain units use mercury activating tubes and must be correctly leveled for maximum accuracy.

4. Do not place the aquastat in the path of a cold-water supply or return line.

5. Be careful. The aquastat is a well built but delicate precision

instrument and is important to the safe operation of the entire hot-water heating system.

**Warm-Air System Control**—An *airstat,* or *air switch,* when installed in the oil burner electrical circuit, limits the operation of warm-air systems.

It does this, as previously described for other controls, by controlling the air temperature within the furnace. The airstat is mounted in the furnace bonnet with a mounting ring or holder supplied by the manufacturer. It is positioned so that the sensing element may accurately detect the changes in air temperature. The standard airstat comes with either a long sensing end or with a heat-feeling capillary tube that matches the particular brand of furnace. The device is fitted into the furnace bonnet in such a way that it can rapidly detect the necessary air changes and control the automatic firing device.

A number of precautions should be observed during the installation of an airstat:

1. Always be careful. The air switch, or airstat, is a well-built but delicate precision instrument and is important to the safe operation of the entire warm-air system.
2. Install the airstat in a level position. Some units have mercury actuating tubes and must be correctly leveled for accuracy.
3. Do not damage the airstat during installation by twisting or bending. Use the template (which usually is packaged with each control) for correctly sizing the installation hole. Be gentle, and use correctly sized tools.
4. Avoid locations in the bonnet where there may be dead-air spots or where air circulation is not totally free.
5. If a capillary sensing element is used, take care not to kink or lead the unit over sharp or wearing objects.
6. Do not place the sensing element on the inner surfaces of the heated furnace or where it may be affected by radiant or reflected heat.

You will note from the preceding paragraphs that the "caution" or "installation" instructions have been repeated separately for each of the individual controls, although many may be repetitious. This was intentional, for the manufacturer's installation and caution instructions are so important that the space and repetition are well justified.

## Limit-Control Sensing Mechanisms

In order to fully comprehend the operation of various limiting controls associated with steam, hot-water, and warm-air systems, it is best to divide the standard control into two sections—the mechanical or sensing section, and the electrical or operating section. Primarily, we shall discuss the sensing mechanism, although we will briefly cover the simple electrical parts of a limit control.

Once the sensing mechanism of the limiting device has been activated by temperatures within the boiler or furnace, the impulse or movement is transmitted to the section of the control that deals with electrical action. The movement of the helix spring, the capillary tube, or the bellows is usually the activating force. The control calls for either more or less heat through a series of gears, cams, levers, contacts, or a multitude of other mechanical arrangements. This motion is then converted into electrical action. One can see, and often hear, this motion through the opening and closing of a switch, the opening and closing of sets of coordinated points, the making and breaking of a circuit in a mercury tube, etc. The limit control electrically starts or stops the burner, depending on the heat demands of the house.

How does the sensing mechanism work? How does it know when to start and when to stop? What are the different kinds of mechanisms which operate a limit control? Three major motivating mechanisms drive the limiting device:

1. A temperature-sensitive bulb is actuated by liquid expansion. When the temperature in the controlled area (boiler-furnace) rises, the fluid in the bulb expands, causing the contacts in the switch mechanism to snap open. As the temperature in the controlled areas cools, the fluid in the sensing tube contracts. When temperatures in the sensing areas drop to the proper control setting, the contacts snap closed, reversing the process and returning the control back to the thermostat.

225

2. A bimetal spring or helix is immersed in the air currents of the furnace, or is covered by a shielding well in the water paths of the hot-water boiler. When the temperature rises in the controlled areas (furnace-boiler), the helix, which is a part of the drive shaft, turns. This shaft may be part of the dial or mercury-actuating mechanism, or it may have an "arm" connected to the shaft, which moves contact points. As the shaft turns, through heating or cooling action of the bimetal helix, the burner is turned on or off according to the requirements of the system or the dial settings.

3. A diaphragm or bellows type of unit that reacts to pressure. A combination of plungers, pivot arms, gears, or cams complements this device. Pressures that rise in the controlled area of the boiler are transmitted almost directly against this diaphragm. Interconnected to the opposite side of the diaphragm are the motivating gears, etc., which then control the "on-off" process of the system through correct dial setting.

## Limit-Control Styles

There are various installation applications and demands placed on limiting devices. Some heating units have, for example, no direct openings for the controlling mechanisms and require one style, while other furnaces require remote applications of these limiting devices. Generally, the following styles may be depended on to meet a major portion of your field requirements:

1. *Surface style.* This limit control, securely clamped on the heating unit in a heat-sensitive position, performs the limiting functions from outside the furnace or boiler area, but by direct contact with the sensing or heat-feeling section of the unit. The motivating and electrical mechanisms are the same for these "clamp-on" or "surface-type" limit controls as for other steam, hot-water, or warm-air devices.

2. *Immersion type.* A well or protective tube (See Fig. 6-18) is first inserted into the boiler as part of the limiting device. The sensing mechanism (helix-capillary, etc.) of the control is then inserted and held secure in the well. The motivating

and electrical mechanisms are identical to those described previously.

3. *Direct immersion style.* This style of limiting control requires no well or protective tube to cover its sensing mechanisms, but is inserted directly into the furnace or boiler. Response to unit temperature changes is fast and accurate with this control. Once again, the mechanisms that control the limiting action (steam, hot water, warm air) are the same as for the preceding styles.

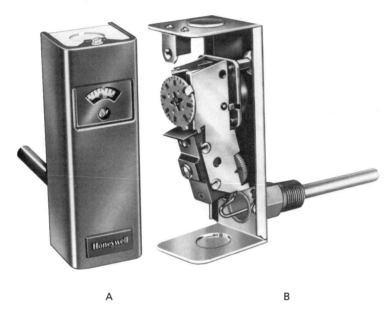

A                    B

Courtesy Honeywell, Inc.

**Fig. 6-18. (A) Immersion aquastat for use with hydronic or forced hot-water heating systems, (B) interior view.**

4. *Remote style.* Occasions arise when the physical control must be in a place apart from the actual heating equipment. There are remote limiting controls designed for these purposes. These devices permit the sensing mechanisms to be positioned in the heating equipment, while the electrical or functioning section of the control is placed elsewhere.

## Additional Control Functions

There are additional functions that controlling devices are called upon to accomplish. Special mention is made of these activities because often the same control, or a modification of the basic limit control, is all that may be necessary. For example, the mercury or the electrical mechanism may be positioned in reverse of standard, or the control may simply be installed in a particular or a special section of the heating system in order to adjust and qualify for this new use. What are these special uses?

**Reverse-Acting Controls**—These devices are used in all heating systems where activation of the pumping or blowing unit is not desired until sufficient steam, hot water, or warm air is generated in the system. Let us use as an example a typical forced warm-air or hot-water system. The water or air is heated within the furnace or boiler by an automatically fired device. These heated products must be transmitted to the living quarters of the residence via a pump or blower. If these mechanisms were to begin operating as soon as the oil burner started, the resulting flow of water or air would be cold and uncomfortable. The *reverse-acting control* does not permit the pump or blower to begin circulation of the water or air *until* the water or air has reached a temperature that will either be practical or comfortable to the occupants. In the case of a steam system equipped with blowers (unit heaters), the *reverse-acting pressuretrol* will not allow the fan, which is normally mounted behind the unit heater's "radiator," to begin operation until sufficient pressure and heat have been built up within the system (Fig. 6-19).

**Low-Limit or Operating Control**—This controlling device permits a unit to function for special purposes such as maintaining boiler water temperatures within set limits. Most summer-winter hookups, for example, use a low-limit control in the circuit to ensure a steady production of domestic hot water.

## Limit-Control Adjustment

The standard limiting control will open its contacts on pressure or temperature *rise* and close its contacts on pressure or temperature *drop*. In order to maintain a comfortable and satisfactory period of control action, each unit has a built-in differential or

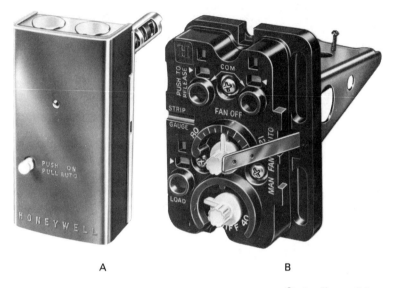

Courtesy Honeywell, Inc.

**Fig. 6-19. (A) Fan and limit control combination for forced warm-air heating systems, (B) interior view.**

range device. The differential is the period between the time the control shuts off because of satisfaction with the particular set temperature, and the time the unit mechanically and electrically calls upon the firing mechanism to resume action. Some controls have nonadjustable differentials ranging from about 5°F to 15°F, while others have differentials that may be manually adjusted to suit the installation circumstance.

Pressuretrols vary in their differentials as the total range and setting are determined on an accumulative basis. There are two settings that must be considered on standard pressure devices. One is to set the unit's desired *cut-in* pressure—the other is to set the desired differential. When the two are added together, the *cutoff* point of the pressuretrol is determined.

All settings, whether steam, hot water, or warm air, depend on the particular system and manufacturer's installation instructions. Always read these instructions carefully. The majority of all controls in the field may be simply set with a screwdriver, pliers, or adjustable wrench. Be careful, however, not to force any dials or gauges.

## Wiring Limit Controls

It is basic, of course, to note that all wiring should be installed according to local and national electrical codes. If a boiler, furnace, or unit manufacturer recommends a particular wiring diagram, then follow such recommendations.

When wiring a limit control, make sure to place it in the *hot side* of the line and to tighten all connecting screws firmly. Never use a low-voltage control in a high-voltage line, and be sure that the control is not externally overloaded. Basic wiring diagrams for hot-water, steam, or warm-air systems may be obtained from any manufacturer's catalogs or service manuals.

## Testing Limit Controls

In order to determine whether a control is functioning properly, the following electrical tests should be performed if limit-control difficulty is suspected:

1. Remove the cover of the limit control.
2. Ground one side of your test light.
3. Turn limiting control to the *on* position.
4. Find the hot line by touching the end of the test lamp to each control terminal. The hot line will be indicated by the test lamp lighting. (If the lamp does not light at either limit control terminal, either the hot line is broken or something else is wrong elsewhere in the circuit.)
5. Touch the test light to the other terminal—the test light should not light if everything is functioning correctly. (If it does light on both terminals service the switch.)

## General Limit-Control Information

Each limit-control manufacturer designs and builds his own particular limiting device in line with field demands, competition, and his firm's creative abilities. In many instances, the limit controls of one firm may be used or interchanged with that of another.

# LIMIT-CONTROL TROUBLES

*Symptom and Possible Cause*     *Possible Remedy*

**Limit Control Does Not Shut Off System When Proper Temperature or Pressures Are Reached**

1. Control wired incorrectly.
2. Adjustment dial defective.
3. Control jammed in *on* position.
4. Control defective or incorrect for the job.
5. Limit control set too high.
6. Pigtail or line filled with sludge or dirt (hot-water or steam system).

1. Wire control according to diagram.
2. Replace unit.
3. Repair or replace as necessary.
4. Replace control with correct unit.
5. Reset to correct limits.
6. Clean pigtail or line.

**Limit Control in *On* Position; Unit Calling for Heat; System Not Functioning**

1. No electricity to control.
2. Control incorrectly wired.
3. Internal control mechanism defective (mercury tube, contacts, etc.).
4. Wiring shorted or defective.
5. Other controls or switches in system defective.

1. Check out wiring and repair.
2. Wire correctly according to diagram.
3. Repair or replace as necessary.
4. Check wiring and repair or replace as necessary.
5. Check all controls and switches for malfunction and repair or replace as necessary.

231

**Limit Control in *On* Position; Unit Calling for Heat; System Not Functioning Cont.**

6. Limit-control mechanism jammed.

7. Adjustment dial broken or defective.

6. Repair or replace as necessary.

7. Repair or replace as necessary.

# TIME/TEMPERATURE CONTROLS

Normally, thermostat and aquastat (or other limiting devices designed to match the equipment in use) combine to control the oil burner operation and home comfort. A new piece of equipment is now available to handle the job. It is a programmed time/temperature control capable of integrating boiler-water temperatures based on changing outside temperatures. The unit also has built-in night setback temperature features and automatic domestic hot-water control.

At one time, high cost dictated that these multipurpose controls be available only for commercial buildings. Today, microcomputers and new electronic designs have lowered the price and size and made the controls feasible for residential installations.

Here's the way the controls work. Sensors, part of the programmed timers, positioned on the outside of the residence, "read" external temperatures and translate the data to the electronic control mechanism. The control automatically resets the boiler-water temperature based on the flow of changing information. This attention to weather, combined with boiler-water temperature control, can effect a fuel savings and increase home comfort.

Night temperature setback with wider time options is another built-in feature of the unit designed to save fuel and cut costs. Control of domestic hot-water boiler operation on an "as needed" of special "timed" basis is an additional money-saving feature.

The new programmed electronic time/temperature controls provide all the items necessary for complete home heating comfort in one unit. Climatic external conditions and basic heat loss characteristics of the individual home are integrated, and the programmed time/temperature control takes over automatically.

## RELAYS

Perhaps the most important single contribution a controlling device can make to any automatic heating installation is combustion safety. This is job number one for the oil burner relay, stack switch, primary or combustion control. Almost fifty years ago, according to manufacturers' records, a "damper flapper" device was used to control the oil burners of that era.

Finally, after much experimentation, the first of a long line of combustion relays was developed. This first combustion control would simply open the electrical contacts of the combustion unit if the current failed. This was not completely safe, as you can well imagine, and not completely automatic; but it was a start. As the years passed and the requirements developed for a safer, sounder, more dependable primary control, a great deal of experimentation by numerous manufacturers followed. In the early 1930s, a "fail-safe" series N10 circuit housed in a one-piece box was developed by the Honeywell Company, which met the requirements of all burners on the market at that time. More experimentation followed, and the cumulative results are evident in a multitude of dependable field-combustion control devices.

What does the future hold? People in the control industry claim that, very soon, combustion controls will be marketed that are capable of sensing the responding to flame failure instantaneously. The final goal of complete combustion safety is within reach.

What does a primary combustion control do? Basically, the device is a combination of several electrical switches, a mass of wires, a number of mechanical movements, and a mounting board with many terminals. This combination of components is connected in such a manner that it operates the oil burner upon response and at the correct moment.

233

A relay will start and stop the combustion unit upon demand by the thermostat or other controlling device. The combustion control (relay) will not allow the burner to operate unless a flame is established on unit startup. Should a low-voltage electrical condition suddenly occur, the stack relay will drop out and stop the combustion unit from operating. On intermittent-ignition types of relays, the stack switch will cut off the ignition spark after a predetermined length of time. If a flame failure occurs during operation, the stack switch will automatically drop out, cutting off the oil burner unit. On certain types of relays, if there is still a demand for unit operation, the combustion control will permit the oil burner to restart after a predetermined time lag or "purge" period.

It should be pretty obvious at this point that the combustion relay is the "brain center" of the automatic heating system. Here, most of the wires on the installation either begin or terminate; and on the terminal block a good share of the unit troubleshooting may be accomplished by the service mechanic.

## Relay Names

Before going any further into the direct operational aspect of combustion devices, perhaps we had best speak about what to call the item. In previous paragraphs we have given the device a number of different titles. Each company naturally has its own brand name or number for the combustion control product. For the sake of familiarization, we will list some common names here and refer to each of them at some point in this chapter.

1. Relay.
2. Primary Combustion Control.
3. Safety Stack Switch.
4. Stack Control.
5. Master Control.
6. Pyratherm.
7. Protectorelay.
8. Stack Switch.

Here are some of the more familiar numbers of controls that you will see in the field.

Honeywell—RA 816/817/116/117
American Standard—CA-701/702/704
White Rodgers—610-630
Mercoid—JM1/JM
Penn—670/680/682
General—5200/5520/5525/5250/5550

## Combustion Control

There are four main sections to the average residential combustion control.

1. The *main body* provides a platform and protection for the integral parts of the device, as shown in Fig. 6-20. All the wiring, terminals, and additional specialty parts are securely mounted within this housing. The entire device, as a unit, is then mounted on the smokestack of the installation.
2. The *helix and clutch assembly* mechanically drives the entire device into action when it senses or reacts to the heat of the combustion unit.
3. The *transformers, relays,* and *wiring assemblies* transfer the electrical impulses of the operating mechanisms into action.
4. The unit *cover* provides protection for the primary control from dirt, dust and physical damage as shown in Figs. 6-21 and 6-22.

On an individual part basis, a stack combustion control consists of:

*Bimetal spring or coil element (helix).* This part, protected by the housing, is placed in the smokestack directly in contact with the hot gases of combustion.

*Clutch assembly.* The mechanical action of the heat-actuated helix is transferred to the contacts through this clutch assembly. The contacts are positioned on this clutch rod and the motion of the heat-actuated helix feeler end prods them into action.

*Motion-ignition relays.* The relays controlling the oil burner motor and ignition operation are mounted on the housing of the stack control. Each is responsible for transmitting electrical energy, on demand, to the combustion installation.

*Reset or safety switch.* Built-in and, in most instances, fully

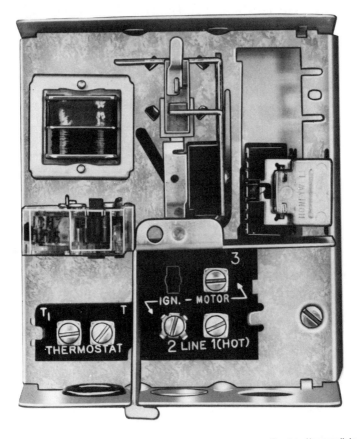

**Fig. 6-20. Interior view of a Honeywell stack switch.**

protected with a special covering, is the heater or *wrap* switch. A buildup of electrical heat through an improper electrical sequence of the combustion cycle will automatically put the safety switch into action. This unit will go on safety and (in most instances) must be manually reset.

*Transformer.* The low-voltage electrical energy for operational control, through such units as the thermostat or aquastat, is transformed at this point into the voltages necessary for unit operation.

Courtesy Honeywell, Inc.

Fig. 6-21. Protectorelay, or stack switch. Reset (safety) button located in center of housing.

## Relay Types

Two distinct types of combustion controls are found on residential installations. The *intermittent relay* (Fig. 6-23) is designed for use in control systems where ignition is required only at the start of each heating cycle.

On a call for heat, both the motor and the ignition circuit are electrically activated. Then, within a specific length of time, the ignition circuit either drops out or is turned off, leaving the motor circuit to continue operation until load demands are satisfied.

The *constant-ignition relay* (Fig. 6-24), on the other hand, is designed to be used in control systems where it is desired to maintain the electric ignition constantly during the entire burner heating cycle. When a demand for heat is made, both the motor and ignition circuits are activated. Those circuits remain on until the heating demands of the residence are satisfied.

## Stack-Control Operation

Following is how the standard stack safety control operates. It should be noted here, however, that because many different

REVERSIBLE MOUNTING FLANGE

FOR CURVED OR

FLAT SURFACES

**Fig. 6-22. Complete stack-switch assembly.**

companies produce these controls, they may differ slightly in sequence of operation.

On a call for heat by the room thermostat or by an operational call by a working control, an electrical circuit is completed. The relay pulls in, energizing the motor and ignition terminals. The rising stack temperatures created by the combustion equipment expand the bimetal element. The element (helix) in expanding mechanically moves the safety control's internal contacts. The circuits in moving jointly *make* a running circuit and *break* the safety heater circuit. Following this, the ignition circuit drops out if the unit is of the intermittent-ignition type.

If, for any of a number of reasons, the combustion heat does not reach the bimetal helix or element, a different sequence will take place. The bimetal will not move nor will the combustion control arms or contacts. Within a predetermined length of time,

Fig. 6-23. Constant-ignition relay panel.

Fig. 6-24. Intermittent-ignition relay panel.

the control heater switch will heat up and shunt the entire unit to lockout. The device will then have to be reset manually and the breakdown condition repaired. Some control manufacturer relays have a different sequence of operation. An example of this is listed below.

When the thermostat or load circuit manufactured by Mercoid is closed (calls for action), the transformer-relay secondary coil moves up, tilting the motor switch to the *on* position. Since the ignition switch is closed with the control in the starting position, the burner starts. As the temperature at the bimetal helix rises in the stack, it causes the bimetal coil to rotate, tilting the safety heater coil from the bimetal loop, and also tilting the ignition switch to the *off* position. When the burner is stopped, either by the thermostat load source, or momentary power interruption, the burner will not be permitted to start until the stack temperature has cooled down sufficiently to return the Pyratherm to the starting or cold position.

Honeywell gives the following operational schedule for the residential stack relays:

The expanding bimetal (helix) pushes the drive shaft to the left and, on contracting, pulls it back. The clutch fingers on the relay are carried by friction with the shaft until unlocked by hitting the stops. In the cold position, the hot contact is open and the cold contact is closed. As the bimetal heats, the hot clutch closes the hot contacts, then the cold clutch lets the cold contacts open. As the bimetal cools, the hot contacts open, then the cold contacts are pulled together. The sequence may vary a bit, but the end result is the same. If, for any reason, the combustion heat does not reach the bimetal element that mechanically drives these mechanisms, the safety lockout is energized.

## Relay Timing Procedures

The *Protectorelay* is the central point of the entire combustion operation and *timing* is of utmost importance. We should know the safety timing of the individual control. How long will it take the relay to discover a faulty combustion operation (e.g., flame failure)? This factor is of vital importance to operational safety. A unit that does not shut off properly and within a predetermined length of time can build up combustion fumes and gases and is potentially dangerous. Here is how to check for safety timing:

1. Turn the main oil burner switch *off.*
2. When the oil burner has been off for about 5 minutes, remove the lead wires from the motor and ignition terminal.
3. Close the main oil burner switch (turn up the room thermostat). This should activate the relay button as it has been disconnected.
4. Make a note of the length of time it takes between the *closing* of the oil burner *on* switch and the time it takes for the stack control to go on safety or *lockout.*

This is the *safety timing period,* and should be about 1½ minutes. Do not forget to turn off the oil burner switch and replace the wire lead to the motor-ignition terminals which you have previously disconnected. Wait a few minutes and then reset the stack switch *reset button* for normal burner operation.

The *scavenger timing* of the individual relay should also be checked. How long will the gases exist in the combustion area after shut down and before the unit begins to operate once again? You can readily realize the safety factor of this particular safety phase. Here's how to check scavenger timing:

1. Allow the burner to run for at least 5 minutes before beginning this test.
2. Turn the oil burner switch *off*, stopping the combustion process. Once completely stopped, return the oil burner switch back to its original *on* position.
3. Make a note of the length of time it takes from the time the oil burner was turned off until the unit comes on again. Keep the thermostat turned up during this procedure.

The time between these two points is the *scavenger timing period* and should be about 1 minute. This may vary slightly with different types of units. A final timing check is the ignition timing period. It is important to know this factor in order to function on an intermittent basis.

Here's how to check the ignition timing:

1. Turn the oil burner *on*.
2. Note the length of time it takes from the establishment of combustion flame to the time it takes the ignition relay to drop out of the combustion circuit.
3. If the time is too short (or too long) a simple adjustment may be made to correct this factor on most units. (See manufacturer's instructions.)

## Rebuilding Defective Relays

Combustion controls can be rebuilt when they become defective. This procedure may be particularly useful when an identical replacement relay is required for a particular installation. There are, however, certain points that should be checked on a rebuilt unit. First, make sure that the rebuilding firm is reputable and not a fly-by-night outfit. Then, ensure yourself that the rebuilt unit can pass the following 11-step checkup program:

1. Is the helix replaced with a new one or just painted? The helix is subject to wear and heat, so for complete new-unit operation and safety, the part must be changed and not just painted.

2. Are the high-voltage points replaced or filed clean? Marks and scratches on the face of the points are signs of unsatisfactory attempts to renew these high-voltage items.

3. If the relay has a mercury tube, has it been replaced if unsatisfactory? An older, defective mercury tube will have a film or glaze on the inside wall of the tube, giving evidence of wear.

4. In a mercury-tube relay, have the leads been replaced? Some companies merely dye these leads in green ink, not bothering to check the wires for breaks and brittleness.

5. Is the finest grade of solder used on all electrical connections? Some cheaper grades of solder and flux begin to oxidize and connections will begin to break off in a relatively short operating time.

6. Is the entire unit free from hums or buzzes? If the low-voltage transformer units do not test out as new, they must be replaced. Failure to do so will result in noises in the relay and eventual early breakdown.

7. Is the safety timing and contact stacking correct and adjusted to rigid specifications? It is important that all adjustments be set according to specifications. This is especially true of the *pyrostat* contacts and safety switch.

8. Are the high-voltage pull-in coils tested on each unit? Each coil, motor, and ignition must check out as new for long life.

9. Are all low-voltage contacts resurfaced? For peak unit efficiency, these contacts should be resurfaced.

10. Is the unit completely disassembled and the wiring checked? Internal relay wiring must be completely checked, for fired-out wiring can cause breakdowns or potential service difficulties. Complete disassembly ensures overall checking of internal wiring and connections on each unit.

11. Is the rebuilt relay outer case and cover spray painted and not just "cleaned up"? For maximum customer satisfaction and company profit, a good, "like-new" paint job is necessary.

A series of pointers should be given consideration before and during installation of the combustion control, as shown in Fig. 6-25. If these are conscientiously followed, your next installation will be that much easier and better.

Fig. 6-25. Combination Protectorelay and aquastat for hydronic system control.

Follow instructions of the manufacturer and his spec sheets.

Check all operating sequences and timing procedures before leaving the installation.

Install stack-mounted controls between the furnace, boiler, and the draft regulator.

Place the helix or bimetal sensing element in the direct path of hot combustion gases.

Keep the relay cover on at all times and screwed securely so that it will not loosen and fall off.

See that all contacts are in their correct starting position before allowing the oil burner to operate.

Do not change any settings that have been made at the factory unless you know it to be absolutely necessary. Always check and recheck the operating sequences of the control.

Do not bend or tamper with any contact blades.

Do not change the positioning of any mercury tubes.

Do not permit the bimetal element to be placed in the path of gases which are hotter than 1000°F.

Do not expect the bimetal element to react to stack temperatures that are relatively cold.

Do not locate the sensing element of the relay in the dead-air path areas of a smoke elbow.

Do not expose the housing, relays, transformers, wires, etc., to excessive radiant heat from the smokestack.

Do not overventilate the combustion control.

Do not install the combustion control in a position where dampness or water may easily get to it.

## INSTALLING THE COMBUSTION CONTROL

Check the preceding list of "do's and don'ts"—there is no sense in doing a job over. Next, select the actual position for the combustion control and the type of device you will use.

1. Use the stack-control mounting plate as a template and mark off the actual position the mounting plate will take on the smokestack.

2. Cut out the designated portion with tin shears. Make sure that there is plenty of clearance for the bimetal element.

3. Using an awl, punch out holes for the metal screws that will secure the mounting plate to the smokestack.

4. Install the piece of smokestack between the boiler and chimney breeching area. Make sure that all dampers are removed from the installation.

5. Loosen the relay holding screw and install the combustion control into the mounting plate. Retighten the screw.

6. If the unit requires leveling, use the proper instruments to ensure an even installation.
7. Wire the unit into the job.

## Wiring the Combustion Control

A number of electrical ground rules should be followed when installing a combustion control. The first, of course, is to adhere to the specific manufacturer's instructions whenever possible.

Choose the correct-size wire for the job. Too light a wire will eventually give you service problems. As a rule, do not use wire smaller than No. 18 for low-voltage wiring work and No. 14 for line voltage work. All connections, splicing, etc., should be neatly and carefully made, soldered, or connected with an approved type of connecting device.

The high-limit control should be connected in the hot line of the combustion control (terminal No. 1). Do not put the high limit in the line to the oil burner motor. Always leave slack wire in connecting the combustion control so that the device may be easily removed for inspection if desired. All wiring must conform to local electrical ordinances.

# WIRE CODE

Every relay, no matter what manufacturer, has a definite numerical wiring code that has been carried through for many, many years. Follow this code in wiring up your installation and in troubleshooting for maximum efficiency.

Terminal No. 1: The hot or line terminal (black wire).
Terminal No. 2: The ground terminal (white wire).
Terminal No. 3: The motor terminal (black wire).
Terminal No. 4: The ignition terminal (red wire).

The above schedule is for an *intermittent-ignition relay* wiring installation. If the installation is to be *constant ignition,* the No. 4 or ignition terminal wire will be placed on the No. 3 terminal along with the motor wire.

## TESTING THE WIRING

In order to determine whether you have wired the relay correctly, use a test lamp.

Terminal No. 1 will test "hot" with the line switch *on.*
Terminal No. 2 or ground, will test "dead" with the line switch *on.*
Terminal No. 3 or No. 4 will test "hot" *only* on a call for heat or operation by the room thermostat or aquastat.

The low-voltage terminals may have many designations such as "T-T," "R-W-B," or "R-W," according to the model and manufacturer. Read the instructions that come with the control.

## REPLACING THE HELIX
## OR BIMETAL ELEMENT

The helix or bimetal element can be changed on combustion relays if necessary. Often, unusually high temperatures or certain basement or furnace conditions will cause the helix to lose its ability to perform. The procedure that follows will allow you to change the bimetal element in the field when necessary.

1. Remove the two mounting screws which hold the U-shaped or spiral bimetal to the relay. If a great deal of difficulty is encountered, heat the screws until they become red hot and then unscrew them.
2. Slide the old helix from the holder.
3. Place the new helix on the relay.
4. Certain bimetals require twisting or winding in order to properly seat the new device.
5. Replace the holding screws.

6. Do not damage or twist any items out of shape when removing or reinstalling the bimetal. Always support the helix holders when removing the screws. Special helix tools are available at supply houses to aid in removal and replacement of the helix.

## RELAY TROUBLES

*Symptom and Possible Cause*     *Possible Remedy*

### Relay Will Not Pull In (no voltage to terminals No. 1 and No. 2 of unit)

1. Entrance switch off.
2. Fuse burned out.
3. Fuse loose in socket.
4. Limit control set too low; not closing or out of adjustment.
5. Relay incorrectly wired.

1. Turn on switch.
2. Replace fuse.
3. Tighten fuse.
4. Set or adjust control

5. Check diagrams and require correctly.

### Safety Switch Contacts of Relay Open

1. Malfunction in sequence.

1. Close contacts by pressing or moving reset button.

### Relay Circuit Open

1. Combustion contacts not in *start* position.
2. Combustion contacts dirty.

3. Combustion relay contact leaf broke.
4. Relay incorrectly wired.

1. Reset manually.

2. Clean contacts by using business card or bond paper between blades.
3. Replace relay.

4. Check diagram and rewire correctly.

247

| Symptom and Possible Cause | Possible Remedy |
|---|---|

**Relay Circuit Open Cont.**

5. Open circuit in internal wiring of relay.
6. Line voltage below required voltage

5. Replace relay.

6. Test with voltmeter. If too low, check with electric company.

**Relay Pulls In but Burner Motor Does Not Start and No Ignition Is Established**

1. Unit incorrectly wired.

2. Line-voltage contacts of relay dirty or out of adjustment.
3. Open circuit in relay.

1. Check diagram and rewire correctly.
2. Clean contacts or adjust as necessary.

3. Replace relay.

**Relay Pulls In, Burner Motor Starts, but No Ignition Is Established**

1. Faulty transformer or ignition system.

1. Repair or replace components in ignition system as necessary.

**Relay Pulls In, Ignition Is Established, but Burner Motor Does Not Start**

1. Defective motor.

1. Repair or replace motor.

**Relay "Locks-Out" on Safety Frequently or Infrequently**

1. Fuel difficulty.

1. Check oil and pump sections. Repair or replace as necessary.

*Symptom and Possible Cause*      *Possible Remedy*

**Relay "Locks-Out" on Safety Frequently or Infrequently Cont.**

2. Ignition difficulty.

3. Flame failure.

4. Improper location of stack relay.

5. Relay helix dirty and soot covered.
6. Relay helix broken, burned out, etc.

2. Check ignition and transformer sections. Repair or replace as necessary.
3. Check 1 and 2 and nozzle section. Repair or replace components as necessary.
4. Reinstall in proper location. Relay should be mounted at least 18 in. from, and on the furnace side of, the draft regulator.
5. Clean helix and adjust flame properly.
6. Replace helix or relay as necessary

**Oil Burner Cycles Too Frequently**

1. Thermostat differential set too close.
2. Improper thermostat heater or heater setting.

3. Limit control setting too low.
4. Limit control differential too close.
5. Dirty or smoky flame.
6. Unstable line voltage conditions.

1. Adjust differential. *See* Thermostat section.
2. Change heater or adjust as required. *See* Thermostat section.
3. Adjust to proper limits.

4. Adjust to proper limits.

5. Adjust flame.
6. Check with voltmeter and report to electric company for correction.

249

*Symptom and Possible Cause*       *Possible Remedy*

**Oil Burner Cycles Too Frequently Cont.**

7. Blower not operating or filters dirty in a warm-air system.

7. Repair blower (pulley, belt, motor, etc.) or replace filters.

**Room Temperature Too Hot or Too Cold Before Burner Starts or Stops**

1. Thermostat differential too wide.
2. Thermostat in wrong location.

1. Adjust differential. *See* Thermostat section.
2. Relocate thermostat.

Control manufacturers indicate that a very high percentage of all controls returned to their factories as defective actually have no defects at all. The percentages are even higher with stack relays. Check out all possible causes of relay breakdown before declaring the unit defective.

# ELECTRONIC RELAYS

Through the years, heating controls for commercial and industrial oil burners followed two lines. The first was the basic sequencing type of control for pressure atomizing equipment, and the second was the full sequencing control for the horizontal rotary type of oil burner.

An example of the basic sequencing control was the R114A Protectorelay developed by Honeywell. This device utilized a separate flame detector in the form of a two-wire stack switch or a two-wire Protectorstat, which operated from the combustion flame's radiant heat. This particular control saw a great deal of use on the commerically sized, pressure-atomizing oil burner. In the event that you run into this type of equipment on the job, the sequence of operation is as follows: On a call for heat, the burner motor, ignition, and oil valve (if used) become energized simultaneously. As soon as the flame is established and proven, the ignition is cut off. In the event of a flame failure, this control provides for accelerated safety shutdown of one half the normal safety switch timing.

An example of the full sequencing control was the R161, also produced by Honeywell. This particular type of control was used with the large, horizontal rotary oil burners. The device incorpoated a time switch that gave adjustable timed ignition and of the delayed opening of the oil valve. In the event that you should run into this type of control on the job, you should understand that the purpose of the timed ignition is to provide a longer ignition period for assuring a dependable light-off of horizontal burner equipment. A delayed oil valve on the model allowed the burner motor to come up to speed before the oil valve was open. There were two basic models of this particular relay. One unit, in the event of flame failure, stopped the oil burner and allowed the device *one* opportunity to restart. The other model locked out on safety as soon as there was a flame failure in the combustion area. The flame-sensing elements for both of these relays was either a stack switch, such as the Pyrostat or the Protectorstat.

Other relays were marketed (and may still be in the field) that varied in sequence only slightly from the first two units mentioned in the previous text. These units, used on commercial burners, were the RA114 and the R161. Both were manufactured by Honeywell and both were typical primary controls designed for the two types of oil burners mentioned previously.

When using a stack switch as the flame detector, there was obviously a delay in recognizing the establishment of flame or a flame failure due to the time required to sense the change in stack temperatures. Even with the Protectorstat, which operated from the radiant heat of the flame, there was a delay in response, although it was much faster than a stack-actuated unit. However, the Protectorstat could be actuated by radiant heat from the hot refractory of the combustion area. In addition, both types of flame-sensing units were subject to fatigue due to extremely high combustion temperatures. There was a real need, therefore, for a means of obtaining faster response to recognition of the flames of combustion, and, even more critical, recognition immediately of a flame loss.

Electronic flame-detection equipment was the obvious answer to the demand for speed of response. With electronic equipment, it was possible to recognize the establishment or loss of flame instananteously—something unheard of with earlier equipment. It was also possible, with electronic equipment, to minimize the effect of radiant heat from hot refractories because the photocell used to prove an oil flame was located outside the combustion chamber. It was not affected by the intense heat that stack switches or radiant diaphragms had previously been subjected to. The end result was a much more reliable operation.

One of the first electronic controls in the Honeywell line, for example, was the R177A. This unit utilized the flame-rectification principle using a photo-emissive photocell to provide a small direct-current signal. This small signal was amplified (stepped up) to a usable level by a vacuumtube, and operated a relay that would cut off the heating of the safety switch. It allowed the relay to go from the starting cycle to the running cycle. Ignition, with this control, was usually interrupted at the same time that the combustion flame was proven. This control provided the basic operating sequence except that now, in the event of a unit flame failure, ignition returned within .8 of a second in an attempt to reestablish the flame and continue the burner in operation. This basic sequence worked very well for the pressure-atomizing oil burner. A number of additional controls superseded the R117A in the Honeywell line. These included the R187, the R887, and the RA 890. These units provided improved designs in relay construction, safety switch construction, and improved components. Other manufacturers in the control field developed their controls along similar lines to provide fast-reacting, electronic response.

This is a good spot to point out that the electronic Protectorelay provided two important features not previously available in the early flame-sensing controls. In the event of a component failure, the relay would go out on safety, and any flame-simulating type of failure would be recognized between burner cycles. This prevented the relay from starting on the next call for heat. However, it required that the electronic network be constantly energized, and therefore a separate limit control location other than the hot line to the relay was required. With the RA890

Protectorelays, for example, an added relay made it possible to give a safe-start component checkout following a power failure, regardless of the duration. Later improvements in this particular control included an addition of a jack in the photocell circuit, permitting a micromameter to be plugged in directly without disturbing the wiring. This made it easier for the serviceman to check out the relay. In the Honeywell line, the RA890E Protectorelay with its basic sequence is one of the standard controls found in the field for commercially sized, pressure-atomizing oil burners where direct spark ignition of the oil is used.

Incidentally, a cutoff feature can be added to the RA890E by using a relay having a double-pole, double-throw overlapping contact. In the event of a flame failure, the oil valve is shut off immediately, and the burner motor continues to run. This provides a post-purge period for the duration of the safety-switch timing. This combination can be obtained in a panel either with or without an additional load relay. It provides a greater load rating than may be presently available on models in the field at this time and on present equipment.

## RELAY OPERATIONAL SEQUENCE

### Normal Sequence Power Off

1. Disconnect switch is open—no power at TR1 (see Fig. 6-26).
2. Disconnect switch is closed—power is supplied to TRI.
3. Vacuum tube heats—component check begins.
4. Flame relay pulls in—FR5 makes contact.

With low-voltage controller only, TR2 is powered, and check relay pulls in. A negative bias is applied to the grid of the tube in the flame-relay circuit, dropping out flame relay.

### Starting Circuit

1. Controller contacts made. With line voltage controller only, check relay pulls in and the flame relay drops out.
2. Load relay pulls in, safety-switch heater is energized, ignition starts, and pilot valve of burner motor is powered.

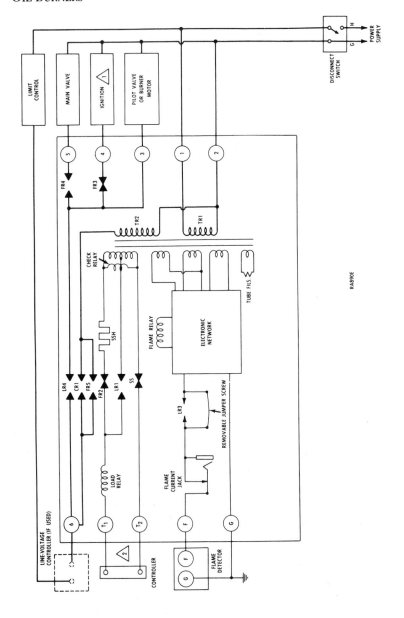

**Fig. 6-26.** Relay

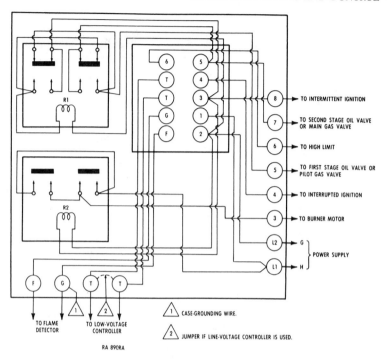

TO INTERMITTENT IGNITION

TO SECOND STAGE OIL VALVE
OR MAIN GAS VALVE

TO HIGH LIMIT

TO FIRST STAGE OIL VALVE OR
PILOT GAS VALVE

TO INTERRUPTED IGNITION

TO BURNER MOTOR

G

POWER SUPPLY

H

TO FLAME
DETECTOR

TO LOW-VOLTAGE
CONTROLLER

1  CASE-GROUNDING WIRE.

2  JUMPER IF LINE-VOLTAGE CONTROLLER IS USED.

RA 890RA

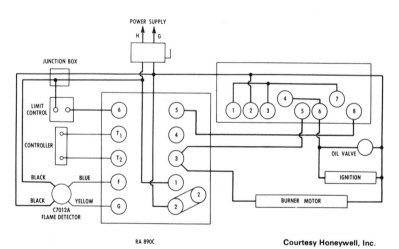

RA 890C

Courtesy Honeywell, Inc.

**schematic diagrams.**

255

## Flame Circuit

1. If flame is proven, flame relay pulls in, safety-switch heater is shunted, main valve opens, and ignition stops.

## Controller Stop

1. Controller contacts break.
2. Load relay drops out, main valve and pilot valve close, burner motor stops, and flame-signal circuit is broken.
3. Sytem is ready for next cycle.
   With low voltage, controller-flame relay drops out. With line voltage, controller-check relay drops out.

When the electronic circuit detects the absence of flame, the flame relay drops out. Terminal No. 5 is then deenergized, and the safety-switch heater is energized. If the ignition is connected to terminal No. 4, the ignition is returned in an attempt to reestablish flame.

If the flame is not reestablished within the safety switch timing, the safety-switch heater breaks the control circuit, the load relay drops out, and terminals No. 3 and 4 are deenergized. Manual reset of the safety switch is required before a new start can be made.

If the flame is not proved before the expiration of the safety-switch timing, the safety switch locks out, breaking the control circuit. Terminals No. 3 and 4 are deenergized. Manual reset of the safety switch is required before a new start can be made.

The flame relay remains in at the end of the running cycle. If the hot refractory is still capable of holding in the flame relay when the controller calls for heat, the flame relay does not drip out as it does under normal conditions. Thus, start-up is prevented until the hot refractory is no longer keeping the flame relay in.

# GENERAL OPERATIONAL INFORMATION

The above sequence was detailed as an example. Each control manufacturer has a definite sequence outlined for his particular electronic controls. It is wise for the serviceman to obtain spec sheets and operational schedules of each of the major manufacturers in the field today. This will provide reference for installations having electronic equipment.

A short while after the first electronic Protectorelay, the R177 was developed by Honeywell. Service people began to realize that a portion of this relay could be used as an electronic switch, enabling electronic flame detectors to be used with other Protectorelays previously using mechanical flame-sensing devices. The R7009A flame-detector relays, developed by Honeywell and later superseded by the R7023A flame-detector relay, were made available with double-pole, double-throw switching action. This was basically the electronic portion of the complete Protectorelay.

The R161, for example, was modified so that in the event of a flame-simulating component failure, the starting circuit of the R161 would be interrupted, and the burner could not be started. The use of the R7023 with the appropriate electronic flame detectors and the R161 enabled a new safety sequence to be added. This proved the pilot *before* the main fuel valve could be opened. It was not feasible to prove the pilot separately before the main fuel was opened with mechanical flame detectors.

Many horizontal rotary oil burners used either a two-position or a modulating motor to vary the firing rate to the load demand. This meant an additional relay was necessary to drive the firing-rate motor back to low-fire or closed position at the end of each firing cycle so that the next burner start could be made at low fire.

The R178 Protectorelay was designed to combine the functions of the R161 with delayed oil valves and timing ignition. The R7023, with provisions for utilizing electronic flame detectors, and the R482C relay, for controlling the firing rate of the oil burner motor, were used. The R178A Protectorelay provided delayed oil valve sequence, adjustable and selectable timed ignition, firing rate motor control, and a 15-second postpurge period.

The R178B Protectorelay was designed as a variation of the above unit. The delayed oil valve sequence was changed to a prepurge sequence with the ignition held off until the oil valve

257

was open. This was an important step in the automatic programming for horizontal rotary oil burners and some of the larger pressure-atomizing units where it was important to prove the pilot before opening the main fuel oil valve.

The R478 Protectorelay was designed to offer a wider range of flexibility for horizontal rotary oil burners and packaged steam generators. This unit provides 30-second prepurge selectability of ignition timing—either 15 or 45 seconds or intermittent ignition. The R478A was for use with flame-rectification flame detectors, like the flame rod, and the photo-conduction photocell. The R478B was designed for use with the lead-sulphite cell. In this system, one flame detector can be used to provide both gas and oil flames. A modification of the R478 is the R4047B, which eliminates the selectivity of sequencing and provides a 30-second post-purge, 15-second ignition timing, high fire at the end of the ignition cycle, and a 30-second post-purge.

Two major factors appear to be influencing control manufacturers today:

1. The response time (response to the presence or absence of heat).
2. The physical size of the device.

For example, one of the big breakthroughs covering both of the above factors was the cadmium-sulfide flame detector. The CdS detector was small enough to mount directly on the oil burner and its response time was immediate. This permitted the manufacturers to do away with a mass of external wiring. It also provided heating-unit designers with controls that would fit the pattern of compact furnaces and boilers.

Improvements in these Protectorelay units continue on a regular basis. For example, the R478 and the R4047 Protectorelay have had their rectifier tubes replaced with more dependable diodes and a special signal light that make service work on these units even simpler. One of the latest oil burner primary controls, the R8185, introduced by Honeywell, is smaller, more compact, and faster reacting than its immediate predecessors, the R8118 and the R866B.

# THE PROGRAMMING RELAY

## Installation Start-Up and Fast Service Check (see Fig. 6-27)

### Installation—

1. Remove any protective cardboard found on switching relays.
2. Set voltage selector link for proper voltage—all three screws must be tight.
3. With power off, install programming relay on base.

### Initial Start-Up Burner—

1. Shut off main fuel valve manually or electrically disconnect main fuel valve.
2. Reset safety switch if necessary.
3. On a modulating burner, hold burner in low-fire position by using the low-fire switch if provided or removing the *blue wire* on the *modutrol* motor.
4. Turn on the power source.
5. With all controls and interlocks made, start oil burner by throwing on-off switch to *on* position.

### Manual Sequencing of Control (R478-M-H)—

A. Continuous Prepurge

   1. Pull timing (top) tube.
   2. Burner motor will run continuously to purge combustion chamber. On an oil installation, this can be used to bleed the air out of the oil lines.
   3. "Purge" lamp will be lighted during this operation.

B. Intermittent Pilot

   1. Used to bleed pilot line, adjust pilot, and check location of flame detector.
      a. Make sure main fuel valve is manually closed or disconnected.
      b. Prop safety switch open with piece of paper.

259

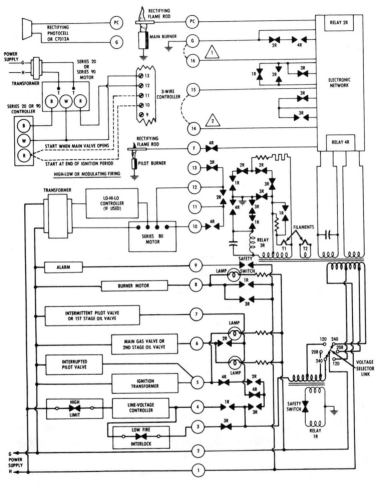

① ON "1 OR 3-MINUTE PREPURGE" MODLE ONLY, A JUMPER BETWEEN TERMINALS G AND 16 PROVIDES 3-MINUTE PREPURGE TIMING; NO JUMPER, 1-MINUTE TIMING.

② JUMPER BETWEEN TERMINALS 14 AND 15 PROVIDES 15-SECOND IGNITION TIMING; NO JUMPER, 30-OR-60-SECOND TIMING, AS SPECIFIED ON ORDER.

SCHEMATIC OF TYPICAL BURNER SYSTEM INCLUDING THE R478A.

**Fig. 6-27. Relay**

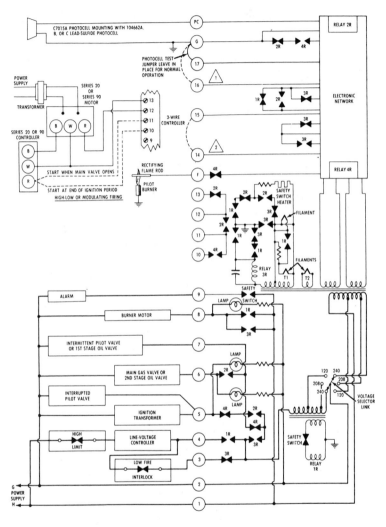

  *c.* Manually push in tab on top relay.

  *d.* Pilot valve and ignition transformer energized. "Pilot Ignition" lamp will light.

  *e.* Pilot and ignition will be powered as long as timer tube is removed.

  *f.* "Flame Proven" lamp will light when detector senses flame.

## C. Main Flame

 1. To check or adjust main flame.

  *a.* Make sure oil burner is in low-fire position.

  *b.* Open or reconnect main fuel valve.

  *c.* Main flame should light smoothly from pilot.

  *d.* Pilot will remain on until timer tube is replaced.

  *e.* To turn off, and restore boiler or burner to automatic operation, replace timer tube, and remove safety switch prop.

## D. Fast Manual Cycling of Programming Relay

 1. Used to run burner rapidly through many starts to determine if pilot ignites and is detected on each cycle.

  *a.* Manually shut off main fuel valve or disconnect it electrically.

  *b.* Block safety switch with piece of paper.

  *c.* If burner is modulating on high-low, hold in low-fire position with switch by removing the *blue wire* to the *modutrol* motor.

  *d.* Make limit and starting circuits "Purge" lamp on.

  *e.* As soon as "Purge" lamp is lighted, push flipper on top switching relay.

  *f.* "Pilot" and "Ignition" lamp lights followed by "Flame Proven" lamp if detector has seen flames.

  *g.* As soon as "Flame Proven" lamp is on, rapidly flick safety switch.

  *h.* "Pilot," "Ignition," and "Flame proven" lamps will go out.

  *i.* As soon as flame relay drops out (2 to 4 seconds), push flipper on top relay for another cycle.

**Fast Check of R478—**

Basically, a programming relay of this type does only two things:

1. It is a timer.
2. It is a flame detector.

Checking either of the above two functions takes only a few minutes. Checking the timing section takes only 30 seconds:

1. Complete the starting and limit circuits.
   a. You will know when this is done because the "Purge" lamp will light.
   b. 30 seconds later, the "Pilot Ignition" lamp should light.

     i.If it does, the timer section is working.
     ii.If it does not, replace the timer (the top tube).

Checking the Flame Detection Unit of the R478:

1. Make sure that there is power to the programming relay, and that the burner is not running (no signal lamp is lit).
2. When checking leak sulphide programming relays, jiggle the tip of your finger on the top terminal while keeping the side of your finger on the chassis (R478B). On the 478A, hold the prongs of the flame simulator against the PC and G terminals instead of using your fingers.
   Make sure the G prong of the simulator is on the G terminal of the R478.
   a. If you hear the flame relay click, the entire electronic flame-detection system is good. (The "Flame Proven" lamp will not light during this test.) Fifteen seconds of tapping on the PC terminal will cause the programming relay to lockout on safety, which is a good check of the safety switch.
   b. If the relay does not pull in, remove the wire to the PC terminal and try tapping the top terminal again (with R478A, apply simulator).
   c. If the flame relay still does not pull in when the PC terminal is tapped, or the simulator is applied, change the lower tubes.

After the detector section of the programming relay has been checked and found good, you can quickly check the flame detector (except for flame rods).

1. Remove the cell and holder from the sighting pipe.
2. Hold a lighted match in front of it:
    *a.* The flame relay should click in.
    *b.* If the flame relay does not pull in, replace the cell or tubes if an ultraviolet (UV) detector is used.

If the programming relay passes both these tests, there is no need to replace it. For more detailed service instructions, use instructions and spec sheets supplied by the individual control manufacturers.

## TIMING SEQUENCE OF A
## FIREYE ELECTRONIC CONTROL

With a gas or oil proven pilot (no connection between terminals No. 6 Unit: UPV-2 system with Type 25RU8, and No. 7). Model 6570 (see Fig. 6-28)

| Timer Rotation Seconds | Dial Indicator | Burner Startup (action) |
|---|---|---|
| 0 | 0 | Operation control closes. Master relay, timer motor and burner motor (terminal No. 8) become energized. Modulator control switches go to high-fire position (10-12 opens; 10-13 closes). |
| 20 | - | Purge air-flow interlock (8 to W closed) must be satisfied for cycle to continue. |
| 42 | - | Modulator control switches go to low-fire position (10-12 opens; 10-13 closes). |
| 53 | × | If, for any reason, flame relay holds in, cycle timer motor stops until lockout switch trips. If low-fire interlock (W to B closed) is not satisfied, motor timer stops until interlock is satisfied. |
| 63 | 1 | Ignition (terminal No. 1) and pilot fire valve (terminals No. 5 and 6) *on.* |
| 70 | A | Ignition (terminal No. 1) *off.* |

| Timer Rotation Seconds | Dial Indicator | Burner Startup (action) |
|---|---|---|
| 75 | 2 | Fuel valve (terminal No. 7) *on* (provided pilot is proven). |
| 90 | 3 | Pilot valve (terminal No. 5) *off.* Modulator control switches go to demand position (10-12 open, 10-11 closed). |
| 105 | Dot (Index) | Pilot valve (terminal No. 6) *off.* End of initiating cycle; timer motor stops. Burner operates until heat demand is satisfied. |

**Burner Shutdown**

| Timer Rotation Seconds | Dial Indicator | Burner Startup (action) |
|---|---|---|
| 105 | Dot (Index) | Operating control opens; master relay and fuel value (terminal No. 7) deenergized; timer motor becomes energized. Modulator control switches go to low-fire position (10-11 open, 10-12 closed). |
| 120 | 0 | Burner motor (terminal No. 8) circuit and cycle timer motor deenergized. |
| | | System is ready for start-up whenever operating control closes again. |

## TIMING SEQUENCE OF A FIREYE ELECTRONIC CONTROL WITH AN UNPROVEN PILOT OR DIRECT SPARK IGNITION

(Terminals No. 6 and No. 7 jumpered). Unit: UVP-2 system with Type 25RUB, Model 6570. (See Figs. 6-29 and 6-30).

| Timer Rotation Seconds | Dial Indicator | Burner Startup (action) |
|---|---|---|
| 0 | 0 | Operation control closes. Master relay, timer motor and burner motor (terminal No. 8) become energized. Modulator control switches go to high-fire position (10-12 opens; 10-13 closes). |
| 20 | | Purge air-flow interlock (B to W closed) must be satisfied for cycle to continue. |
| 42 | | Modulator control switches go to low-fire position (10-13 opens; 10-12 closes). |

| Timer Rotation Seconds | Dial Indicator | Burner Startup (action) |
|---|---|---|
| 53 | × | If, for any reason, flame relay holds in, cycle timer motor stops until lockout switch trips. If low-fire interlock (W to B closed) is not satisfied, motor timer stops until interlock is satisfied. |
| 63 | 1 | Ignition (terminal No. 1) and fuel valve (terminal No. 7) *on.* |
| 70 | A | Ignition (terminal No. 1) *off.* If flame has not been established and detected, fuel value is deenergized. |
| 75 | 2 | No action. |
| 90 | 3 | Modulator control switches go to demand position (10-12 open, 10-11 closed). |
| 105 | Dot (Index) | End of the initiating cycle; timer motor stops. Burner operates until heat demand is satisfied. |
| | | **Burner Shutdown** |
| 105 | Dot (Index) | Operating control opens; master relay and fuel value (terminal No. 7) deenergized; timer motor becomes energized. Modulator control switches go to low-fire position (10-11 open, 10-12 closed). |
| 120 | 0 | Burner motor (terminal No. 8) circuit and cycle timer motor deenergized. |
| | | System is ready for start-up whenever operating control closes again. |

# SUGGESTED SPECIFICATIONS FOR FLAME SAFEGUARD CONTROL FOR AUTOMATIC COMMERCIAL-INDUSTRIAL BURNERS

Each automatically fired oil burner should be equipped with an electronic combustion safety and programming control that is UL listed, FM approved, and meets with the requirements of FIA. This control should provide the following:

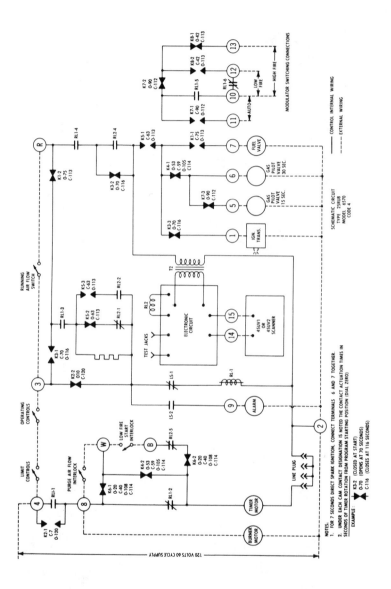

**Fig. 6-28. Fireye electronic control circuit.**

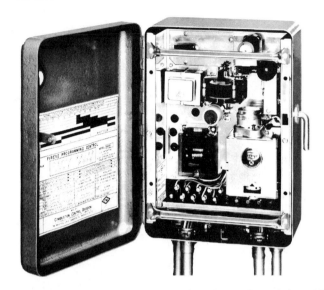

Courtesy Electronic Corp. of America

Fig. 6-29. Typical industrial control used on industrial-size automatic heavy oil burner.

Courtesy Electronic Corp. of America

Fig. 6-30. Large-boiler installation safeguarded by electronic control equipment.

1. The control should accomplish a safe-start component check during each start, which will prevent the burner from firing under any condition that causes the flame relay to assume and hold its energized position due to the presence of an actual flame, a flame-simulating component failure, or a mechanical failure.

2. A programmed purging cycle with provision for directing air dampers to or toward wide open position, connections for purge rate interlock to assure purging at or above a specified airflow rate, provision for directing the air dampers back to low-fire position, and connections for an interlock to assure that the dampers have returned to a low-fire position before a lighting attempt is permitted.

3. A pilot establishing period of not more than 10 seconds.

4. A pilot-providing period that necessitates proving pilot flame only (with ignition spark off) before energizing the main fuel valve circuit.

5. Limited trial-for-ignition of main flame restricted to 15 seconds for oil or gas and 30 seconds for heavy oil only.

6. A running interlock circuit for connection of running airflow interlock, high or low fuel-pressure interlocks, etc. Opening of the circuit during prepurge should effect an automatic recycling or during the firing period should initiate a safety shutdown.

7. A post-purge period of 15 seconds following a normal shutdown and 60 seconds or more following a safety shutdown.

8. Safety shutdown following flame failure, with fuel and ignition circuits deenergized in not more than 4 seconds.

9. The control system should recycle automatically under control of the operating control, and when power is restored following power failure, manual reset should be required following any safety lockout.

The control should permit direct connection of safety limit switches, operating controls, starting interlocks, fuel temperature and pressure switches, running interlocks, and lockout alarms. The pilot and main flames should be monitored by an ultraviolet sensitive flame scanner which should not be activated by hot refractory.

The control system should be designed for 120-volt operation with one side grounded. All switching should be accomplished in the hot circuit. The control and/or scanner should have the following features:

1. The program timing should be accomplished by a cam-driven, heavy-duty switch assembly readily accessible for inspection. The timing periods must not vary more than 5 percent through an ambient temperature range of 0°F to 125°F and through a supply range voltage of plus 10 percent or minus 15 percent of normal line voltage.

2. The contacts in the fuel valve circuit should be of weld-resistant tungsten alloy material.

3. The safety lockout switch should be temperature compensated and contain alarm contacts rated at not less than 50 VA at 120 volts.

4. The flame-relay circuit of the flame-safeguard control must incorporate a latch circuit which prevents the flame relay from becoming energized following a safety shutdown, until a lockout has occurred and manual reset has initiated a complete restart.

5. Test jacks should be provided for direct connection of a DC voltmeter to measure flame signal voltage.

6. The control chassis should be of plug-in design to facilitate replacement without disconnecting any external wiring.

7. The scanner should mount on and sight through a ¾-in. standard pipe.

8. The control should be suitable for operation over an ambient temperature range of 0°F to 125°F.

9. The scanner should be suitable for operation over a temperature range of 0°F to 200°F, as measured on the mounting hub.

Specifications suggested by Electronics Control Corporation of America, Combustion Control Division.

## ADDITIONAL ELECTRONIC UNITS

The serviceman may also come upon other types of electronic units in his work in the field. One of these units uses the principle of ultraviolet light for flame detection. The device may be used with existing flame-rectification Protectorelays. The R4075 maximum safety relay features the continuous component check while the burner is in operation. Prior to this particular relay, no Protectorelay could check for flame simulating failures while the burner was in operation. This particular control provides for maximum safety for those gas-fired installations having long or continuous firing periods.

The lead-sulphide system of flame detection does not respond reliably, at all times, in the presence of hot refractory and the problems involved with the supervision of individual burners on multiple burner installations. With the ultraviolet system of detecting ultraviolet radiation of combustion flames, hot refractory is no longer a problem. In addition, this system for the first time permitted simple and reliable flame-detection application on multiple burner applications. Because the ultraviolet detector can be mounted without regard for refractory backgrounds, each burner on a multiple installation can be supervised at a point where adjacent burner flames would not be seen.

A number of control manufacturers produce electronic relay equipment for the oil burner industry. The controls of each of these companies should be studied thoroughly so that the service mechanic has a working knowlege of the equipment before going on the job. Various types of relays, equipment installations, and related devices are shown in Figs. 6-31 through 6-37.

Courtesy Electronic Corp. of America

Fig. 6-31. Electronic combustion control used on commercial oil burner.

Courtesy Electronic Corp. of America

Fig. 6-32. Oil burner assembly with Fireye electronic control.

## ELECTRONIC CONTROL SERVICE AND TROUBLESHOOTING

### General

1. Fireboxes and flues must always be free of unburned gases before lighting the oil burner.
2. A component check always occurs when power is restored after interruption. The electronic relay cannot be energized until check is satisfactorily completed.
3. Always pull the disconnect switch before loosening or tightening the mounting screws.
4. Replace all relay covers before leaving the job.
5. On any service call, check the controller for approximately correct calibration and differential. Make sure the relay con-

Courtesy Electronic Corp. of America

Fig. 6-33. Fireye technicians at work testing various oil burner installations.

tacts are clean, the mounting screws and heater plug (if used) are tight.

6. Before assuming that the relay or some other component unit of the system is defective, make sure that wiring is correct and oil burner is properly adjusted.

7. Never use oil on any part of the relay.

8. When cleaning the oil burner, automatically clean the flame-detector device.

9. Since there is a minimum of moving parts in the relay, the unit should not deteriorate in use. Preventative maintenance, such as periodic inspections of the flame electrode (if one is used on the particular unit), annual replacement of vacuum tubes, and check of burner adjustment and flame characteristics may forestall unnecessary oil burner shutdowns.

273

**Fig. 6-34. Panel for programmed energy-saving hydronic control system. Unit automatically "watches" domestic hot-water, home heating, and boiler water temperatures.**

## No Heat

After checking the controller, start from the relay to locate the trouble. Observe action of the relay while an assistant changes the controller settings.

1. Check for safety lockout. Operate the reset switch several times. If the contacts are dirty, the resulting contact wiping may clean them.
2. Check for voltage across terminals No. 1 and No. 2.

274

Courtesy Heat-Timer Corporation

Fig. 6-35. A micro-processor heating control designed for hot-water heating systems in large installations. Unit features electronic clock with different setback levels and temperature control linked to outside temperatures.

3. Check mounting screws for tightness.
4. Check for open circuits in the wiring to the controller or at terminals.
5. If the Protectorelay responds but the burner does not start, check fuel supply, valves, ignition and thermal overload circuit.

## Relay Chatter

Load relay chatter may result from extreme low voltage (notify power company), or from loose connections (tighten). Flame

Fig. 6-36. Photocell and oil burner relay.

Fig. 6-37. Burner-mounted cad cell primary control.

276

relay chatter may result from improper combustion (adjust oil burner) or soot or carbon on flame detector (clean and correct cause).

Relay contacts may be cleaned by pushing a piece of hard-surfaced paper between the closed contacts, or by spraying with a commercial contact cleaner-restorer.

## Overheating

Observe Protectorelay response when the controller setting is changed. Look for short circuits in the controller wiring. Inspect the limit control. If the flame relay holds in continuously or fails to pull in and drop out when the line switch is closed and power is available to terminal No. 6, install a new vacuum tube. If this does not cure the problem, install a new Protectorelay.

## Lockout

If the flame relay does not pull in with flame established:

1. Make sure that there is a steady flame signal to the flame detector. If excess air or other difficulties cause the flame to float away from the oil burner, the flame relay is unable to pull in.
2. Make sure that the flame detector is in proper alignment.
3. Insert a new vacuum tube. If the new tube produces no change, reinstall the old tube unless it has been in service over one year.
4. Install a new Protectorelay.
5. Check wiring from flame detector to Protectorelay.

*Note:* Checking the flame circuit is easier and quicker with a micromameter to read the flame current. Use of the meter is recommended on every call to detect marginal conditions before a trouble call develops. Normal operation requires a flame signal of at least 2 microamperes. A flame-simulator part is available from the manufacturer to use in checking the Protectorelay. If the Protectorelay operates with the flame simulator held across F and G terminals, the trouble is in the flame detector or its wires. If the upper screw (connected in parallel to LR3) is removed, the load relay must be powered or held in manually to complete flame circuit. *Never* leave the flame simulator connected between F and G terminals.

It is important to repeat that the above troubleshooting guide covers just one particular type of electronic control. Space does not permit discussing each individual model and brand of electronic relay at present on the market. The above troubleshooting information should provide a sufficient amount of background material so that with a guide or manufacturer's spec sheets before him, a serviceman will be able to adequately troubleshoot most equipment in the field today.

## SUMMARY

There are three different styles and shapes of motors: split-phase, capacitor-start, and shaded pole. Many factors determine the durability and performance of any motor. These factors are: rigid, sturdy motor housings; type and design of drive shaft armature and overload protection; and size and quality of wire used in the windings. The rated horsepower of any motor; the revolutions per minute (rpm); and the voltage, amperage, and cycles are very important when selecting a particular motor to do the job.

A thermostat sends electrical impulses to the heating equipment, which starts or stops the operation of the equipment. A dial or scale is set to a predetermined room temperature. This is activated by a bimetal strip of coil spring that expands or contracts to room temperature. The movement closes a set of contacts or tilts a mercury bulb that completes the electrical circuit.

There are many types of thermostats, including some with clock-timing devices which automatically control nighttime temperatures, and low-voltage and high-voltage units that offer many deluxe advantages.

A limit switch is needed to control burner operation. A furnace can heat up too much if the operation is too frequent or too long. A limit switch stops the burner, even though the thermostat is calling for more heat. When the fan circulates enough air through the furnace to carry away the heat, the limit switch permits the thermostat to continue operation and ask for more heat.

There are basically two types of steam limit switches. The pressuretrol and aquastat controls regulate the pressure limits in the boiler and water lines. Steam builds up and generates heat more rapidly than the distribution system can carry it to the rooms. When this occurs, the burner will shut off, allowing the steam pressure to lower; when pressure has dropped, these controls will allow the burner to operate again.

A control or limit switch called the airstat is installed in the warm-air system and controls the air temperature within the furnace. It is positioned so that the sensing element feels the air temperature change and controls the automatic firing of the furnace.

In later years, electronic relays were used and developed to accelerate safety shutdown when malfunction occurred in the furnace. It was possible with electronic equipment to minimize the effect of radiant heat because a photocell was located outside and away from the combustion chamber.

## REVIEW QUESTIONS

1. Explain the purpose of an overload switch.
2. What are the visual checks to make on a rebuilt electric motor?
3. What are the three basic types of electric motors?
4. What is meant by rpm of a motor?
5. Explain the purpose of a thermostat.
6. What is the advantage in using a clock-controlled thermostat?
7. Why is proper location for a thermostat necessary?
8. What are the advantages of a low-voltage thermostat?
9. What purpose does a weather-watching thermostat serve?
10. How often should a thermostat be cleaned and inspected?
11. What is the purpose of the limit control?
12. Explain the operation of the pressuretrol control.
13. Explain the reverse-action limit control.

14. What are the advantages in using the electronic relays?
15. What is the sensing device called that is used on controls and relays?
16. What are the two general types of relays?
17. Explain constant ignition.
18. What can cause relay chatter?
19. Is electronic flame detection the answer to the demands for speedy response in combustion units? Why?
20. Explain intermittent ignition.

# CHAPTER 7

# Oil Storage

Fuel oil is an integral part of all oil heating installations. Most cities have specific rules and regulations governing the installation of oil tanks, piping, and auxiliary fuel storage equipment. It is important that the service mechanic adhere strictly to all local regulations. Infractions can be costly.

There are two kinds of fuel oil storage installations. These are the inside (cellar) fuel storage unit and the outside (buried) underground fuel storage installation. Inside storage tanks are generally 275-gal. capacity; outside underground tanks are generally 550-, 1000-, and 1500-gal. capacity. These tanks must be Underwriter Approved. Certain manufacturers produce storage tanks with odd capacities.

# UNDERGROUND STORAGE TANKS

Specific regulations usually govern underground storage tank installations. These regulations, local in nature, include distance from buildings and the depth the tank is to be buried. Usually 2 ft. beneath the surface of the ground is satisfactory (see Fig. 7-1). If the soil is sandy and the tank might rise when empty, the entire unit should be anchored. This is accomplished with cement. Underground tanks should be painted with several coats of tar or asphaltum paint as a protection. The tank or piping should never be exposed to coal ash or cinders as these substances can be corrosive.

## Installing the Underground Tank

Select a suitable spot for tank installation. Do not place the unit in the driveway. Have the area where the tank is to be placed excavated to the proper depth, width, and length. Allow a number of extra feet in width and length for ease of lowering. Clear the entire base area under the tank of stones or protruding rock. Gently lower the tank into the excavation. Allow a pitch of about 3 in. with the low end of the tank being opposite the area

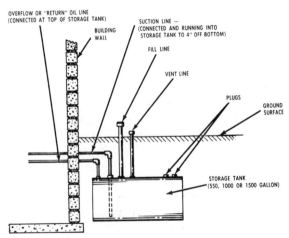

Fig. 7-1. Underground storage tank.

that will be used for the suction line. If you have the proper equipment, cap the tank completely after lowering and test the unit for leaks using a pressure test. At this point, fill the tank with fuel oil (this will prevent the tank from floating in case a water or rain condition exists before covering). Cap, pipe, and vent the various openings at the tank top and backfill the space around the buried storage tank. Pipe joints should be made with swing joints in the event of strain or tank shifting. Do not splice piping that runs underground. The tank should have a fill pipe 2 in. in diameter, a vent pipe at least 1 in. in diameter, and properly sized suction and return lines. Refer to manufacturer's fuel pump spec sheets for proper line sizes. It may also have a connection for a remote-reading fuel gauge. See Fig. 7-2.

Courtesy Petrometer Corp.

**Fig. 7-2. Remote-reading fuel gauge for underground tanks.**

If the top of the underground oil storage tank is higher than the oil inlet on the oil burner, the suction line should be installed so that it inclines slightly to the point where it enters the boiler room. At the point that it enters the boiler room from the outside, an anti-siphon valve should be installed on the line to prevent the storage tank from siphoning the oil back when the oil burner shuts off. A good shutoff valve should be installed between the anti-siphon valve in the boiler room and the oil burner. A ball check valve should be installed between the antisiphon valve and the oil storage tank.

The underground tank suction should be installed so that it is approximately 3 to 4 in. off the bottom of the tank. This will prevent the line from picking up sludge and water collections that will accumulate during use. Remember not to bury underground storage tanks too deep. Depth can affect fuel pump vacuum and draw. Avoid water, rock, and mud spots for tank installations. Make sure that fill and vent lines are pitched correctly and will not collect rain water, subsequently running it into the storage tanks.

# INSIDE STORAGE TANKS

Inside storage tanks are installed singly or in tandem units in basements or boiler rooms (see Fig. 7-3). When joined together, the total capacity is 550 gal. In this type of installation, fuel oil is fed to the burner by *gravity flow*. In certain cities and areas, regulations govern the installation of inside storage tanks. Service mechanics are advised to heed all area regulations.

Easy-to-read tank gauges and combination vent-alarm signal gauges are available for inside tank installations (Figs. 7-4, 7-5, 7-6, and 7-7).

## Installation Procedure

A suitable level area is first selected for the tank installation. It should be located as close as possible to an outside wall for fill

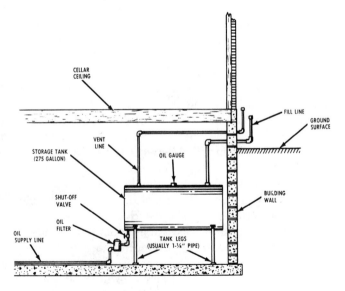

Fig. 7-3. Inside storage tank.

Fig. 7-4. Tank gauge installed on inside fuel storage tank.

Fig. 7-5. Inside fuel oil storage tank gauge.

285

Fig. 7-6. Combination ventalarm and tank gauge for inside oil storage tanks.

Fig. 7-7. Ventalarm or whistling tank-filling alarm for inside oil storage tanks.

and venting convenience. The spot should be clear of combustible areas. Tank legs (usually 1¼-in. pipe), which raise the tank off the cellar floor, steady the tank, and give it sufficient height for gravity flow, are attached next. A good shutoff valve (easily accessible) is connected to the bottom of the fuel storage tank as shown in Fig. 7-8. The entire unit should now be piped for venting and filling. A gauge that calculates the oil supply is installed on the tank. The fill line, connected to the top of the storage tank, should be a minimum of 2 in. in diameter. The vent line, also positioned at the tank top, should be a minimum of 1 in. in diameter, and should be capped so that water cannot run into the line and tank.

The standard 275-gal. tanks are usually made of 12- or 14-gauge metal. Their sizes are 22 in. wide × 44 in. high × 79 in. long, or 26 in. wide × 42 in. high × 72 in. long. All fuel storage tanks should be Underwriter Approved.

Courtesy General Filters, In.

Fig. 7-8. Shutoff valve at bottom of inside fuel storage tank with oil filter in place.

287

# TANDEM TANK HOOKUPS

The 275-gal. fuel storage tanks may be hooked up in tandem style. It is suggested that the service mechanic check local regulations on tandem hookups (see Fig. 7-9). Assuming that local codes permit this type of hookup, the tank fill and vent lines are joined together so that only one feed line and one vent line are needed outside for both units. One oil gauge will also suffice for both tanks. For maximum safety, both storage tanks should have their own shutoff valves with supply piping connected through a tee to the oil burner. Service mechanics should follow installation instructions set forth earlier in this chapter for inside storage tanks.

**Additional Devices**—Additional devices such as whistle vents and fast-fill units may be installed on both inside and outside oil storage tanks. These devices whistle during the fill process and alert the oil truck driver, by sound, to the tank's capacity. This can speed up the filling process and ensure spill-free deliveries. The smart service mechanic will see that a fuel filter is installed

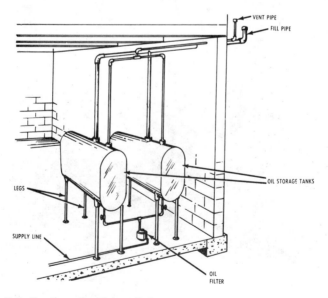

**Fig. 7-9. Tandem oil tank installation.**

between the oil supply and the fuel pump. This filter can short-stop dirt and foreign materials from entering both the fuel pump and nozzle area; see Fig. 7-10. The filter element within the filter body should be changed regularly. Various filters are shown in Figs. 7-11, 7-12, and 7-13.

## SUMMARY

A good oil storage supply system is an important part of the oil heating installation. An even flow of clean oil must be supplied at all times to the furnace in order to have an efficient, troublefree heating system. This is why proper tank installation and line filters are very important to any oil furnace.

There are two types of fuel oil storage installations: inside (basement) and outside (buried) underground. Underground tanks must be sealed from moisture and anchored to keep them from floating to the surface.

Courtesy W. G. B. Oil Clarifier, Inc.

**Fig. 7-10. Filter installation on fuel storage tank.**

Courtesy Eddington Metal Specialties Co.

**Fig. 7-11. Replacement fuel oil filter element and oil filter case.**

Proper venting pipe and filler pipe are very important to uninterrupted fuel flow. A shutoff valve and fuel filter should always be connected at the bottom (outlet) of the storage tank.

Underground tank capacity is generally 550, 1000, and 1500 gal., while the inside storage tanks are 275 gal. Inside tanks may be hooked up in tandem style, which would store approximately 550 gal.

## REVIEW QUESTIONS

1. What gauge metal is used to make the inside storage tanks?
2. Name the two kinds of tank installations.
3. How deep should an outside tank be buried?
4. What precautions are taken to protect an outside tank from moisture?

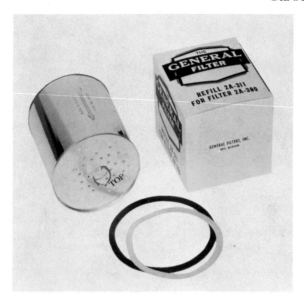

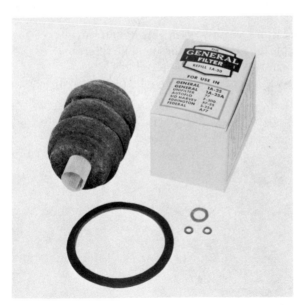

Fig. 7-12. Oil filter elements.

Fig. 7-13. An oil line filter designed for extra protection of nozzles in oil burner applications of 2:00 gallons per hour or less.

5. What size diameter pipe should be used for venting and filling?
6. What is the capacity in gallons of an inside tank? An outside tank?
7. What is the purpose of an anti-siphon valve?
8. What is the purpose of the fuel line filter?
9. Is a whistle vent important? Why?
10. Where should a shutoff valve be placed? Why?

CHAPTER 8

# Commercial
# Oil Burners

The first question one may ask about commercial oil burner equipment is, Who uses this equipment? A glance down the main street of any town is all you need to discover heavy oil equipment users in your area. The greenhouses, laundries, schools, apartment houses, churches, and large buildings of every description will easily fill a prospect list. The list can further be enhanced when you consider the many operations that still use hand-fired equipment—the numerous apartments and greenhouses requiring equipment replacement because of age—the economy-minded public housing and building programs at present using a high-priced fuel, and the multitude of new schools, churches and institutions going up daily.

As a point of interest, you should know that heavy oils do not necessarily have to be stocked at local oil plants. Most major oil suppliers maintain convenient depots where transports pick up the heavy oil product and move it directly to the consumer.

# FUEL OIL

No. 4 fuel oil is generally used for commercial oil burners not equipped with preheating facilities. This oil has a heat value of about 145,000 Btu per gallon and is considered one of the finer of the heavy oils.

No. 5 fuel oil, although a product of medium viscosity, is also used for commercial applications. The heat value of this fuel ranges from 145,000 to 150,000 Btu per gallon. It is interesting to note that the delivery of this heavy oil or commercial fuel is accomplished in the same manner and with the same simplicity as the lighter No. 2 or domestic fuels.

No. 6 fuel oil, or bunker C oil, is the heaviest commercial fuel oil. When cold, it is almost of solid consistency. The Btu content is approximately 152,000 Btu per gallon. The flue is maintained in the storage tank in a preheated condition, so that when it is required, it can be moved through the piping to the oil burning unit. Storage temperature range is just a little below the 100°F mark. The fuel temperature is raised even further (to approximately 180°F) before it enters the combustion equipment.

# HEAVY OIL EQUIPMENT

Surprisingly enough, a great deal of the heavy oil burner's integral parts, accessory equipment, and component items are similar to those found in burners using No. 2 oil and respond equally well to good service procedure. Naturally, the parts and equipment vary, but with practice, study, and application these service problems are certainly surmountable. See Figs. 8-1, 8-2, and 8-3.

### Gun-Type Heavy Oil Equipment

Suppose we discuss the different types of common heavy oil and commercial equipment found in the field today.

Fig. 8-1. Pressure-atomizing gun-type oil burner for industrial use.

Fig. 8-2. Industrial gun-type burner. Note low-high fire-control unit on left side of burner and electronic control.

295

**Fig. 8-3. Installing a commercial oil burner.**

The first style of heavy oil burner is a close kin to the standard-chassis gun burner we have become so familiar with in No. 2 equipment. Three important design features differentiate this equipment from the gun-type burners we know in domestic work.

First is the method of fuel burning, or so-called atomization. One type of these burners prepares the commercial oil for combustion by sending it into the combustion area treated and then "atomizing" it under pressures of about 140 psi. This type of equipment uses standard No. 2 nozzles in order to arrive at the required gallon-per-hour firing rates. Still another type of burner (low-pressure atomizing) permits a portion of the heavy oil and air to be premixed prior to the entrance into the combustion chamber at low pressures. The firing rate is determined by burner design, size, nozzle, and special firing system permitting varying gallonage in certain types of equipment.

The second design feature difference encountered in heavy oil burners is their operation and control through electronic safety (maximum unit protection) devices. These electronic safety controls, part and parcel of all modern heavy oil equipment, are quick sensing and positive acting in the event of flame failure, ignition difficulties, or other burner breakdowns.

Design difference number three permits certain gun-type heavy oil burners to maintain a flexible firing-rate control. Through special linkage, garage, and equipment, these burners may either be manually or automatically controlled in their range of firing (high fire-low fire). This permits, in certain instances, a unit to be automatically started at a low firing rate, gradually and automatically switched to its maximum output as combustion and boiler conditions demand.

The normal firing range for heavy oil burner is about 25 GPH (gallons per hour), but certain manufacturers do have units with higher outputs.

## Horizontal Rotary Heavy Oil Equipment

The outstanding difference between the gun and the horizontal rotary heavy oil burner that we cover next is the ability of gun-type units to function without the special combustion chamber extras required on horizontal rotary equipment.

Probably the most common heavy oil burner equipment in operation in the field today is the horizontal rotary heavy oil burner. These units differ from their gun counterparts in their method of oil atomization and air supply. The safety of the unit itself is under the same rigid control of electronic equipment. Atomization of the heavy oils is accomplished by feeding the commercial grades of fuel into an open horizontal cup, rotating at high speeds. When the burner is in operation, the centrifugal action of the finely machined rotating cup causes the oil to cling evenly to the inner surfaces. The cup is designed with a taper that causes the oil to move forward until it reaches the front end where it leaves the cup and is flung at high speeds into the combustion areas a fine mist. Primary air is supplied by a fan, mounted on the same shaft as the spinning cup, and driven by the same motor. The primary air leaves the air cone also at a high speed, comes in contact with the fuel, and its velocity helps to further atomize the oil. The action of the primary air tends to carry the flame forward and provides shape to the combustion fire. Secondary air is admitted through a hinged and linked door below the burner and beneath the combustion chamber proper.

### The High-Pressure Atomizing Burner

The final common commercial burner using heavy oil makes use of a high-pressure atomizing burner as its means of combustion. The unit is simplicity itself, consisting of a firing-delivery line with a nozzle at the boiler or combustion end. It is connected to a fuel pump at the discharge side. The heavy oil is pumped through these lines under high pressure, as compared with the two previously discussed types of equipment. Combustion air is supplied artificially through connected delivery tubes. The flow of both is controlled by valves. As with both other types of heavy oil burners, the equipment is completely controlled by modern electronic equipment.

## IGNITION

Heavy oil equipment can be lit-off in a number of ways. The unit may have No. 2 pilot burner. These, as you know, are lit-off by a standard transformer ignition system. The heavy oil burner may use a gas pilot flame for the ignition start-up, or, if properly sized, the heavy burner may be started through a common transformer ignition device. In previous chapters, we covered electronic controls. These devices monitor, watch, and guard heavy oil equipment. If, for example, a combustion flame is not established within a very, very short time after ignition, the control will shut down the oil burner system until the unit is checked and repaired.

## HEATING OIL

Some grades of heavy oil are so thick that they require heating or "preheating" before they can make their way to the oil burner equipment. Other oils require varying amounts of preheating. The process is about the same for all. The piping carrying the flue is surrounded by a jacket. Through this jacket flows a warming agent. This may be hot water or may be an electrical coil charged with the problem of bringing the fuel up to the proper temperatures. This warm-up process can extend from the interior of the fuel storage tank to the nozzle body of the oil burner itself.

Preheating temperatures must be controlled, for if they were allowed to get too hot, the oil would vaporize. In order to handle this problem, controls are placed in the lines carrying the heating mediums. These devices automatically maintain the correct temperatures for preheating the fuel.

## ADDITIONAL HEAVY OIL EQUIPMENT

Filters are used extensively on heavy oil installations. They are used to remove the impurities that may be found in the oil. Valves and gauges also form an integral part of heavy oil installations. The gauges indicate to the serviceman the various temperature and pressure conditions of the fuel and its agents within the piping complex. The valves provide a means of controlling the flow of the oil.

Certain industries require specific types of heavy oil equipment to meet selected heating needs. For example, certain portions of the baking, drying, and melting industries require a heavy oil burner where the burner can be hand operated and controlled. These units are generally air-spraying types of burners using air pressures ranging from ½ psi to 100 psi (pounds per square inch.)

The best way to learn all you can about new equipment is to contact the manufacturer and obtain instruction booklets and specification sheets covering the particular installation. The information outlined in this chapter should be of valuable assistance in helping you identify and select equipment for specific jobs (see Figs. 8-4, 8-5, and 8-6).

## SUMMARY

Commercial oil burners are used in great numbers in churches, schools, apartment houses, and large family clubhouses.

Fig. 8-4. An industrial-commercial oil burner—front, or firing, view.

Much about heavy oil burners is similar to (except for size) home-type units. There are three basic differences between the two units: method of fuel burning, control devices, and a flexible firing rate.

Probably the most common heavy oil burner in use today is the horizontal rotary heavy oil burner. Oil is fed into open horizontal cups rotating at high speed. The oil is distributed evenly to the inner surface of the combustion chamber by centrifugal action of the horizontal cups.

Another type of commercial oil burner is the high-pressure atomizing burner. Oil is pumped through lines under high pressure. The combustion air is also supplied through tubes and is controlled completely by electronic equipment.

Some heavy oils are so thick that they must be preheated before they can move through the pipe to the oil burner. This is

Courtesy Industrial Combustion

**Fig. 8-5.** Side view of an industrial-commercial burner showing swing-away air housing that provides easy access to nozzle, scanner, and other mechanical parts.

accomplished by electric heating coils wrapped around the pipe or by hot water in a jacket surrounding the oil pipe.

## REVIEW QUESTIONS

1. What determines the firing rate on heavy oil burners?
2. What type of commercial oil burners is most commonly used?
3. What are the differences between heavy oil burners and home units?
4. Name the different ways a heavy oil burner fuel can be lit-off.
5. What grades of fuel oil must be preheated?
6. What is the Btu rating of Nos. 4, 5, and 6 fuel oil?

301

Courtesy Peabody Gordon-Piatt

**Fig. 8-6. Industrial oil burner, rear view.**

7. What are the most important design features of heavy oil burners?
8. Where would you find heavy oil burners in use?
9. What are the three important extra features found on most good heavy oil burners?
10. To what temperature is heavy oil heated before delivery?

# CHAPTER 9

# Troubleshooting

With this information as background reference, and the types of service calls covered in this chapter, you should be able to adequately handle any service problem that arises.

## SERVICE CALLS

The series of service calls that follow account for a major portion of the service work you will be called on to handle. In addition, each chapter in this book that deals with the component parts of an oil burner system (motors, nozzle, controls, etc.) contains a section that covers "troubleshooting."

### Servicing the No-Heat Call

On a *no-heat* service call, follow service steps 1 to 23. Carry out steps 1 to 5 on each and every service call.

The service call is complete *only* when the trouble spot has been satisfactorily located and solved.

Complete each step *before* going on to the next.

**Service Steps—**

1. Answer the service call immediately.
2. If you are in the business of oil burner service, be prepared to provide good service 24 hours a day.
3. Arrive equipped to do the job quickly and efficiently.
4. Courtesy and congeniality are good for public relations.
5. Do a clean job from start to finish.
6. Measure the oil supply—do not second-guess.
7. Check residence thermostat. Be sure it is set well above room temperatures.
8. Inspect stairwell oil burner emergency switches for *on* position.
9. Look for blown or defective fuses in the main oil burner switch box.
10. Inspect combustion areas of the boiler or furnace. Sight-smell for evidence of oil impregnation.
11. Open relay cover, and using a test lamp, test across terminals No. 1 and No. 2.
12. If test lamp does not light up, check for break or open circuit in the limiting control, switches, low-water cutoff, and wiring.
13. If test lamp *lights up*, individually test terminals No. 1, No. 2, and No. 3 of the relay (one prod of test light to specific terminal and the other prod to ground surface). *Only* terminal No. 1 should test *live* with burner operative. If other terminals light up test lights, the wiring relay is not correct.
14. If test lamp *lights up*, short-out thermostat at terminals. If relay still does not pull in, restep relay points and check helix for dirt or wear. Visually check all relay points for wear.
15. If test lamp *lights up*, press or reset stack switch safety or lockout button.
    *a.* If relay does not pull in, change unit.
    *b.* If relay pulls in, go on to following steps.
16. Stack switch "clappers" pull in—burner functions.

17. After *stack-switch thermostat terminals* have been shorted out, check for:
    a. Dirty thermostat contacts.
    b. Loose thermostat connections.
    c. Defective or broken low-voltage wiring.
    d. Defective thermostat.

    If unit short cycles, check for:
    a. Boiler water level and cutoff.
    b. Thermostat and limit differentials.
    c. Hot contacts of stack switch.
    d. Dirty thermostat contacts.

18. After stack-safety lockout switch has been reset, check for:
    a. Defective oil burner motor.
    b. Defective oil spray pattern.
    c. Defective burner ignition.
    d. Improper flame pattern.
    e. False safety shutdown.

19. Use combustion testing equipment. If there is any possibility of the unit being out of adjustment, use your combustion testing equipment.

20. If burner functions but there is no ignition or light-off, check for:
    a. Loose or defective high-tension wires.
    b. Broken, dirty, or defective porcelains.
    c. Weak or defective transformer.
    d. Loose or broken wiring at stack-switch terminals No. 2 and No. 4.

21. If the burner motor functions but there is no spray of oil, disconnect oil tube firing line. If oil flows from pump discharge port, check for:
    a. Dirty or defective nozzle.
    b. Obstruction in oil tube firing line.
    c. Dribble-proof valve or other line adapter stuck.

22. If the burner motor functions but there is no spray of oil, disconnect oil tube firing line. If *no oil* flows from pump discharge port, check for:
    a. Leaks in oil line.
    b. Off position of oil valve.

  *c.* Defective motor/pump couplings.

  *d.* Pump pressure.

  *e.* Loss of prime in fuel pump.

  *f.* Pump vacuum.

  *g.* Defective fuel pump.

  *h.* Clogged strainers.

23. If the burner motor is inoperative, check for:

  *a.* Overload reset button position.

  *b.* Frozen fan/pump/motor shaft.

  *c.* Loose or defective wiring.

  *d.* Wires broken or loose at stack switch terminals No. 2 and No. 3.

  *e.* Loose motor wiring.

  *f.* Defective motor.

## Servicing the Insufficient-Heat Call

On an *insufficient-heat* call, follow service steps 1 to 20.

Carry out steps 1 to 5 on each and every service call.

The service call is complete only when the trouble spot has been satisfactorily located and solved.

Complete each step *before* going on to the next.

### Service Steps—

1. Answer the service call immediately.
2. If you are in the business of oil burner service, be prepared to provide good service 24 hours a day.
3. Arrive equipped to do the job quickly and efficiently.
4. Courtesy and congeniality are good for public relations.
5. Do a clean job from start to finish.
6. Look at the flame size (nozzle). Is it too small? Is it the correct angle? Is it the right spray pattern? Is it dirty or clogged? Is the nozzle loose? Is the nozzle defective? Change or clean nozzle if any of the above conditions exists.
7. Test fuel pump. Is the oil pressure too low? Is the fuel pump undersized? Is the bypass valve stuck? Is the drive coupling slipping? Is the pressure resulting valve stuck? Make necessary adjustments or repairs to the fuel pump.
8. Inspect combustion chamber for:

    *a.* Flame obstruction (carbon buildup).

    *b.* Correct firebox size.

    *c.* Proper construction and materials (quick heating).

9. Check unit for:
   *a.* Dirty or clogged strainers.
   *b.* Leak in suction oil line.
   *c.* Dirty or clogged foot valve.
   *d.* Partially closed oil valve.

10. Check oil supply for:
    *a.* Water.
    *b.* Poor quality.
    *c.* Sludge.

11. Check thermostat for:
    *a.* Too low a setting.
    *b.* Improper installation.
    *c.* Dirty contacts.
    *d.* Misadjustment or miscalibration.
    *e.* Defective unit.

12. Check limit control for:
    *a.* Incorrect setting.
    *b.* Defective operation.

13. Test voltage circuits for:
    *a.* Motor not operating at proper speed.
    *b..* Voltage fluctuation.
    *c.* Incorrect voltage.
    *d.* Low voltage.

14. Check for:
    *a.* Excessive combustion air.
    *b.* High draft condition.
    *c.* Heavy air infiltration.
    *d.* Dirty blower blades.
    *e.* Excessive temperatures.
    *f.* Poor burner construction.

15. Use combustion testing equipment. If there is any possibility of the units being out of adjustment, use your combustion testing equipment.

16. Inspect boiler or furnace for:
    *a.* Undersized unit.

      *b.* Dirty heating surfaces.

      *c.* Improperly pitched piping.

      *d.* Mains or trunks too small.

      *e.* Unit not suited to oil firing.

      *f.* Dirty or oily water in unit.

      *g.* Piping too small.

      *h.* Domestic hot-water load too great.

      *i.* Piping of ducts running through cold air areas.

17. Inspect radiation for:

      *a.* Undersize.

      *b.* Units blocked or covered.

      *c.* Valves or registers partially closed.

      *d.* Defective or clogged vent valves.

      *e.* Wrong type of radiation.

18. Inspect steam systems for:

      *a.* Water line too high.

      *b.* Trapped or poorly pitched piping.

      *c.* *Pressuretrol* set too low or incorrectly.

      *d.* Defective *pressuretrol.*

      *e.* Defective or missing quickvent valves.

      *f.* Uninsulated piping.

      *g.* Low-water cutoff improperly adjusted.

19. Inspect warm-air systems for:

      *a.* Dirty filters.

      *b.* Blowers too small.

      *c.* Fan/limit control set too low or incorrectly.

      *d.* Defective fan/limit control.

      *e.* Broken or loose belt.

      *f.* Loose blower pulley.

      *g.* Incorrectly operating blower motor.

      *h.* Insufficient air supply.

20. Inspect hot-water systems for:

      *a.* *Aquastat* set too low or incorrectly.

      *b.* Defective *aquastat.*

      *c.* Insufficient water in system.

      *d.* Undersized radiator valve orifices.

      *e.* Defective circulator.

      *f.* Undersized circulator.

      *g.* Partially closed flow-control valve.

      *h.* Airbound radiators.

## Servicing the Overheat Call

On an *overheat* service call, follow service steps 1 to 11. Carry out steps 1 to 5 on each and every service call.

The service call is complete *only* when the trouble spot has been satisfactorily located and solved.

Complete each step *before* going on to the next.

### Service Steps—

1. Answer the service call immediately.
2. If you are in the business of oil burner service, be prepared to provide good service 24 hours a day.
3. Arrive equipped to do the job quickly and efficiently.
4. Courtesy and congeniality are good for public relations.
5. Do a clean job from start to finish.
6. Adjust flame size. Check for:
   * a. Oversized nozzle. Install correct-size nozzle.
   * b. Excessive fuel pump pressure. Adjust.
   * c. Afterdrip at nozzle caused by loose nozzle or nozzle body. Tighten.
   * d. Sticking bypass valve in fuel pump. Repair, adjust, or replace.

7. Inspect electrical system for:
   * a. Room thermostat set too high.
   * b. Incorrectly installed thermostat.
   * c. Thermostat out of calibration.
   * d. Dirty or defective thermostat.
   * e. Shorted low-voltage wiring.
   * f. Limit control set too high.
   * g. Dirty or defective limit control.
   * h. Incorrectly installed limit control.
   * i. Too great a demand for domestic hot water.
   * j. Aquastat set too high.
   * k. Aquastat in wrong position.
   * l. Too much equipment on water line.
   * m. Incorrectly operating combustion control.
   * n. Incorrectly wired combustion control.

8. Check boiler or furnace for oversize.
9. Check radiators or registers for oversize.

309

10. Check for constant-running blower fan or circulator pump.
11. Check for flow-control valve in hot-water system stuck in open position.

## Servicing the Heating-Unit Call

On a *heating-unit service call,* follow service steps 1 to 14. Carry out steps 1 to 5 on each and every service call.

The service call is complete *only* when the trouble spot has been satisfactorily located and solved.

Complete each step *before* going on to the next.

### Service Steps

1. Answer the service call immediately.
2. If you are in the business of oil burner service, be prepared to provide good service 24 hours a day.
3. Arrive equipped to do the job quickly and efficiently.
4. Courtesy and congeniality are good for public relations.
5. Do a clean job from start to finish.
6. For a steam system not delivering enough heat, check for:
   - *a.* Undersized boiler.
   - *b.* Too high a water level.
   - *c.* Boiler not suited to oil firing.
   - *d.* Insufficient radiation.
   - *e.* Undersized steam riser and branch piping.
   - *f.* Dirty boiler water.
   - *g.* Dirty interior surface in boiler.
   - *h.* Inadequate vent valves.
   - *i.* Lack of piping insulation.
   - *j.* Excessive domestic hot-water load.
7. For a steam system delivering no heat, check for:
   - *a.* Closed radiator hand valves.
   - *b.* Closed motorized valves.
   - *c.* Inoperative motorized main valve.
   - *d.* Water level too high.
   - *e.* Water level too low.
   - *f.* Low-water cutoff.
8. For a steam system delivering too much heat, check for:

    *a.* Oversized boiler.

    *b.* Motorized valve not closing properly.

9. For a warm-air system not delivering enough heat, check for:

    *a.* Undersized furnace.

    *b.* Furnace not suited to oil firing.

    *c.* Undersized ducts.

    *d.* Defective fan-control device.

    *e.* Blower belt or pulley slipping or off.

    *f.* Dirty air filters.

    *g.* Inadequate return-air openings.

    *h.* Undersize warm-air registers.

    *i.* Dirty furnace surfaces.

    *j.* Blocked or covered registers.

    *k.* Uninsulated ducts.

10. For a warm-air system delivering no heat, check for:

    *a.* Register closed in room.

    *b.* Damper or valve closed in trunk line.

    *c.* Blower not functioning.

11. For a warm-air system delivering too much heat, check for:

    *a.* Oversized blower fan.

    *b.* Blower fan running constantly.

    *c.* Motorized damper valve stuck in open position.

12. For a hot-water system not delivering enough heat, check for:

    *a.* Undersize boiler.

    *b.* Boiler not suited to oil firing.

    *c.* Undersize main risers.

    *d.* Inadequate vent valves.

    *e.* Dirty boiler water.

    *f.* Insufficient radiation.

    *g.* Lack of piping insulation.

    *h.* Domestic hot-water load too great.

    *i.* Insufficient water in boiler.

    *j.* Airbound radiation.

    *k.* Partially closed flow-control valve.

    *l.* Dirty boiler surfaces.

      *m.* Blocked or covered radiation.

      *n.* Waterlogged expansion tank.

13. For a hot-water system delivering no heat, check for:
    - *a.* Closed radiator hand valves.
    - *b.* Closed motorized main valve.
    - *c.* Inoperative motorized main valve.
    - *d.* Flow-control valve stuck in closed position.
    - *e.* Circulator pump not functioning.

14. For a hot-water system delivering too much heat, check for:
    - *a.* Oversized boiler.
    - *b.* Circulator pump running constantly.
    - *c.* Flow control valve stuck in open position.

## Servicing Miscellaneous Calls

On *miscellaneous* service calls, follow service steps 1 to 9.

Carry out steps 1 to 5 on each and every service call.

The service call is complete *only* when the trouble spot has been satisfactorily located and solved.

Complete each step *before* going on to the next.

Miscellaneous service calls include: cold-residence-between-cycles call, uneven-heat-distribution call, odor-smoke-and-soot calls, and high-fuel-consumption call.

### Service Steps—

1. Answer the service call immediately.
2. If you are in the business of oil burner service, be prepared to provide good service 24 hours a day.
3. Arrive equipped to do the job quickly and efficiently.
4. Courtesy and congeniality are good for public relations.
5. Do a clean job from start to finish.
6. For a *cold-between-heating cycles* call, check for:
    - *a.* Improperly installed thermostat.
    - *b.* Thermostat out of adjustment.
    - *c.* Dirty thermostat.
    - *d.* Wrong type of thermostat.
    - *e.* Slowly reacting combustion control.
    - *f.* Incorrectly adjusted fan control.
    - *g.* Too small a combustion flame.
    - *h.* Fuel pump or nozzle not "atomizing" oil correctly.

    *i.* Water level too high in boiler.

    *j.* Dirty or greasy water in boiler and piping.

    *k.* Improper venting air valves.

7. For an *uneven-heat-distribution* call, check for:
   - *a.* Thermostat installed in wrong location.
   - *b.* Improperly adjusted thermostat.
   - *c.* Limit-control setting too low.
   - *d.* Too small a combustion flame.
   - *e.* Lack of radiation in certain areas.
   - *f.* Radiators and/or registers in wrong location.
   - *g.* Lack of water in hot-water systems.
   - *h.* Airbound radiators in steam or hot-water systems.
   - *i.* Defective piping or ductwork.
   - *j.* Excessive heat loss for existing radiation.
   - *k.* Radiator air valves not venting properly.
   - *l.* Defective quickvent valves on mains.
   - *m.* Lack of quickvent valves on mains.

8. For an *odor-smoke-and-soot* call, check for:
   - *a.* Defective electrodes.
   - *b.* Defective high-voltage transformer.
   - *c.* Low voltage in house service.
   - *d.* Too close a differential in thermostat.
   - *e.* Incorrectly set or positioned nozzle.
   - *f.* Oversized nozzle.
   - *g.* Worn, dirty, or loose nozzle.
   - *h.* Obstructions in combustion chamber.
   - *i.* Incorrectly sized combustion chamber.
   - *j.* Incorrectly constructed combustion chamber.
   - *k.* Excess air to combustion chamber.
   - *l.* Oil leaks or spills near furnace.
   - *m.* Defective fuel pump (cutoff valve leaking or bypass valve stuck).
   - *n.* Lack of proper chimney draft.
   - *o.* Overbaffled heating unit.
   - *p.* Closed damper or wide-open draft regulator.
   - *q.* Insufficient air supply to furnace or boiler room.

9. For a *high-fuel-consumption* call, check for:
   - *a.* Thermostat in wrong location.

b. Thermostat set too high.

c. Thermostat for domestic hot water set too high.

d. Leak in hot-water line.

e. Limit control set too high or too low.

f. Incorrect combustion chamber size.

g. Incorrectly constructed combustion chamber.

h. Obstruction in combustion chamber.

i. Worn or dirty nozzle.

j. Wrong size nozzle.

k. Inferior grade of fuel oil (test at laboratory and match specifications if you have any doubts about quality).

l. Excess air into unit.

m. Oversized furnace or boiler.

n. Undersized furnace or boiler.

o. Unit not designed for automatic firing.

p. Dirty interior water surfaces.

q. Dirty exterior surfaces.

r. Defective valves.

s. Lack of valves.

t. Inadequate or incorrect room radiation.

u. Water level too high in steam systems.

v. Clogged air filters in warm-air systems.

w. Poor or uninsulated building construction.

x. High draft condition.

y. Uncontrolled draft condition.

## COMPLETING THE OIL BURNER INSTALLATION

This book has discussed the component parts that go into an oil burner installation. Each component has been treated on an individual basis. The oil burner units have been discussed in detail including design, service, installation, and troubleshooting.

We have now reached the point where we can bring all the loose ends together and tie a complete *installation knot*. In order to do this adequately, we will use the individual chapters as background reference.

## Designing an Oil Burner Installation

Use the accompanying chapter charts, or other references, to determine the installation Btu requirements.

Select the proper size, type, and brand of oil burner for the installation based on these findings and other background information you have collected.

## Purchase Equipment

List the requirements necessary for the installation. Purchase this equipment. Bring it to the job. A great deal of time can be saved by making sure that all necessary units and supplies are on the job.

Select the oil burner for the installation.

Select the oil tank, piping and auxiliary equipment for the installation. (See Chapter 7 on Oil Storage for know-how.)

Select the combustion chamber material for the installation. (See Chapter 3 on Combustion for know-how.)

Select the proper controls for the installation. (See Chapter 6 on Controls—Thermostats, Limit Controls, Relays—for know-how.)

Select the wiring material, switches, etc., for the installation. (See Chapter 6 on Electric Wiring for know-how).

1. Construct combustion chamber. (See Chapter 3 on Combustion for know how.)
2. Install oil tank and piping. (See Chapter 7 on Oil Storage for know-how.)
3. Install the oil burner in combustion area of boiler and furnace. Hook up fuel lines.
   a. Make sure that the burner is level (if standing type) on the basement floor and secure.
   b. Install with draft tube set approximately ½-in. back from the combustion chamber inner well.
   c. Seal all openings surrounding the draft tube with asbestos cement.
4. Wire unit up. (See Chapter 6 on Electric Wiring for know-how.)

5. Adjust.
   a. Electrodes. (See Chapter 5 on Ignition Systems for know-how.)
   b. Nozzles. (See Chapter 4 on Nozzles for know-how.)
   c. Fuel pump. See Chapter 4 on Fuel Pumps for know-how.)

6. Test-fire the installation.
   a. Test controls.
   b. Test wiring.
   c. Test combustion equipment.

7. Check installation for combustion efficiency. (See Chapter 3 on Combustion for know-how.)
8. Remove excess equipment, wiring, old parts, etc., from job.
9. Clean up work area.
10. Fill out a record card covering all work and parts that went into installation for future information.

## Firing Rate for an Installation

1. *Method A*
   a. Add up the Btu heat loss of each room in the home.
   b. If radiation is already installed, total up the Btu output of each radiator, register, baseboard strip, etc.
   c. Add up the Btu figures for all of the rooms *or* add up the Btu figures for all of the radiation in the house.
   d. Add to this the following allowances. These allowances have been designed to take in piping, pickup, and loss and duct considerations:

      i. *Gravity hot-water unit installation*—Large: Add 15% to total figure. Small: Add 20% to total figures.
      ii. *Forced hot-water unit installations*—Large: Add 20% to total figures. Small: Add 30% to total figures.
      iii. *Gravity hot-water unit installations*—Large: Add 30% to total figures. Small: Add 40% to total figures.

   e. Add these figures to arrive at a total. Divide this number by 100,000. (This figure represents Btu per gallon at approximately 73% efficiency.) The figure you arrive at will be the necessary gallon per hour (GPH) rate and complementary firebox size.

*Example:* A Btu heat loss of 90,000 has been calculated for a residence. A forced hot-water system is in use in the home. Add allowance of 30% (90,000 × 30% = 27,000). The total house heat loss is now 90,000 plus 27,000 = 117,000 Btu per hour. Divide Btu heat loss (117,000) by 100,000 (factor). The results are 1.2 GPH firing rate.

f. You can now match the nozzle size and the combustion chamber size. Do not forget to include an allowancefor domestic hot water in your calculations if excessive demands are made.

2. *Method B*

a. Repeat the Btu heat loss calculations which were outlined in Method A.

b. If the unit is a forced hot-water system, divide the total Btu heat loss by 75,000. The result will be the GPH requirements of the installation.

c. If the unit is a forced warm-air system, divide the total Btu heat loss by 75,000. The result will be the GPH requirements of the installation.

d. If the unit is a steam system, use 1 GPH firing rate for each 200 sq. ft. of standing radiation, or ⅓ GPH for each 100 sq. ft. of measured heat loss.

e. You can now match the nozzle size and the combustion chamber size. Do not forget to include an allowance for domestic hot water in your calculations if excessive demands are made.

## SPECIAL COMBUSTION HEADS

Design advances have been made in the handling of oil burner parts during the past few years. These include equipment such as the shell combustion head and flame retention heads. These *heads* control the air at the end of the oil burner's firing tubes, producing a unique airflow pattern (see Figs. 9-1, 9-2, and 9-3). This pattern conforms closely to the oil-spray pattern and permits complete mixing of oil and air in the proper amounts for efficient combustion. The air handling portions of this equipment can be adjusted to give an efficient mixing over a wide variety of conditions. This is accomplished through a control knob that moves a primary air cylinder back and forth with respect to the fixed secondary air cone. The primary air cylinder encloses the firing assembly and conducts the air to the flame front. Air holes around the back of the primary air cylinder admit a metered amount of air. This stabilizes the flame and controls the flame burning distance from the nozzle. These air holes can be opened or closed by rotating a primary air ring or by a rod from the back of the oil burner.

Fig. 9-1. Adjusting combustion head.

The cone at the end of the primary air cylinder directs air to the flame front. It keeps the nozzle cool by shielding it from the combustion chamber heat. The secondary air cone directs air into the oil spray. The spiral collar behind the secondary air cone

Fig. 9-2. Packing around combustion head prior to installation.

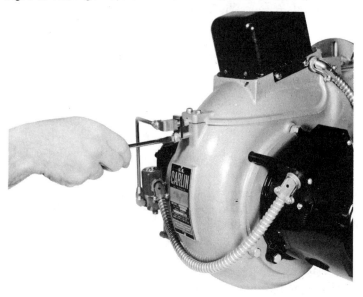

Fig. 9-3. Adjusting combustion head on one model oil burner.

gives a spinning motion to the air as it envelops the oil spray. Fan air supply is separated into two streams—a slow-moving primary air and a fast-moving stream of secondary air. These streams of air are recombined in the correct proportion at the end of the burner blast tube in and around the oil spray. The overall effect of this unit is a more stable combustion flame that eliminates wavering or flame floating. This is especially important with fast-acting electronic controls (see Figs. 9-4 and 9-5).

## TOOLS OF THE TRADE

In the preceding pages we've detailed the methods for installing and servicing oil burner equipment—the *how-to* sections. Each of these operations requires a specific tool to do the job correctly. The following paragraphs deal with these *tools of the trade*, and offer a bit of advice on transporting these tools and auxiliary equipment to and from the particular job or installation.

Service truck equipment can be divided into seven categories:

1. Replacement parts: fuel pumps, relays, motors, etc.
2. New replacement parts: nozzles, copper tubing, filters, etc.
3. Tools of the trade required for service and installations.
4. Boiler and furnace cleaning equipment: vacuum cleaners, brushes, scrapers, etc.
5. Testing equipment: $CO_2$ set, gauges for fuel pump testing, etc.
6. Chemicals and cement products including boiler seals, boiler cleaners, and furnace and retort cements.
7. Miscellaneous items: fire extinguishers, hand cleaners, rags, etc.

An oil burner service vehicle, whether it be a car or truck, may carry over 500 individual pieces, some large, some small, but all requiring a secure storage spot. In dollars and cents, a service vehicle outfitted with the parts listed will have an inventory investment of approximately $1000.

Here's a recommended list of parts, equipment, and tools to carry with you. Keeping a modest supply on hand will save you time and money running back and forth to supply houses. In

Courtesy Field Division of Heico Inc.

Fig. 9-4. Making a final air adjustment.

Courtesy Field Division of Heico Inc.

Fig. 9-5. Attention to detail is important when installing oil heating equipment such as a draft regulator.

addition, you will be able to handle almost any service job directly and from your own supply.

**Category No. 1**—Replacement Parts:

1 Sundstrand fuel pump, CW, 2-hole attachment—left port.
1 Sundstrand fuel pump, CW, 2-hole attachment—right port.
1 Sundstrand fuel pump, CCW, 2-hole attachment—left port.
1 Sundstrand fuel pump, CCW, 2-hole attachment—right port.
1 Thermostat—3-wire low-voltage—select controls dominant in your area.
1 Thermostat—2-wire low-voltage.
1 Clock thermostat.
1 High-voltage thermostat.
4 Stack switches—assorted.
1 Webster fuel pump, CW, left port.
1 Webster fuel pump, CW, right port.
1 Webster fuel pump, CCW, left port.
1 Webster fuel pump, CCW, right port.
1 High-voltage aquastat.
1 Low-voltage aquastat.
1 Pressuretrol.
1 Fan and limit control.
1 Airstat limit control.
1 Reversible two-hole motor.

**Category No. 2**—New Replacement Parts:

1 Package 50 assorted oil burner nozzles.
1 Package assorted ignition terminals.
1 Package assorted couplings.
1 Package fuel pump gaskets.
1 Tank hum eliminator.
1 Circulator coupling.
1 50-ft. coil $\frac{3}{8}$-in. copper tubing.
1 50-ft. coil $\frac{1}{4}$-in. copper tubing.
2 Slip-on vent caps.
3 Air cones—assorted sizes.
3 Assorted stabilizers.

  6 Gauge glasses (steam boiler repairs).

  1 Package assorted gauge glass washers (steam boiler repairs).

  1 Package assorted ignitors.

  1 Spool ignition wire (100 ft.).

10 Assorted filter elements.

  1 Filter unit complete.

  1 Oil burner switch.

10 Assorted household fuses.

12 Air bleeder valves (hot-water system repairs).

25 Assorted copper flare fittings.

  1 Tankit repair unit.

  1 Roll electrical tape.

  8 Assorted Fustats.

  1 Transformer kit (assorted).

  1 Sundstrand pump kit (assorted).

  2 Firomatic check valves.


**Category No. 3**—Tools of the Trade:

1 Tool box.

1 25-ft. drop light with extra outlet.

1 Flaring kit.

1 8-in. pipe wrench.

1 10-in. pipe wrench.

1 Hacksaw and blades.

1 Side-cutting pliers.

1 Long-nosed pliers.

1 Telescopic flame mirror.

1 Grip pliers.

1 Low-voltage thermostat tester.

1 High-voltage tester.

1 Oil can.

1 Pressure and vacuum hand pump.

1 Nozzle extractor.

1 Gauge glass cutter (steam boiler work).

1 Sludge pump (to remove water and sludge from oil tanks).

1 Ball-peen hammer.

1 Soft-face hammer.

1 8-in. shank screw driver.

1 Adjustable screw driver.
1 Pocket screw driver.
1 Set of allen wrenches (6-in.).
1 Set box wrenches.
1 Set open-end wrenches.
1 6-in. adjustable wrench.
1 8-in. adjustable wrench.
1 Flashlight.
1 Shop knife.
1 Wire stripper.
1 Fan puller.
1 Fuel-pump valve wrench.

**Category No. 4**—Boiler Cleaning Equipment:
1 Vacuum cleaner and assorted items.
1 Respirator.
1 Set of flue and boiler brushes.

**Category No. 5**—Testing equipment:
1 Mini-Volt meter.
2 Clip adaptors.
1 Complete $CO_2$ kit.
1 Set of room thermometers.
1 0- to 30-in. vacuum gauge (fuel pump testing).
1 0- to 300-psi pressure gauge (pump testing).
1 Quick test adapter for above gauges.
1 Air velocity meter (forced warm-air work).

**Category No. 6**—Chemicals and Cement:
1 Jar water-finding paste.
1 Quart can boiler treatment.
1 Quart can boiler sealer.
1 Can odor neutralizer.
1 5-lb. can oil-spill cleaner.
1 30-lb. can of retort cement.
1 5-lb. can furnace cement.
1 2-lb. can soot destroyer.
1 Can nozzle-cleaning solution.

**Category No. 7**—Miscellaneous:
1 5-lb. fire extinguisher.

1 Portable transfer pump (fuel and water).
1 Safety cutoff valve and adapter.
1 Can hand cleaner.
1 Expansion tank drainer (forced hot-water systems).
1 Tube Permatex gasket cement.
1 Can Liquid Wrench.
1 Can motor oil.

Keep your tools in good repair. Remember to take your tools with you after you have completed the job. Leaving tools behind on a job is not only costly in dollars and cents, but can be costly in lost time on the next job.

If possible, mark tools with your name and address. Lost tools are more apt to be returned when the owner's name is inscribed.

When you remove a part or use up a chemical, make sure that you replace the item on your next trip back to the office or the supply house. This too can save time and trouble on the next job.

## REVIEW QUESTIONS

1. What service steps should be performed when you receive a service call for insufficient heat?
2. List just a few parts needed to do service work.
3. What are the servicing procedures for an overheating service call?
4. What are the procedures for checking a defective thermostat?
5. List a few tools needed in service work.
6. What procedure should be followed on a no-heat service call?
7. What would be the first check made on a heating unit that was operating satisfactorily but had no heat?
8. What happens to a heating system if the limit control is set too low?
9. Is the location important when installing a thermostat?
10. What procedure is followed to check the firing rate of the burner gun?

CHAPTER 10

# Fuel Consumption
# Heating Costs

In times of rising fuel costs, inflation, and potential or threatened shortages, one of the questions often asked of heating people is: "How much fuel will this house consume over the coming cold weather season?"

## CALCULATING FUEL CONSUMPTION

The simplest way to make this fuel consumption determination is to apply the degree-day formula. This is an engineering formula developed about 40 years ago, and it is still applicable. It has a number of basic components. These include the *normal annual heating degree days* for the area in which you are doing the calculating, the Btu *heat load of the residence* you are working with, and the *outdoor design temperature*. Item number one is available from most fuel supply companies or from the area weather service. You may have to do a bit of quick calculating to find item number two, or the homeowner may have this information available from the people who have installed the system. If the unit is a standard development type or specially designed house, the building architect should have this data. Item number three is a practical comfort factor.

All you need to know is how low the temperature drops in the area where you are doing the calculations. In addition, the "degree-day" method depends on a number of specific established engineering factors. The tables that follow automatically take into account these factors—items such as insulation of the residence, internal heat gains, and wind.

The degree-day formula begins with a basic assumption. This is that heat from specific outside sources (those apart from the residence's unit) will provide the necessary residential warmth until outside temperatures fall below 65°F. At this point, fuel consumption begins and our calculations start.

The ASHAE Guide, one of the bibles of the heating, air conditioning, and ventilating industries, has a number of prepared tables designed to provide established calculations. These tables take into consideration the factors mentioned previously.

Table 10-1 establishes a series of numerical factors for heating systems with *varying operational efficiencies*. This table is

**Table 10-1. Unit Fuel Consumption per Degree Day per 1000 Btu Design Heating Loss**

| Fuel | Utilization—Efficiency | | |
|------|------|------|------|
| | 60% | 70% | 80% |
| Fuel Oil In Gallons 141,000 Btu | 0.00405 | 0.00347 | 0.00304 |

designed specifically for outside design temperatures of from 65°F to 0 degrees. Table 10-2 was produced to provide the necessary calculations when temperatures in an area are known to *fall below 0 degrees*. Both tables assume that residential fuel oil is in use in the heating system having a heating output of 141,000 Btu per gallon (No. 2 fuel oil).

### Table 10-2. Outside Design Temperatures

| Temperature | Outdoor Design Temperatures (0°F and Below) | | |
| --- | --- | --- | --- |
| | 0°F | –10°F | –20°F |
| Correction Factors | 1.000 | 0.875 | 0.778 |

*EXAMPLE (Using Tables 10-1 and 10-2):* A residence has a *heat loss of 150,000 Btu.* The *outside design temperature* for the region is –10°F. The known *annual degree days* in the sample area is 5111 (normal heating degree days). The unit in the residence is *operating at 80% efficiency.*

$$\frac{150,000 \times .00304 \times 5111}{1000} = 2331 \text{ gallons}$$

2331 gallons *divided by .875*

( –10°F correction factor—Table 10-2)

= 2964 gallons—annual fuel consumption of residence

Here is the way the formula works:

1. Multiply the *known residence heat loss* (example—150,000 Btu × the *Unit Fuel Consumption per Degree Day per 1000 Btu Factor* (Table 10-1, example—.00304 – 80%) × the *Established Number of Degree Days* per season in the area where you are doing the calculating (example—5111 dd).
2. Divide this figure by 1000.
3. If the design temperature requirement is below 0°F, divide the above figure by the proper correction factor in Table 10-2 (example— – 10°F—0.875).

## COMPETITIVE FUEL COSTS

Electric heat and oil heat proponents have been battling each other for years about the relative heating costs of the respective fuels. Chart 1 (below) gives you factors necessary for comparing two fuels and permits you to easily calculate the cost of heating for each type of fuel. Determine the actual cost per gallon of fuel oil and the actual cost per Kwh of electricity in you area to make the necessary comparisons.

## CHART 1

To convert *electric baseboard heat fuel consumption to hydronic (hot water) baseboard heat fuel consumption:*

Multiply Kwh × .033

This will give you the number of gallons of fuel oil used by the oil-fired boiler.

To convert *electric furnace fuel consumption to hydronic (hot water) baseboard heat:*

Multiply Kwh × .028

This will give you the number of gallons of fuel oil used by the oil-fired boiler.

To convert *electric ceiling cable fuel consumption to hydronic (hot water) baseboard heat fuel consumption:*

Multiply Kwh × .03

This will give you the number of gallons of fuel oil used by the oil-fired boiler.

To convert the quantity of *electricity used by a heat pump to hydronic (hot water) baseboard heat fuel consumption:*

Multiply Kwh × .052

This will give you the number of gallons of fuel oil used by the oil-fired furnace.

To convert *electric baseboard heat fuel consumption to warm-air oil-fired furnace fuel consumption:*

Multiply Kwh × .039

This will give you the number of gallons of fuel oil used by the oil-fired warm-air furnace.

To convert an *electric furnace fuel consumption to an oil-fired furnace fuel consumption:*

*Multiply Kwh* × .032

This will give you the number of gallons of fuel oil used by the oil-fired furnace.

To convert *electric ceiling cable fuel consumption to oil-fired warm-air furnace fuel consumption:*

Multiply Kwh × .034

This will give you the number of gallons of fuel oil used by the oil-fired warm-air furnace.

To convert an *electric heat-pump fuel consumption to oil-fired warm-air furnace fuel consumption:*

Multiply Kwh × .061

This will give you the number of gallons of fuel oil used by the warm-air oil-fired furnace.

Here is how to apply Chart 1. A residence has a known use of 20,000 Kwh of electricity. You want to know how many gallons of fuel oil the home will use with an oil-fired boiler. The house currently has electric baseboard heat (or electric baseboard heat is being considered for the installation). From the formula in Chart 1 (electric baseboard to hydronic baseboard), multiply Kwh × .033. Kwh in this instance is 20,000. 20,000 × .033 = 660 gal. of No. 2 fuel oil. Suppose that a Kwh of electricity in your area costs 6¢ and a gallon of fuel costs 40¢. 20,000 Kwh × 6¢ = $1200.00; 660 gal. fuel oil × 40¢ = $264.

## HOT-WATER FUEL COSTS

Another area of real concern to many individuals is the cost of producing domestic hot water for their homes. There are three major fuels used to produce the hot water used for all household washing processes. These fuels are electricity, gas, and fuel oil. In order to accurately and equitably provide a comparison of the three fuels, it is necessary to start with a set of common denominators:

1. We will base our calculations on a family of four people.
2. The individuals will use 100 gal. of hot water daily.
3. The equipment for heating the hot water, in all instances, will be an automatically fired hot-water heater with a storage capacity of 30 gal.
4. The test period will be one month.

Table 10-3 shows the results of the test.

## Table 10-3. Typical Fuel Costs

| Type of Fuel | Hot Water Heated In a 15-Minute Period In a 30-Gal. Storage Tank | Heating Units Required To Produce 3000 Gal. of Hot Water | Estimated Unit Fuel Cost | Monthly Costs For Fuel |
|---|---|---|---|---|
| Electric hot-water heater | 5 gal. | 732 Kwh electric | $4.30* Kwh | $31.48 |
| Gas hot-water heater | 8 gal. | 34 Therms gas | 42ᶜ* therm | $14.28 |
| Oil-fired hot-water heater | 30 gal. | 24 gal. | 40ᶜ gal. | *$9.95 including approx. 35ᶜ for burner operation |

*Fuel costs in different sections of the country vary. Use the exact cost of fuel in your area to make accurate determinations.

## HOW OIL DEALERS KEEP TRACK OF CUSTOMER FUEL CONSUMPTION

The majority of oil dealers throughout the nation depend on "degree days" to monitor the quantity of fuel each of their customers consume. The system has two obvious benefits. It assures the homeowner of a steady, uninterrupted supply of fuel oil, year-round, without any of the inconvenience of "run-outs." It organizes the dealer's delivery system in such a way that he can forecast and route fuel oil deliveries to best suit the company's operation. The system can be manually or automatically operated.

A "degree day" is the measurement of the daily outdoor *mean* temperatures and their relationship to the homeowner's daily fuel consumption. The starting point of all calculations is a 65°F outdoor temperature.

The system is simple. First, we determine the *known outdoor high-temperature reading for the day*. This can be obtained from a standard high-low outdoor thermometer, an automatic temperature recorder, or the area weather bureau. Next, we repeat the process and determine the *known outdoor low-temperature reading for the day*. These *two figures are now added together* and the *total divided in half*. The result is the *day's mean temperature reading*. The mean *temperature reading is subtracted from 65°F*, which is our constant degree-day starting point. The result will be the day's *degree days*.

*Example:*

| | |
|---|---|
| High Temperature Reading for day: | 60°F |
| Low Temperature Reading for day: | 40°F |
| Total of both temperature readings: | 100°F |
| Divide total by (2) | ÷ 2 |
| Mean daily temperature: | 50°F |
| Established degree-day starting point: | 65°F |
| Subtract day's mean temperature(example) | − 50°F |
| Total degree days for this day ................ | 15 |

Each degree day calculated on a daily basis is now logged in a book (or automatically calculated in a degree-day computer). The procedure is repeated on a daily basis throughout the heating season (September 15 through April 30). Each day, the temperature findings are recorded and the degree-day calculations established. The day's total is added to the preceding one. *The totals will be the cumulative degree days for the year.*

When the above information is established, the goal is to find out exactly *how many "degree days"* each residence or residences can get out of *each gallon of fuel purchased. This figure is known as the "K" factor, or consumption factor.* Once it is established for the individual residence, it will usually remain fairly constant. *Each house will have a different "K" factor* depending on such items as inside temperatures, number of people in residence, position of thermostat, or number of windows left open.

*The "K" factor is determined* by establishing the *exact number of gallons of fuel oil* that have been *consumed between two consecutive deliveries* to the residence. The gallons used figure is divided into the total number of degree days that have elapsed during the two known dates. The resulting "K" factor is *the number of degree days that one gallon of fuel oil will provide* for the residence.

*Example:*

Total number of gallons of oil consumed:
November 1 to December 15:       203 gal.
Number of *degree days* calculated between
November 1 and December 15:      406 degree days
Divide 203 (gal.) into 406 (degree days)    2.0 K factor

You now have a method established for *determining the degree days for a particular area* of the country and *the "K" factor for an individual residence.* With this information, you will *know how much fuel oil a particular home will consume* in a *specific period of time.* Replenishment of fuel oil in storage tanks can now be safely based on this information. If you have anything to do with delivery of the fuel oil, you should be aware that a "reserve" figure should be established for each size oil tank. This is the quantity of fuel oil that should remain in the storage tank; a safety figure at which point the supply should be replenished. The following calculations will give you a safe "reserve" figure for various size oil storage tanks:

A 275-gal. fuel oil tank should have— 65 gal. in reserve

A 550-gal. fuel oil tank should have—150 gal. in reserve

A 1000-gal. fuel oil tank should have—250 gal. in reserve

A 1500-gal. fuel oil tank should have—300 gal. in reserve

Remember to deduct the reserve gallons from the total number of delivered gallons in the fuel storage tank. This will give you the actual number of usable gallons. If you are interested in determining exactly how many usable *degree days* of oil you have, multiply the number of usable gallons times the "K" factor.

*Example:*

An oil tank has 200 *usable gal.*
The residence's *"K" factor is 2.0.*
200 × 2.0:   400 Usable Degree Days Oil

In actual practice, fuel dealers make the system useful by *projective future of next-time customer deliveries* in advance. As indicated previously, not only does this "protect" the residence against running out of fuel at an inconvenient time but also permits the fuel oil dealer to plan routes, schedule labor, and keep the company operation far better organized. Here is how the degree system is put into actual practice by a fuel supply company:

1. Each residence has *an established "K" factor.* This factor is used to develop the *"degree days of usable oil" available to each residence* on the system.
2. Each day of the heating season, degree days are accumulated and logged either in a book or by automatic degree-day computer. *These daily degree days are added to the degree days of usable oil* of the individual residence.
3. The resulting figure will be the *degree day next delivery.*

*Example:*

Degree days of usable fuel oil (individual residence):   400
Accumulated degree days to date:   446
Degree days next delivery (individual residence):   846

When degree day (846) rolls around, it is time to roll out the fuel oil truck and dispatch it to the individual residence.

If the home heating equipment also is used to *produce domestic hot water* (washing hot water), it is *necessary to compensate for fuel consumption during the period when heat is not being produced.* When *degree days are not being logged* and domestic hot water is being produced, use the following chart to compensate. The degree days calculated are cumulative and should be added to regulate residence consumption.

*Add 6 degree days*
when mean temperature (degree-day system) is 62°F or higher.
*Add 5 degree days*
when mean temperature (degree-day system) is 58°-61°F.
*Add 4 degree days*
when mean temperature (degree-day system) is 54°-57°F.
*Add 3 degree days*
when mean temperature (degree-day system) is 50°-53°F.
*Add 2 degree days*
when mean temperature (degree-day system) is 46°-49°F.
*Add 1 degree day*
when mean temperature (degree day system) is 43°-45°F.

If the residence appears to be using an excessively large amount of domestic hot water, add additional degree days.

A great many homes are "heat sneaks" when it comes to cold-weather heating comfort and winter heating costs. *Warmth, amply generated by the heating system, sneaks out of loose-fitting windows and doors and through unheated attic floors.* Often, this escaping heat can account for a sizable portion of the residential heating bill. Proper wall insulation is not enough.

There is a relatively simple solution to the "heat sneak" problem, and it will pay for itself in lower fuel bills and greater heating comfort for residents of the house. The answer, according to knowledgeable heating specialists, is the installation of storm windows, storm doors, and proper insulation on the attic floor of the residence. The savings can be even more effective if the house is air conditioned. Just as heat is retained during the winter months by proper insulation, storm windows, and doors, cool air generated by air conditioned equipment is kept inside the house longer and not lost as rapidly to the outside during the warm weather months.

A large amount of the savings generated depends on the type of insulation used. Insulation is rated on its R value. This is a tested engineering determination of the efficiency of the insulating product. The higher the R rating, the more effective the insulating value. Insulation with an R-7 rating, for example, does not have the same effectiveness as that of a piece of insulation with an R-30 rating. Insulation batts with a minimum R-19 rating are usually suggested for attic floors.

To give you an idea of the dollar effectiveness of insulation, Table 10-4 points out the potential savings possible with various types of installed insulation. *The sample home is 1200 sq. ft. in size* and has an unheated attic. The dollar figures represent the potential *annual dollar savings* that can be *achieved* with insulation of various ratings. The price of *fuel oil* used to compute the sample chart was *40¢ per gallon*. Move your cost-saving calculations upward as the price of fuel escalates.

### Table 10-4. Typical Heating Costs Savings

| Area of Country | Average Annual Degree Days | Annual Cost Savings Using Insulation with an (R) Factor of: | | | |
|---|---|---|---|---|---|
| | | R-7 | R-11 | R-19 | R-30 |
| Northwest | 8300 | $508 | $551 | $566 | $604 |
| Midwest | 6100 | $374 | $406 | $432 | $446 |
| East Coast | 4200 | $255 | $276 | $292 | $302 |

In order to calculate your own potential savings with high R-factor insulation, storm windows, and doors, use the "average annual degree day" figures for the area closest to the number in your area. This information is available from your local oil dealer, weather bureau, or public utility. In many instances, it is possible to install your own insulation in your attic. You can use mineral wool, batts, or blankets of insulation to do the job. The performance of the individual insulation is usually printed on the packaging. Remember—the higher the R number, the more insulation the material provides. Do not base your selection necessarily on the *thickness of the material* but instead on the R factor or the manufacturer's specifications on the package.

Use the same caution and judgment when selecting storm windows and doors. Be sure that the units are installed properly and well sealed at all joints. A storm window or door that does not fit properly will permit heat to "sneak" out. A well-installed window or door can cut in half the amount of heat lost through the glass surfaces.

## ABOUT OLDER HEATING EQUIPMENT

Many residential heating units currently in operation have seen years of service. Large numbers of these older systems were sized and installed using what is today considered outdated information. Some of the jobs are even the results of "rule-of-thumb" formulas.

It has been estimated that upward of 75 percent of the older heating installations are overfired in relation to the basic system requirement. In addition, if oil-fired, a majority of these boiler and furnace units were usually installed with nozzles sized to the boiler or furnace capacity rather than to the actual measured system requirements.

In this age of high fuel costs, we often find heating systems that are up to 50 percent larger in capacity than needed. One might even find jobs in the field that go 100 percent over the mark. Some of the "high number" calculations are the result of using piping-loss figures that have changed considerably, according to engineering studies. Updated baseboard installations and conversion of gravity to force hot-water systems, for example, can be an important factor in lowering installation calculations. Boilers handling these upgraded systems may actually offer a greater heating capacity than previously calculated and considered available. Modern oil burners with better oil-preparation equipment and more efficient combustion, and units that operate with a zero smoke, result in hotter boiler heating surfaces and lower operating costs.

The wise service procedure to follow is to test heating units for their efficiency, calculate heat loss on the basis of upgraded engineering figures, and either make the necessary equipment modifications or replace the unit entirely.

## List of Manufacturers

If you require some technical data or want specialized information for a particular job, there are many firms nationwide producing oil heating equipment that will be pleased to respond to your request. Manufacturers in each major equipment category are listed below:

## Circulators

Bell & Gossett–ITT
8200 North Austin Avenue
Morton Grove, IL 60053

Grundfos Pumps
2555 Clovis Avenue
Clovis, CA 93612

Taco, Inc.
1160 Cranston Street
Cranston, RI 02920

## Combustion Chambers

Industrial Petrolic Corp.
20-45 128 Street
College Point, NY 11356

Lynn Products Company
400 Boston Street
Lynn, MA 01905

Monogram Products, Inc.
731 North 35 Street
Philadelphia, PA 19104

## Combustion Testing Equipment

Bacharach—United Technologies
625 Alpha Drive
Pittsburgh, PA 15238

Lynn Products, Inc.
400 Boston Street
Lynn, MA 01905

## Control Manufacturers

American Stabilis (Enertorol)
Industrial Park
Lewiston, ME 04240

Electronic Corporation of America
1 Memorial Drive
Cambridge, MA 02142

General Electric Company
1 River Road
Schenectady, NY 12306

Heat-Timer Corporation
10 Dwight Place
Fairfield, NJ 07006

Honeywell, Inc.
Honeywell Plaza
Minneapolis, MN 55408

Johnson Controls, Inc.
2221 Camden Court
Oak Brook, IL 60521

White Rodgers Division
Emerson Electric Company
9797 Reavis Road
St. Louis, MO 63123

## Flue/Chimney Equipment

Field-Division of Heico, Inc.
Mendota, IL 61342

Flair Manufacturing Company
600 Willets Path
Hauppauge, NY 11718

Metalbestos Systems/Selkirk Metalbestos
P.O. Box 372
Nampa, ID 83651

Trionic Industries
6720 Allentown Boulevard
P.O. Box 6212
Harrisburg, PA 71765

Ultimate Engineering Corp.
200 West Central Street
Natick, MA 01760

## Fuel Pumps/Oil Burner

Sundstrand Hydraulics
2210 Harrison Avenue
Rockford, IL 61101

Webster Electric Company
1900 Clark Street
Racine, WI 53403

## Heating Units

Axeman-Anderson Company
233 West Street
Williamsport, PA 17701

Burnham Corp.
P.O. Box 3079
Lancaster, PA 17604

Lennox Industries
P.O. Box 400450
Dallas, TX 75240

New York Steel Boiler Company
Colmar, PA 18915

Oneida Royal Inc.
109 North Warner Street
Oneida, NY 13421

Peerless Heater Company
Spring & Schaeffer Streets
Boyertown, PA 19512

Slant Fin Corporation
100 Forest Drive at East Hills
Greenvale, NY 11548

H. B. Smith Company
57 Main Street
Westfield, MA 01085

Tekton (HS TARM)
Conway, MA 01341

Thermo Products, Inc.
North Judson, IN 46366

Utica Radiator Corp.
2201 Dwyer Avenue
Utica, NY 13501

Williamson Company
3330 Madison Road
Cincinnati, OH 45209

## Heating Units—Auxiliary Equipment

Gorton Heating Corp.
546 South Avenue E.
Cranston, NJ 07016

ITT Fluid Handling Division
4711 Golf Road
Skokie, IL 60076

Thermiser Vent Control Systems
1900 South Michigan Avenue
Chicago, IL 60616

A. Y. McDonald Corp.
P.O. Box 508
Dubuque, IA 52001

## Ignition Equipment

Crown Engineering Corp.
Timberlane
Marlboro, NJ 07746

Hydrovalve Co. Inc.
1310 Rockaway Parkway
Brooklyn, NY 11236

## Motors—Oil Burner

General Electric Company
1 River Road
Schenectady, NY 12306

Jefferson Electric Co.
840 South 25th Avenue
Bellwood, IL 60104

Marathon Electric Co.
Randolph and Cherry Streets
P.O. Box 1407
Wausau, WI 54401

Universal Electric Co.
Owosso, MI 48867

## Nozzle—Oil Burner

Danfoss, Inc.
16 McKee Drive
Mahwah, NJ 07430

OIL BURNERS

Delavan Manufacturing Company
P.O. Box 969
Bamberg, SC 29003

Hago Nozzles
1120 Globe Avenue
Mountainside, NJ 07092

H. Harsch & Co. Inc.
Whitehouse Station, NJ 08889

Monarch Manufacturing Company
2513 East Ontario Street
Philadelphia, PA 19134

Wm. Steinen Manufacturing Company
East Halsey Road
Parsippany, NJ 07054

## Oil Burner Manufacturers

Environmental Ltd. AERO
37 Hanna Avenue
Toronto, Ontario
Canada M6K 1X2

R. W. Beckett Corp.
P.O. Box 1289
Elyria, OH 44036

Carlin Manufacturing Company
Windsor, CT 06095

Industrial Combustion Inc.
4465 North Oakland Avenue
Milwaukee, WI 53211

Peabody Gordon-Piatt
P.O. Box 650
Winfield, KS 67156

Pressure Jet Burner Systems Inc.
P.O. Box 70
Exeter, NH 03833

Ray Burner Corporation
1301 San Jose Avenue
San Francisco, CA 94112

Waltham Products, Inc.
1214 Bennington Street
East Boston, MA 02128

Wayne Home Equipment Company
Scott & Fetzer Co.
801 Glasgow Avenue
Fort Wayne, IN 46803

## Oil Burner—Auxiliary Equipment

Guardian Industries, Inc. (Couplings)
1215 East 2nd Street
Michigan City, IN 46360

Hydrovale Company (Couplings)
1310 Rockaway Parkway
Brooklyn, NY 11236

Pioneer Products Company (Pulleys)
666 Sugar Lane
Elyria, OH 44035

Revcor Manufacturing Company (Blower Wheels)
251 Edwards Avenue
Carpenterville, IL 60110

Torrington Manufacturing Company (Blower Wheels)
Torrington, CT 06790

## Rebuilts (Oil Heating Equipment)

Eveready Burner Supply Co.
416 North Wantagh Avenue
Bethpage, NY 11714

Sid Harvey Industries, Inc.
605 Locust Street
Garden City, NY 11530

Wholesale Heating Co.
516 Lackawana Avenue
Scranton, PA 18503

N. H. Yates and Company
117C Church Lane
Cockeysville, MD 21030

## Tank Gauges, Oil—Auxiliary Equipment

General Filters, Inc. (Filters)
43800 Grand River Avenue
Novi, MI 48050

Klemm Products (Filters)
1700 West Irving Park Road
Chicago, IL 60613

Krueger Sentry Gauges (Gauges)
1056 West Mason Street
P.O. Box 3003
Green Bay, WI 54303

Petrometer Corp. (Gauges)
1807 Gilford Avenue
New Hyde Park, NY 11040

Scully Signal Company (Oil Fill Signal)
70 Industrial Way
Wilmington, MA 01887

## Transformers

Dongan Electric Company
2981 Franklin Street
Detroit, MI 48207

Kenyon Magnetics, Inc.
1057 Summit Street
Jersey City, NJ 07307

# Index

**Over a Century of Excellence
for the Professional
and
Vocational Trades and the Crafts**

Order now from your local bookstore
or use the convenient order form
at the back of this book.

# AUDEL

**These fully illustrated, up-to-date guides and manuals mean a better job done for mechanics, engineers, electricians, plumbers, carpenters, and all skilled workers.**

## CONTENTS

## ELECTRICAL

### HOUSE WIRING (Sixth Edition)
ROLAND E. PALMQUIST

*5 1/2 x 8 1/4 Hardcover 256 pp. 150 Illus.*
*ISBN: 0-672-23404-1 $14.95*

The rules and regulations of the National Electrical Code as they apply to residential wiring fully detailed with examples and illustrations.

### PRACTICAL ELECTRICITY
(Fifth Edition)
ROBERT G. MIDDLETON;
revised by L. DONALD MEYERS

*5 1/2 x 8 1/4 Hardcover 512 pp. 335 Illus.*
*ISBN: 0-02-584561-6 $19.95*

The fundamentals of electricity for electrical workers, apprentices, and others requiring concise information about electric principles and their practical applications.

### GUIDE TO THE 1987 NATIONAL ELECTRICAL CODE
ROLAND E. PALMQUIST

*5 1/2 x 8 1/4 Hardcover 664 pp. 225 Illus.*
*ISBN: 0-02-594560-2 $22.50*

The most authoritative guide available to interpreting the National Electrical Code for electricians, contractors, electrical inspectors, and homeowners. Examples and illustrations.

### MATHEMATICS FOR ELECTRICIANS AND ELECTRONICS TECHNICIANS
REX MILLER

*5 1/2 x 8 1/4 Hardcover 312 pp. 115 Illus.*
*ISBN: 0-8161-1700-4 $14.95*

Mathematical concepts, formulas, and problem-solving techniques utilized on-the-job by electricians and those in electronics and related fields.

### FRACTIONAL-HORSEPOWER ELECTRIC MOTORS
REX MILLER and
MARK RICHARD MILLER

*5 1/2 x 8 1/4 Hardcover 436 pp. 285 Illus.*
*ISBN: 0-672-23410-6 $15.95*

The installation, operation, maintenance, repair, and replacement of the small-to-moderate-size electric motors that power home appliances and industrial equipment.

### ELECTRIC MOTORS
EDWIN P. ANDERSON;
revised by REX MILLER

*5 1/2 x 8 1/4 Hardcover 656 pp. 405 Illus.*
*ISBN: 0-672-23376-2 $14.95*

Installation, maintenance, and repair of all types of electric motors.

### HOME APPLIANCE SERVICING (Fourth Edition)
EDWIN P. ANDERSON;
revised by REX MILLER

*5 1/2 x 8 1/4 Hardcover 640 pp. 345 Illus.*
*ISBN: 0-672-23379-7 $22.50*

The essentials of testing, maintaining, and repairing all types of home appliances.

## TELEVISION SERVICE MANUAL (Fifth Edition)
ROBERT G. MIDDLETON;
revised by JOSEPH G. BARRILE

*5 1/2 x 8 1/4   Hardcover   512 pp.   395 Illus.*
*ISBN: 0-672-23395-9   $16.95*

A guide to all aspects of television transmission and reception, including the operating principles of black and white and color receivers. Step-by-step maintenance and repair procedures.

## ELECTRICAL COURSE FOR APPRENTICES AND JOURNEYMEN (Third Edition)
ROLAND E. PALMQUIST

*5 1/2 x 8 1/4   Hardcover   478 pp.   290 Illus.*
*ISBN: 0-02-594550-5   $19.95*

This practical course in electricity for those in formal training programs or learning on their own provides a thorough understanding of operational theory and its applications on the job.

## QUESTIONS AND ANSWERS FOR ELECTRICIANS EXAMINATIONS (Ninth Edition)
ROLAND E. PALMQUIST

*5 1/2 x 8 1/4   Hardcover   316 pp.   110 Illus.*
*ISBN: 0-02-594691-9   $18.95*

Based on the 1987 National Electrical Code, this book reviews the subjects included in the various electricians examinations—apprentice, journeyman, and master. Question and Answer format.

---

## MACHINE SHOP AND MECHANICAL TRADES

---

## MACHINISTS LIBRARY
**(Fourth Edition, 3 Vols.)**
REX MILLER

*5 1/2 x 8 1/4   Hardcover 1352 pp. 1120 Illus.*
*ISBN: 0-672-23380-0   $52.85*

An indispensable three-volume reference set for machinists, tool and die makers, machine operators, metal workers, and those with home workshops. The principles and methods of the entire field are covered in an up-to-date text, photographs, diagrams, and tables.

### Volume I: Basic Machine Shop
REX MILLER

*5 1/2 x 8 1/4   Hardcover   392 pp.   375 Illus.*
*ISBN: 0-672-23381-9   $17.95*

### Volume II: Machine Shop
REX MILLER

*5 1/2 x 8 1/4   Hardcover   528 pp.   445 Illus.*
*ISBN: 0-672-23382-7   $19.95*

### Volume III: Toolmakers Handy Book
REX MILLER

*5 1/2 x 8 1/4   Hardcover   432 pp.   300 Illus.*
*ISBN: 0-672-23383-5   $14.95*

## MATHEMATICS FOR MECHANICAL TECHNICIANS AND TECHNOLOGISTS
JOHN D. BIES

*5 1/2 x 8 1/4   Hardcover   342 pp.   190 Illus.*
*ISBN: 0-02-510620-1   $17.95*

The mathematical concepts, formulas, and problem-solving techniques utilized on the job by engineers, technicians, and other workers in industrial and mechanical technology and related fields.

## MILLWRIGHTS AND MECHANICS GUIDE
**(Third Edition)**
CARL A. NELSON

*5 1/2 x 8 1/4   Hardcover   1,040 pp.   880 Illus.*
*ISBN: 0-672-23373-8   $24.95*

The most comprehensive and authoritative guide available for millwrights, mechanics, maintenance workers, riggers, shop workers, foremen, inspectors, and superintendents on plant installation, operation, and maintenance.

## WELDERS GUIDE (Third Edition)
JAMES E. BRUMBAUGH

*5 1/2 x 8 1/4   Hardcover   960 pp.   615 Illus.*
*ISBN: 0-672-23374-6   $23.95*

The theory, operation, and maintenance of all welding machines. Covers gas welding equipment, supplies, and process; arc welding equipment, supplies, and process; TIG and MIG welding; and much more.

## WELDERS/FITTERS GUIDE
JOHN P. STEWART

*8 1/2 x 11   Paperback   160 pp.   195 Illus.*
*ISBN: 0-672-23325-8   $7.95*

Step-by-step instruction for those training to become welders/fitters who have some knowledge of welding and the ability to read blueprints.

## SHEET METAL WORK

JOHN D. BIES

*5 1/2 x 8 1/4   Hardcover   456 pp.   215 Illus.*
*ISBN: 0-8161-1706-3   $19.95*

An on-the-job guide for workers in the manufacturing and construction industries and for those with home workshops. All facets of sheet metal work detailed and illustrated by drawings, photographs, and tables.

## POWER PLANT ENGINEERS GUIDE (Third Edition)

FRANK D. GRAHAM;
revised by CHARLIE BUFFINGTON

*5 1/2 x 8 1/4   Hardcover   960 pp.   530 Illus.*
*ISBN: 0-672-23329-0   $27.50*

This all-inclusive, one-volume guide is perfect for engineers, firemen, water tenders, oilers, operators of steam and diesel-power engines, and those applying for engineer's and firemen's licenses.

## MECHANICAL TRADES POCKET MANUAL
### (Second Edition)

CARL A. NELSON

*4 x 6   Paperback   364 pp.   255 Illus.*
*ISBN: 0-672-23378-9   10.95*

A handbook for workers in the industrial and mechanical trades on methods, tools, equipment, and procedures. Pocket-sized for easy reference and fully illustrated.

---

## PLUMBING

---

## PLUMBERS AND PIPE FITTERS LIBRARY
### (Fourth Edition, 3 Vols.)

CHARLES N. McCONNELL

*5 1/2 x 8 1/4   Hardcover   952 pp.   560 Illus.*
*ISBN: 0-02-582914-9   $59.95*

This comprehensive three-volume set contains the most up-to-date information available for master plumbers, journeymen, apprentices, engineers, and those in the building trades. A detailed text and clear diagrams, photographs, and charts and tables treat all aspects of the plumbing, heating, and air conditioning trades.

**Volume I: Materials, Tools, Roughing-In**

CHARLES N. McCONNELL;
revised by TOM PHILBIN

*5 1/2 x 8 1/4   Hardcover   304 pp.   240 Illus.*
*ISBN: 0-02-582911-4   $19.95*

**Volume II: Welding, Heating, Air Conditioning**

CHARLES N. McCONNELL;
revised by TOM PHILBIN

*5 1/2 x 8 1/4   Hardcover   384 pp.   220 Illus.*
*ISBN: 0-02-582912-2   $19.95*

**Volume III: Water Supply, Drainage, Calculations**

CHARLES N. McCONNELL;
revised by TOM PHILBIN

*5 1/2 x 8 1/4   Hardcover   264 pp.   100 Illus.*
*ISBN: 0-02-582913-0   $19.95*

## HOME PLUMBING HANDBOOK
### (Third Edition)

CHARLES N. McCONNELL

*8 1/2 x 11   Paperback   200 pp.   100 Illus.*
*ISBN: 0-672-23413-0   $13.95*

An up-to-date guide to home plumbing installation and repair.

## THE PLUMBERS HANDBOOK
### (Seventh Edition)

JOSEPH P. ALMOND, SR.

*4 x 6   Paperback   352 pp.   170 Illus.*
*ISBN: 0-672-23419-x   $10.95*

A handy sourcebook for plumbers, pipe fitters, and apprentices in both trades. It has a rugged binding suited for use on the job, and fits in the tool box or conveniently in the pocket.

## QUESTIONS AND ANSWERS FOR PLUMBERS EXAMINATIONS (Second Edition)

JULES ORAVITZ

*5 1/2 x 8 1/4   Paperback   256 pp.   145 Illus.*
*ISBN: 0-8161-1703-9   $9.95*

A study guide for those preparing to take a licensing examination for apprentice, journeyman, or master plumber. Question and answer format.

---

## HVAC

---

## AIR CONDITIONING: HOME AND COMMERCIAL
### (Second Edition)

EDWIN P. ANDERSON;
revised by REX MILLER

*5 1/2 x 8 1/4   Hardcover   528 pp.   180 Illus.*
*ISBN: 0-672-23397-5   $15.95*

A guide to the construction, installation, operation, maintenance, and repair of home, commercial, and industrial air conditioning systems.

## HEATING, VENTILATING, AND AIR CONDITIONING LIBRARY
**(Second Edition, 3 Vols.)**
JAMES E. BRUMBAUGH
*5 1/2 x 8 1/4 Hardcover 1,840 pp. 1,275 Illus.*
*ISBN: 0-672-23388-6 $53.85*

An authoritative three-volume reference library for those who install, operate, maintain, and repair HVAC equipment commercially, industrially, or at home.

**Volume I: Heating Fundamentals, Furnaces, Boilers, Boiler Conversions**
JAMES E. BRUMBAUGH
*5 1/2 x 8 1/4 Hardcover 656 pp. 405 Illus.*
*ISBN: 0-672-23389-4 $17.95*

**Volume II: Oil, Gas and Coal Burners, Controls, Ducts, Piping, Valves**
JAMES E. BRUMBAUGH
*5 1/2 x 8 1/4 Hardcover 592 pp. 455 Illus.*
*ISBN: 0-672-23390-8 $17.95*

**Volume III: Radiant Heating, Water Heaters, Ventilation, Air Conditioning, Heat Pumps, Air Cleaners**
JAMES E. BRUMBAUGH
*5 1/2 x 8 1/4 Hardcover 592 pp. 415 Illus.*
*ISBN: 0-672-23391-6 $17.95*

## OIL BURNERS (Fourth Edition)
EDWIN M. FIELD
*5 1/2 x 8 1/4 Hardcover 360 pp. 170 Illus.*
*ISBN: 0-672-23394-0 $15.95*

An up-to-date sourcebook on the construction, installation, operation, testing, servicing, and repair of all types of oil burners, both industrial and domestic.

## REFRIGERATION: HOME AND COMMERCIAL (Second Edition)
EDWIN P. ANDERSON;
revised by REX MILLER
*5 1/2 x 8 1/4 Hardcover 768 pp. 285 Illus.*
*ISBN: 0-672-23396-7 $19.95*

A reference for technicians, plant engineers, and the home owner on the installation, operation, servicing, and repair of everything from single refrigeration units to commercial and industrial systems.

---

## PNEUMATICS AND HYDRAULICS

---

## HYDRAULICS FOR OFF-THE-ROAD EQUIPMENT (Second Edition)
HARRY L. STEWART;
revised by TOM PHILBIN
*5 1/2 x 8 1/4 Hardcover 256 pp. 175 Illus.*
*ISBN: 0-8161-1701-2 $13.95*

This complete reference manual on heavy equipment covers hydraulic pumps, accumulators, and motors; force components; hydraulic control components; filters and filtration, lines and fittings, and fluids; hydrostatic transmissions; maintenance; and troubleshooting.

## PNEUMATICS AND HYDRAULICS (Fourth Edition)
HARRY L. STEWART;
revised by TOM STEWART
*5 1/2 x 8 1/4 Hardcover 512 pp. 315 Illus.*
*ISBN: 0-672-23412-2 $19.95*

The principles and applications of fluid power. Covers pressure, work, and power; general features of machines; hydraulic and pneumatic symbols; pressure boosters; air compressors and accessories; and much more.

## PUMPS (Fourth Edition)
HARRY STEWART;
revised by TOM PHILBIN
*5 1/2 x 8 1/4 Hardcover 508 pp. 360 Illus.*
*ISBN: 0-672-23400-9 $15.95*

The principles and day-to-day operation of pumps, pump controls, and hydraulics are thoroughly detailed and illustrated.

---

## CARPENTRY AND CONSTRUCTION

---

## CARPENTERS AND BUILDERS LIBRARY (Fifth Edition, 4 Vols.)
JOHN E. BALL; revised by TOM PHILBIN
*5 1/2 x 8 1/4 Hardcover 1,224 pp. 1,010 Illus.*
*ISBN: 0-672-23369-x $43.95*

Also available as a boxed set at no extra cost:
*ISBN: 0-02-506450-9 $43.95*

This comprehensive four-volume library has set the professional standard for decades for carpenters, joiners, and woodworkers.

**Volume I: Tools, Steel Square, Joinery**
JOHN E. BALL; revised by TOM PHILBIN
*5 1/2 x 8 1/4 Hardcover 384 pp. 345 Illus.*
*ISBN: 0-672-23365-7 $10.95*

**Volume II: Builders Math, Plans, Specifications**
JOHN E. BALL; revised by TOM PHILBIN
*5 1/2 x 8 1/4 Hardcover 304 pp. 205 Illus.*
*ISBN: 0-672-23366-5 $10.95*

**Volume III: Layouts, Foundations, Framing**
JOHN E. BALL; revised by TOM PHILBIN
*5 1/2 x 8 1/4 Hardcover 272 pp. 215 Illus.*
*ISBN: 0-672-23367-3 $10.95*

**Volume IV: Millwork, Power Tools, Painting**
JOHN E. BALL; revised by TOM PHILBIN
*5 1/2 x 8 1/4   Hardcover   344 pp.   245 Illus.*
*ISBN: 0-672-23368-1   $10.95*

## COMPLETE BUILDING CONSTRUCTION (Second Edition)
JOHN PHELPS; revised by TOM PHILBIN
*5 1/2 x 8 1/4   Hardcover   744 pp.   645 Illus.*
*ISBN: 0-672-23377-0   $22.50*

Constructing a frame or brick building from the footings to the ridge. Whether the building project is a tool shed, garage, or a complete home, this single fully illustrated volume provides all the necessary information.

## COMPLETE ROOFING HANDBOOK
JAMES E. BRUMBAUGH
*5 1/2 x 8 1/4   Hardcover   536 pp.   510 Illus.*
*ISBN: 0-02-517850-4   $29.95*

Covers types of roofs; roofing and reroofing; roof and attic insulation and ventilation; skylights and roof openings; dormer construction; roof flashing details; and much more.

## COMPLETE SIDING HANDBOOK
JAMES E. BRUMBAUGH
*5 1/2 x 8 1/4   Hardcover   512 pp.   450 Illus.*
*ISBN: 0-02-517880-6   $23.95*

This companion volume to the *Complete Roofing Handbook* includes comprehensive step-by-step instructions and accompanying line drawings on every aspect of siding a building.

## MASONS AND BUILDERS LIBRARY (Second Edition, 2 Vols.)
LOUIS M. DEZETTEL; revised by TOM PHILBIN
*5 1/2 x 8 1/4   Hardcover   688 pp.   500 Illus.*
*ISBN: 0-672-23401-7   $27.95*

This two-volume set provides practical instruction in bricklaying and masonry. Covers brick; mortar; tools; bonding; corners, openings, and arches; chimneys and fireplaces; structural clay tile and glass block; brick walls; and much more.

**Volume I: Concrete, Block, Tile, Terrazzo**
LOUIS M. DEZETTEL; revised by TOM PHILBIN
*5 1/2 x 8 1/4   Hardcover   304 pp.   190 Illus.*
*ISBN: 0-672-23402-5   $13.95*

**Volume 2: Bricklaying, Plastering, Rock Masonry, Clay Tile**
LOUIS M. DEZETTEL; revised by TOM PHILBIN
*5 1/2 x 8 1/4   Hardcover   384 pp.   310 Illus.*
*ISBN: 0-672-23403-3   $13.95*

## WOODWORKING

## WOOD FURNITURE: FINISHING, REFINISHING, REPAIRING (Second Edition)
JAMES E. BRUMBAUGH
*5 1/2 x 8 1/4   Hardcover   352 pp.   185 Illus.*
*ISBN: 0-672-23409-2   $12.95*

A fully illustrated guide to repairing furniture and finishing and refinishing wood surfaces. Covers tools and supplies; types of wood; veneering; inlaying; repairing, restoring, and stripping; wood preparation; and much more.

## WOODWORKING AND CABINETMAKING
F. RICHARD BOLLER
*5 1/2 x 8 1/4   Hardcover   360 pp.   455 Illus.*
*ISBN: 0-02-512800-0   $18.95*

Essential information on all aspects of working with wood. Step-by-step procedures for woodworking projects are accompanied by detailed drawings and photographs.

## MAINTENANCE AND REPAIR

## BUILDING MAINTENANCE (Second Edition)
JULES ORAVETZ
*5 1/2 x 8 1/4   Hardcover   384 pp.   210 Illus.*
*ISBN: 0-672-23278-2   $9.95*

Professional maintenance procedures used in office, educational, and commercial buildings. Covers painting and decorating; plumbing and pipe fitting; concrete and masonry; and much more.

## GARDENING, LANDSCAPING AND GROUNDS MAINTENANCE (Third Edition)
JULES ORAVETZ
*5 1/2 x 8 1/4   Hardcover   424 pp.   340 Illus.*
*ISBN: 0-672-23417-3   $15.95*

Maintaining lawns and gardens as well as industrial, municipal, and estate grounds.

## HOME MAINTENANCE AND REPAIR: WALLS, CEILINGS AND FLOORS

GARY D. BRANSON

*8 1/2 x 11   Paperback   80 pp.   80 Illus.*
*ISBN: 0-672-23281-2   $6.95*

The do-it-yourselfer's guide to interior remodeling with professional results.

## PAINTING AND DECORATING

REX MILLER and GLEN E. BAKER

*5 1/2 x 8 1/4  Hardcover  464 pp.   325 Illus.*
*ISBN: 0-672-23405-x   $18.95*

A practical guide for painters, decorators, and homeowners to the most up-to-date materials and techniques in the field.

### TREE CARE (Second Edition)

JOHN M. HALLER

*8 1/2 x 11   Paperback   224 pp.   305 Illus.*
*ISBN: 0-02-062870-6   $9.95*

The standard in the field. A comprehensive guide for growers, nursery owners, foresters, landscapers, and homeowners to planting, nurturing and protecting trees.

### UPHOLSTERING (Updated)

JAMES E. BRUMBAUGH

*5 1/2 x 8 1/4  Hardcover  400 pp.   380 Illus.*
*ISBN: 0-672-23372-x   $15.95*

The essentials of upholstering fully explained and illustrated for the professional, the apprentice, and the hobbyist.

---

## AUTOMOTIVE AND ENGINES

---

## DIESEL ENGINE MANUAL
**(Fourth Edition)**

PERRY O. BLACK;
revised by WILLIAM E. SCAHILL

*5 1/2 x 8 1/4  Hardcover  512 pp.   255 Illus.*
*ISBN: 0-672-23371-1   $15.95*

The principles, design, operation, and maintenance of today's diesel engines. All aspects of typical two- and four-cycle engines are thoroughly explained and illustrated by photographs, line drawings, and charts and tables.

## GAS ENGINE MANUAL
**(Third Edition)**

EDWIN P. ANDERSON;
revised by CHARLES G. FACKLAM

*5 1/2 x 8 1/4   Hardcover   424 pp.   225 Illus.*
*ISBN: 0-8161-1707-1   $12.95*

How to operate, maintain, and repair gas engines of all types and sizes. All engine parts and step-by-step procedures are illustrated by photographs, diagrams, and troubleshooting charts.

## SMALL GASOLINE ENGINES

REX MILLER and MARK RICHARD MILLER

*5 1/2 x 8 1/4  Hardcover   640 pp.   525 Illus.*
*ISBN: 0-672-23414-9   $16.95*

Practical information for those who repair, maintain, and overhaul two- and four-cycle engines—including lawn mowers, edgers, grass sweepers, snowblowers, emergency electrical generators, outboard motors, and other equipment with engines of up to ten horsepower.

## TRUCK GUIDE LIBRARY (3 Vols.)

JAMES E. BRUMBAUGH

*5 1/2 x 8 1/4   2,144 pp.   1,715 Illus.*
*ISBN: 0-672-23392-4   $45.95*

This three-volume set provides the most comprehensive, profusely illustrated collection of information available on truck operation and maintenance.

**Volume 1: Engines**
JAMES E. BRUMBAUGH

*5 1/2 x 8 1/4   Hardcover  416 pp.   290 Illus.*
*ISBN: 0-672-23356-8   $16.95*

**Volume 2: Engine Auxiliary Systems**
JAMES E. BRUMBAUGH

*5 1/2 x 8 1/4   Hardcover  704 pp.   520 Illus.*
*ISBN: 0-672-23357-6   $16.95*

**Volume 3: Transmissions, Steering, and Brakes**
JAMES E. BRUMBAUGH

*5 1/2 x 8 1/4   Hardcover  1,024 pp.   905 Illus.*
*ISBN: 0-672-23406-8   $16.95*

---

## DRAFTING

---

## INDUSTRIAL DRAFTING

JOHN D. BIES

*5 1/2 x 8 1/4   Hardcover   544 pp.    Illus.*
*ISBN: 0-02-510610-4   $24.95*

Professional-level introductory guide for practicing drafters, engineers, managers, and technical workers in all industries who use or prepare working drawings.

## ANSWERS ON BLUEPRINT
## READING (Fourth Edition)

ROLAND PALMQUIST;
revised by THOMAS J. MORRISEY

*5 1/2 x 8 1/4   Hardcover   320 pp.   275 Illus.*
*ISBN: 0-8161-1704-7   $12.95*

Understanding blueprints of machines and tools, electrical systems, and architecture. Question and answer format.

---

## HOBBIES

## COMPLETE COURSE IN STAINED GLASS

PEPE MENDEZ

*8 1/2 x 11   Paperback   80 pp.   50 Illus.*
*ISBN: 0-672-23207-1   $8.95*

The tools, materials, and techniques of the art of working with stained glass.

## DATE DUE

| | |
|---|---|
| SEP 1 8 1990 | NOV 1 9 1994 |
| OCT 1 7 1990 | MAR 2 1 1995 |
| NOV 2 4 1990 | DEC 5 1995 |
| DEC 2 7 1990 | SEP 1 9 1997 |
| MAR 1 1991 | OCT 1 5 1997 |
| NOV 1 3 1991 | MAY 2 6 1998 |
| MAR 1 2 1992 | JUL - 8 1999 |
| APR 1 0 1992 | SEP 2 6 2000 |
| APR 1 0 1992 | MAR 1 9 2004 |
| | APR 9 2004 |
| JUN 2 4 1992 | JY 23 04 |
| MAR 2 6 1993 | SE 07 04 |
| SEP 1 7 1993 | JUL 1 7 2006 |
| NOV - 2 1993 | JUN 1 2 2012 |
| NOV 2 9 1993 | |
| MAR 1 3 1995 | |

#47-0108 Peel Off Pressure Sensitive